Can you hear the drums

Letters from Zimbabwe 2000–2004

Cathy Buckle

Published by Catherine Buckle

P.O. Box 842

Marondera, Zimbabwe

cbuckle.zim@gmail.com

www.cathybuckle.co.zw

©Catherine Buckle 2013

Revised edition 2022

ISBN: 9798847355933

All rights reserved. No part of this publication may be reproduced, stored in a retrieval system or transmitted in any form by any means– electronic, mechanical, photocopying, recording or otherwise –without prior written permission of the copyright holder.

Design and typesetting: Graham van de Ruit

Cover photograph: Zambezi Valley, ©Lucy Broderick 2010 (www.lucybroderickphotography.blogspot.com)

Fiery necked nightjar illustration: ©MargaretRShattock

ALSO BY CATHY BUCKLE

WILD AND BEAUTIFUL ZIMBABWE
1. Zimbabwe's Timeless Beauty: The 2022 Collection
2. Zimbabwe's Timeless Beauty: The 2021 Collection
3. Rundi: Walking with Elephants
4. Imire, the Life and Times of Norman Travers

5. LIFE DURING POLITICAL CRISES IN ZIMBABWE
1. African Tears
2. Beyond Tears
3. Surviving Zimbabwe
4. Sleeping Like a Hare

EYEWITNESS HISTORY – ZIMBABWE
1. Can You Hear the Drums
2. Millions, Billions, Trillions
3. When Winners are Losers
4. Finding our Voices

To subscribe to Cathy's blog
www.cathybuckle.co.zw
Kindle, paperback or hardback versions
www.amazon.com/author/catherinebuckle

For many years Cathy Buckle wrote under the pseudonym 'The Litany Bird'. The Litany Bird is a Fiery necked Nightjar, its call seems to say 'Good Lord Deliver Us'.

*Dedicated to the people of Zimbabwe,
lest we forget.*

INTRODUCTION

Late in February 2000 after spending the day locked indoors and part of it hiding under the desk in my study, I sent one email to seven friends and family members describing what was happening. Little did I know they passed my letter on to their family and friends and so the news gathered momentum.

In the weeks that followed, I continued relating the story, describing a situation that was incomprehensible to all who followed it. Before long dozens and then hundreds of people were asking to receive the letter. Within months the letters were being printed in newspapers, read on radio stations and published on websites in many countries.

That is how Letters from Zimbabwe began. It is not just another story about farmers and land invasions, it is the story of all of us, black, white and brown, and what happened in Zimbabwe.

Can You Hear the Drums covers the years from 2000 to 2004. It is the first of two books that tell the story of Zimbabwe through the eyes of a mum, an ordinary woman living in a small country town. Some of the letters are sad and frightening, others are absurd, touching and funny but all describe how we survived and how we never gave up hope for our beloved homeland.

The first decade of the new millennium in Zimbabwe are years that must never be repeated. Can You Hear the Drums has been compiled so that we never forget and so that future generations, in Zimbabwe and elsewhere, can learn from our history and not have to endure the heart-breaking times we lived through.

Cathy Buckle

(The Litany Bird)

Marondera

Zimbabwe

2013

Part One 2000

Dear Family and Friends

6 March 2000. Hondo

On Wednesday morning I found out that I was on the unofficial list of farms to be squatted and that Stow Farm would be invaded on Sunday morning. The list was actually a poster erected at a nearby beerhall calling on our communal neighbours to gather at our gate at 0800 on Sunday morning with an axe, a badza (hoe) and an ID card so that they could choose the pieces of our land that they wanted.

In the four days between learning that our 433 hectare farm was going to be taken over and the actual event, I went through hell. Alone on the farm with my seven year old son I didn't have the first idea what to do.

Having paid almost a million dollars for the farm barely a decade ago and then spent almost four million dollars stocking the land with sheep and cattle, we are about to lose everything. This is not a cropping farm; a third of the land is muddy vleis and fragile swamps, the remainder is stony ground and largely unpalatable sourveld. To the passer-by, our thousand acres of grass probably looks great but every winter we spend at least two hundred thousand dollars on stockfeed to keep the animals alive. Everything about this farm is an uphill struggle.

When our one and only local war veteran, the son of the Chief in the neighbouring village, attempted to drum up support for his invasion on Sunday, he was laughed at. 'Ah, but its only stones there,' the locals said. This particular war veteran has already received his $50,000 veterans' gratuity from the government, gets a $2,000 government pension every month and has already been given a farm in Beatrice.

The four days prior to Sunday became ones of complete chaos and confusion. The gossip, rumours, false alarms and advice came thick and fast. Frantically making arrangements to make sure that the farm workers and their families would be safe, that the livestock wouldn't get in the way and that the house was secure, I thought I was ready. Trying to explain all this to my seven year old son Richie wasn't easy. His best friends in grade three at the nearby Government school are all Shona speaking black children. His best friend when he's at home is Linnet, the daughter of our farm foreman. The two kids have breakfast, lunch and supper together as if they were joined at the hip. Richard and Linnet are inseparable, together they wander the farm and have their adventures.

It was even harder to wave goodbye to Richie as I shipped him off to my sister Wiz's house on Saturday morning. With tears streaming down my face I waved goodbye and they were hardly out of the driveway when one of the farm workers came running down through the gum trees.

'Hide yourself! They are coming now,' she screamed.

My hands were shaking so badly that it seemed to take forever to clip the padlock on the gate closed. I ran into the house begging the dogs to follow me. And then it started.

HONDO, HONDO, HONDO! (WAR) the men at the gate shouted again and again. They started singing and whistling. The dogs were going mad, barking, howling and scratching at the doors to get out. I closed all the curtains and locked myself in my study, sat down on the floor and put my hands over my head. After about ten minutes it went quiet and that was even more frightening. I didn't know where they had gone or what was happening. For almost two hours nothing happened and then the shouting started again, further away this time. Peeping out of the lounge curtains I saw thirty to forty people streaming across our fields. They chose plots of our land that they wanted, marking their places with stones, sticks and wooden pegs.

Are you serious? Presidential prize winner

'Zimbabwe's President Robert Mugabe has won Z$100,000 (US$2,639) in a promotional draw carried out by a local bank for its clients, the institution said on Thursday. Zimbabwe Banking Corporation, part of the Financial Holdings Limited stable, said Mugabe's name had been drawn on Wednesday out of thousands of qualifying account holders who participated in the promotion.

'Master of Ceremonies Fallot Chawawa could hardly believe his eyes when the ticket drawn for the Z$100,000 prize was handed to him and he saw His Excellency RG Mugabe written on it,' the bank said in a statement.' (Reuters)

14 March 2000. From 'our half' of the farm

There were about fifty invaders on the farm today but they didn't come to the house, instead they broke down the gate we use to cross the main road when we take the cattle for dipping. The invaders sat under a tree in the field and one big man seemed to be addressing them. We stayed locked up all day and by the time it got dark there were only a dozen or so people left and they camped out around a fire in the field by our tobacco barns. Much of the time the squatters seem to be drunk or high on drugs and they are now selling plots on our farm for between Z$20 and Z$50 each. They take the money they've made selling plots on our farm to the local beerhall where they get themselves worked up for the next day. All the workers are terrified of them and say they've been warned to stop tipping us off and telling us what is going to happen. CNN phoned and said they wanted to come out and take pictures and do a story but I said no; cameras attract attention and this might bring even more squatters.

The squatters have chosen 49 plots on our farm and say it's now their land. The bulk of the people have gone but have left five men as guards in a bright blue tent which they've pitched in the middle of one of our rotational grazing paddocks about five hundred metres from our house.

I've had to move all our cattle out of the fields that the invaders have taken over. All the cattle are now right up close to the house; I don't know how long the grazing will hold out. The grazing on the bottom of the farm that we used to lease out to our neighbour Micky is now in what the invaders call 'liberated land.' Micky has had to take his cattle away which has left him with a big problem: a hundred and seventy cattle and no grass for them to graze and it has left us with more lost income.

After many phone calls asking for help I finally got a visit from the Marondera police today but they did nothing. They say they can't act until they receive instructions from their superiors so they very carefully wrote everything down and then left.

Today the men in the blue tent hoisted a Zimbabwe flag in the field to show that it is 'liberated land.' We go to bed at night knowing that they are there on our land sitting around a campfire fuelled by our wood, and we can do nothing about it. The main war veteran stopped us yesterday as we drove out of the gate. He said that we shouldn't worry, they only want to share our land and there wasn't going to be any violence until they received further instructions from the party. Not a very comforting thought coming from a man reeking of beer.

IN THE NEWS

~*17th March 2000* A High Court Order declares land invasions illegal and instructs Police to evict invaders within 24 hours. The Order is ignored.

~*17th March 2000* Lands and Agriculture Minister, Kumbirai Kangai, is arrested in the investigation into a multi-million dollar fraud at the state-run Grain Marketing Board.

~*1st April 2000* Hundreds of war veterans assault peace marchers in Harare with sticks and stones. It is the biggest protest ever held against President Mugabe and Zanu PF. The police do nothing to stop the assaults by war vets but fire teargas to disperse marchers.

~*10th April 2000* President Mugabe issues a 'declaration of war' against the MDC.

~*13th April 2000* A second High Court Judge declares farm invasions illegal and orders police to remove invaders. The Order is ignored.

17 April 2000. No More Adjectives

There are no more adjectives to describe the situation on farms. This weekend in Macheke (40km from here) farmer, Dave Stevens, was abducted from his property by war veterans. Five neighbouring farmers gave chase to try and rescue him. When they were shot at by the war vets, the five took refuge in the Murehwa Police Station but were abducted from there by war veterans and taken to ZEXCOM (the war vets' headquarters) in Murehwa town. Dave Stevens was shot and killed and the other five farmers were very badly beaten; all are now in our little Marondera hospital. Dave's house on Arizona Farm has been ransacked and burned and the whole workers' village has been looted and burned. A convoy of over fifty farmers has evacuated the Macheke area and most are now in Marondera town. The evacuation has come as close as Peterhouse School (15km outside Marondera).

During the week we've had the usual seven men living in the blue tent in our field with people wandering in and out at will. On Tuesday morning a grey pickup truck arrived loaded with timber off cuts and a prefabricated shack was put up about fifty metres from the nearest house in the workers' compound. Through the grape vine we learnt that this is to be the squatters' beerhall. Squatters' huts are sprouting like mushrooms, there are over a dozen now, all being built with our trees; over a hundred and forty have been chopped down so far. Further down the farm a group of men have started digging pits and are excavating clay and moulding bricks. I phoned an Inspector in the Marondera police and told him about the beerhall and brickmaking and he laughed. When I asked to speak to someone higher up he fobbed me off and when I demanded an RRB number (proof that I had made an official complaint) he told me there was no need.

On Saturday morning the usual crowd of invaders started arriving on the farm and by 10.30 there were about two hundred people in our fields. A white car arrived and we heard that someone from CID told the invaders that this farm was not on the list to be acquired by the government. The CID man told the people they were being conned and should challenge Edward (the main war vet) to account for all the money he had taken from them. Aside from paying Edward for the plots on our farm, the squatters have also each been paying him $20 a week to look after their plots. It turned out that if anyone missed a weekly roll call, Edward had re sold their plot to someone else and now there are two hundred very angry people on our farm. There's a war going on down there on our land. The CFU (Commercial Farmers Union) are still telling us to keep calm and say they are sure that law and order will prevail. We are not convinced.

IN THE NEWS

~*18th April 2000* Zimbabwe's 20th Independence Anniversary. President Mugabe declares white Zimbabweans to be enemies of the State.

22 April 2000. Starting to Sink in

For us and hundreds of farmers around the country it has finally started to sink in that this is not going to go away; it's not going to stop and no one's going to help us. Subsequent to the murder of Dave Stevens and torture of five of his neighbours in Macheke, our entire district went into shock and then panic. Marondera town is full to bursting with homeless farmers wandering around in shock. The town is crawling with journalists and reporters. Outside our Marondera CFU office we've had BBC, CNN, SKY, SABC, ABC, Reuters, the Daily News and Paris Match. Everywhere you walk in town there are foreigners with huge fluffy microphones, desperate for someone to interview. None of us have got anything to say anymore.

The violence after the murder of Dave Stevens raged down from Macheke, exactly as we had feared. It rippled down to the Ruzawi road where gangs of two hundred armed thugs over ran almost the entire Ruzawi River area, took over a local security company outpost and the farmers evacuated. Then the violence came right to the boundaries of Marondera town and gangs rampaged along the North Road which is less than two kilometres from the centre of town. There were horrific beatings in farm workers villages and people in the area said the screams could be heard three kilometres away. From there the gangs moved onto the Bridge Road, about ten kilometres from where we are, and there were more beatings of farm workers. At that point two of our neighbours left and we are now only a couple of farms away from the front line of this horrific violence against farm workers by war vets and government supporters.

Worse horrors are also unfolding in Matabeleland where war veterans stormed the Bulawayo farmyard of Martin Olds. They shot him through the windows and then threw petrol bombs into the house until Mr Olds was forced to crawl out where he was shot and killed. The CFU say over three hundred and fifty farmers in the area have evacuated and are only going back to their farms in groups during the day. Violence rippled nearer to Harare, with areas of Ruwa, Arcturus and Enterprise overrun with roving gangs of looting, burning thugs. The scenes of workers houses being savagely stoned and burnt and the owners' dogs being beaten to death by war vets have left us horrified at the brutality and abomination of it all.

Welcome diversion. Bees in the bedroom

Part of the ceiling in the spare bedroom has started to collapse and there's sticky ooze on the wall. I know I can't put this off any longer and must do something about it. Bees have been slipping in and out of the ceiling all day every day for a very long time. The crack in the outside wall used to be thin and the bees had to queue up and go in one at a time, in single file. In the last year, the crack has got longer and now there are major bee-workings going on in the ceiling.

The bed, curtains and carpet were replaced with ladders, newspaper and an old table and early in the morning a tin of smoking rubber was strategically positioned to persuade the bees to move out. As the sun rose and the smoke penetrated, the bees poured out of the crack in their thousands. When they stopped we got to work.

Starting away from the site of the sticky ooze, we opened up an inspection hatch in the ceiling and gradually began to pull the boards down. Massive honeycombs completely filled the space between the tin roof and the beams on top of the walls. In the torchlight the honeycombs looked eerily frightening and yet strangely fantastic like something in a science fiction film. There were six huge slabs of honeycomb which we pried off with planks and sticks. Some of the combs held onto the tin roof with surprisingly strong waxy threads. One by one the honeycombs thumped solidly into the big plastic baby bath waiting below. One comb was very pale in colour and quite soft to the touch but the rest were a dark dirty brown, waxy and very heavy. The last slab of honeycomb leaked thick golden ooze as it reluctantly peeled away, dangled and finally tumbled down. Two men staggered under the weight of the baby bath and there were no shortage of takers for the many kilos of honey oozing out.

IN THE NEWS

~*22nd April 2000* A bomb thrown from a passing car explodes five metres from the front door of the Daily News offices in Harare.

30 April 2000. The Gods are Angry

The violence against white farmers has abated and the attention has been turned to black farm workers. Last Sunday helicopters and light aircraft witnessed and caught on film a huge group of war veterans and squatters burning down a farm on the Lilifontein Road in Wedza. The mob ran amok in the workers village, burning, beating and looting, destroying livelihoods and property in a couple of hours. The world's cameras captured the most horrific pictures of people with broken arms and legs and one poor woman who'd had petrol thrown over her and been set alight. They have lost everything, their possessions, jobs, homes and dignity. God knows how they will survive.

Meanwhile farmers have been left outraged at the recent deal brokered between the CFU and Chenjerai Hunzvi, the leader of the war veterans. The deal is that squatters are allowed to stay on farms but say they won't commit any more acts of violence. In return for this, we farmers have been told we may no longer support the opposition political party or own, wear or give out MDC T shirts or membership cards. We will also be required to attend Zanu PF rallies where we will be berated for being 'bad Zimbabweans.' There have been three of these rallies in our neighbourhood in the last three days; a neighbour attended one, scared of repercussions if he didn't go, and came back with all the stories. That meeting was chaired by three local war vets who introduced themselves as Koochie, Prince and Satan. The names said it all.

About a month ago, a week after the first High Court Order instructed invaders to get off farms but they didn't, we had a terrific storm with high winds and a lot of rain. The squatters in our field had their tent flattened and they evacuated overnight. When a second High Court ruling was made ordering war vets off farms but still they didn't go, we had another huge storm: No electricity for twenty four hours, thunder, lightning, heavy rain and hail. The next morning our squatters were still there but only just and the workers said: 'the Gods are angry.' How must they be now after what happened in Wedza?

On the lighter side

Sign at a river crossing: Take note: When this sign is submerged, the river is impassable.'

7 May 2000. Doors Locked and Mouths Shut

This week, winter suddenly arrived and night-time temperatures plummeted. After days of mist, drizzle and strong, cold winds, something strange was going on down in our fields. The squatters began packing up and all morning they streamed backwards and forwards carrying out their pots, blankets, the flag and finally the tent. Unbelievably they have re located to the front garden of the butchery over the road from us, planting their flag in the lush lawn inside the butchery's security fence. They've put the tent up for show but have demanded that the butchery owner gives them a 'proper house' and are now installed in an empty farmhouse behind the butchery.

Last week their liberating of the butchery over the road only lasted two days. The war vets took their tent down then brought it back again. They can't seem to make up their minds what to do. It is getting really cold now so they seem to be sleeping at the butchery and making cursory checks of their investment over on our land during the day.

The war vets superiors arrived one evening this week and a long, loud shouting match ensued. The end result was the arrival of a pick-up truck loaded with asbestos roof sheets which trundled across our fields. A few of our big gum trees were cut down and used for roof timbers and the asbestos sheets were laid on top of some old abandoned, derelict houses near our small stock dam. This is where the war vets now intend to stay apparently.

Yesterday afternoon our local war vet, Edward, emerged from a minibus with his head swathed in bandages, limping and bent over. Apparently local villagers had got very annoyed that Edward wasn't guarding their plots on our farm anymore and demanded their money back. When he told them he didn't have their money, they lured him down to the nearby beerhall where he was set upon and beaten badly. He came back yesterday with reinforcements. A white Peugeot stopped outside our store and four big men got out, one armed with a rifle, and they set off into the nearby village to find the people that had assaulted Edward. We can only hope that everyone keeps their doors locked and mouths shut.

We spent Monday and Tuesday loading a third of our prime breeding cows and our two pedigree Brahman bulls onto slaughter trucks. We didn't get paid anywhere near what they were worth but at least now we can keep going for a few more months. Our workers look at us every day with increasing worry and distress on their faces; we have to keep reassuring them that we're not going anywhere, just trying to find ways to pay the bills and survive. In the last three weeks they've watched most of our household being packed into boxes and moved to Marondera town. We are all desperate for an election so that we can get back to normal. Living permanently on the edge is getting very harrowing and even if we lose everything, it will be better than this incessant fear.

IN THE NEWS

~*7th May 2000* The SADC Lawyers Association calls on the Zimbabwe government to uphold the law in the country and address the land issue within the framework of the constitution of the country and relevant laws.

14 May 2000. Sacrificial Lambs

The week started on a terrible note with the murder of Alan Dunn, a Beatrice Farmer. Unarmed, he was beaten to death by a gang of thugs while his wife and children hid inside the house, completely helpless, unable to do anything. Around the country there have been ongoing incidences of violence against farmers and farm workers and it is becoming worryingly clear that these squatters, war lords and paid thugs are out of control, not going to listen to anyone and are getting away with any crime you can think of. Police continue to stand by and watch rape, murder, assault, arson and looting. On Friday, the CFU leaders met with President Mugabe who, for the first time, agreed that the violence has to stop. The next day the beatings continued, including the assault of a Pastor and fifteen workers on a farm in Wedza.

Twelve rural schools on the Mutare side of Marondera were closed barely a day after the new term opened this week; teachers were chased away and children terrorized by government supporters. Some schools haven't opened at all and those that have are being protected twenty four hours a day by security guards behind locked gates.

Sixty seven Marondera farmers were called to an emergency meeting yesterday and we met in the newly refurbished Ruzawi Club. Two weeks ago farm invaders raided the clubhouse, stole all the booze, smashed the counter tops and fridges and trashed the place.

I have never seen such low morale, utter depression and resigned despair as there was at the farmers meeting. Many winter crops are not being planted, tobacco seed beds are not being established, vegetable seedlings not being started and there is huge destocking of beef and dairy cattle. We were told at the meeting that President Mugabe is very concerned about hunger and that it's up to the farmers to decide which farms the government can have. In order to prevent the mass handing over of two thousand farms to war veterans by the government, we were all asked to complete a thirty point questionnaire, the results of which are to be collated and given to Mr Mugabe on Monday.

Basically the questionnaire was all about who's had enough, who wants to sell and who's prepared to be a sacrificial lamb. It's all such a farce because although 35% of farmers in one small area of Marondera say they are happy to leave their farms, it has to be done with compensation. But compensation, we were told, is not an issue that's been discussed yet because there isn't any money. What the government have suggested is that farmers would be given an IOU and then, funds permitting, we would be paid out over a five or ten year period. These comments were met with scorn and disgust. What hope would any of us have of ever being paid and how would we survive in the interim?

Zimbabwe humour. Car bumper sticker

One person, one vote (may not apply in certain towns)

21 May 2000. Sins of the Fathers

A date has finally been announced! Parliamentary elections will take place on the 24th and 25th June and if this week is anything to go by, the violence is going to get much, much worse in the five week run up to elections.

The attention has now turned to anyone daring to want change. School teachers have been dragged out of classrooms, nurses out of clinics and doctors out of hospitals. They are publicly beaten, their homes trashed or burned, their lives threatened. Harare and other cities are bursting at the seams with people fleeing to relative safety, many living out in the open because they have nowhere else to go. All over the country, the campaign for votes has gone door to door: they come in the night, rattling gates, breaking windows, banging on doors, demanding to see proof of allegiance to the ruling party.

On farms and in neighbouring communal areas, Zanu PF continues to hold all night, compulsory re-education meetings. People are forced to attend, sing chimurenga songs and denounce the MDC, the whites, Britain and anyone else deemed to be an enemy. Attacks and invasions of farms continue; over 1,500 properties are now affected.

It's an awful thought, but when this began three months ago and they were bashing the whites, it was almost understandable. Perhaps, I thought, we are paying for the sins of our fathers and grandfathers but now the rent-a-mob is bashing everyone who doesn't support Zanu PF, regardless of their skin colour.

At home on the farm it was another traumatic start to the week with Richie more terrified than ever of going to school on Monday morning. I went to see his teacher and we had a long talk. Richie and many of the other children are totally traumatized after events of the last three months. Because it's all we ever talk about, the children can't help but know that something really bad is going on. Ages ago I tried to explain it to Richie by saying that some people wanted a farm but because they didn't have one of their own, they had decided to have ours; but not to worry, I said, because the police were going to come and make these bad men go away. His teachers are keeping a special eye on him and we keep reinforcing the fact that Mum and Dad are going to be fine, nothing's going to happen to us and we'll be there to pick him up every afternoon at 5pm. The school have just put an evacuation plan in place and Richie came home on Tuesday looking visibly relieved. 'Mum, there's a letter in my case about what we're going to do if the war vets come to the school!' he announced gaily. Now that it was out in the open, his eight year old mind had been able to put things into perspective.

Welcome diversion. The friendly jackal

Late in the afternoon when the shadows are lengthening and twilight paints the sky golden orange, a little jackal comes running along the fence down the farm driveway. It's a dog on a mission, trotting purposely along, nose to the ground, heading towards the feed sheds and chicken runs. He's on the hunt for rats, mice, fruit and berries and, given half the chance he'll have eggs for dinner, if I haven't locked the cages up securely.

I've never seen the jackal calling but I've heard it often enough. The sound in the night is eerie, undoubtedly made worse by the legends planted in my brain as a child at boarding school when the nuns would warn us against bunking out to visit boys by saying the 'rabid jackals' would get us!

Sometimes the jackal lets out a startled, high pitched scream as it trots around the farmyard, other times it's more of a whining or squeaky, high-pitched chattering interspersed with yips and yaps. Whenever I see the jackal on the driveway it reminds me of the 'friendly jackal' encounter we had when Richie was a toddler. One evening I was doing the last egg collection of the day and Richie was outside the cage singing one of his tuneless, endless, made-up songs. He didn't like coming in the cage with me because the hens pecked at his legs and he was quite happy playing in the dust outside. I looked up when his singing suddenly changed to giggling and saw a jackal following him round and round the hen house. As Richie ran faster, so the jackal trotted faster and it wasn't obvious who was chasing who. Even though it looked very innocent and the jackal wasn't being aggressive, I wasn't taking any chances. Dropping the egg basket I raced out of the cage shouting and clapping my hands. The jackal raced away and Richie burst into tears complaining bitterly at the departure of his friend the jackal.

IN THE NEWS

~24th May 2000 Using the Presidential Powers (Temporary Measures) Act, President Mugabe empowers the Zanu PF government to seize farms without paying compensation.

28 May 2000. Waiting for the Letter

President Mugabe has signed into law the compulsory acquisition of white owned commercial farms. Compensation will only be paid for the improvements: housing, buildings, boreholes, dams and fencing. The only problem is that the government haven't got any money to pay that compensation so they say they will pay one quarter of the improvements value on acquisition, another quarter two years later, and the balance after five years. Belated payments will attract 4% interest which is complete and utter insanity as the cost of borrowing money is now over 50%. However, we have no say in the matter as it's now law.

For the time being President Mugabe says he's only going to take the 841 farms that were listed for resettlement in 1997/98. Our farm was never on that list. War veteran leader, Chenjerai Hunzvi was asked this week if he would instruct his men to move off all the other farms that are squatted. He laughed and said that this would depend on the CFU and the owners of the 841 farms; he said he would wait to see if they would accept the new law and vacate their homes.

Marondera is bracing for a Star Rally this weekend which we believe is to be addressed by Mr Mugabe. All week groups of youths have been going door to door in Marondera town, throwing stones on roofs, rattling gates and threatening people with looting and burning if they don't attend the rally. My sister in town has had three such visits this week, two at night and one during the day and said they are pretty terrifying. She has stayed locked in with the curtains closed and while the reign of terror moves into the towns, still the Police do nothing.

One big truck load of about 100 youths went into our neighbouring communal land earlier in the week. They apparently had a list of all opposition supporters and were going to go and re-educate these people. We don't know what happened as no one is saying anything anymore and everyone you see these days either won't greet you or simply puts a finger to their lips. These same trucks have also been going farm to farm and demanding donations in the form of mealie meal, meat and money, accompanied by the threat of burning and beating if you don't comply.

The war vets visited Watershed College in Marondera this week and instructed the Headmaster that all teachers must attend the Star Rally this weekend in Marondera or face the consequences. What would you do if you were in charge of six hundred kids and had that responsibility to contend with? The same message has been passed on to Digglefold School where Richie goes and of course the kids have had to endure another week of terror and what ifs.

We were warned there was a big meeting scheduled to take place in our field this Saturday and for the first time in three months decided to go out for the day. There is nothing more soul destroying than watching these huge gatherings of two hundred plus people wandering all over our farm so we packed up the braai and took ourselves off with our neighbours to a little game park on the other side of town. When we got to the gate of the game park, instead of asking the attendant where the animals were, the question was: any war vets here?

5 June 2000. The Week From Hell

This has been the week from hell. It started on Monday morning when three war veterans arrived at the gate. Our resident war vet, Edward, has apparently been ousted after found to be illegally selling plots of land and has been replaced by these three new war vets, two women and a man.

The three war vets said they needed meat, maize meal, fuel, transport and money in order to muster support for a 'mini-star-rally 'they are having on Friday afternoon in a rural village nearby. The mini rally is apparently to make sure that everyone attends the main rally on Saturday morning which is to be addressed by the President. After a frightening ten minutes I eventually sent them packing saying I wouldn't give anything without an official letter and receipt. The three were not happy with my attitude, were confused as to why I wanted anything official. Didn't I know who they were, what they would do to me, they asked? They left, complaining loudly saying they'd be back when they expected donations from me or I'd have to face the consequences.

Tuesday morning they were back with a letter, handwritten in one of the school exercise books that I sell in the farm store. The letter was from 'The War Veterans, Watershed Road Headquarters' and addressed to 'All Commercial Farmers.' It said all farmers are required to donate meat, maize meal, fuel, transport and money for the two rallies to be held at the weekend. The three war vets also had a brand new receipt book and I suddenly had no more excuses.

Clutching at straws I asked to see all their war vet ID cards which they flashed and I said I wanted to take their cards inside and record all their names and numbers. They weren't too happy with that but I stuck to my guns saying that I must know who I was dealing with. Amazingly they relented and I retreated into the house with their ID cards, my hands shaking and icy sweat dripping down my arms.

Eventually I went back out and gave them Z$300 (approx. £5).

'It's not enough,' they said, 'give more.'

I launched into an emotional speech about how we were on the verge of bankruptcy because for three months our land had been occupied, littered with huts and shacks and that they've 'liberated' all our grazing and water. I said I was being forced to feed 70 cattle and 100 sheep out of a bag; that all the trees which I sell as poles and firewood were being cut down and stolen and all the fences were being removed. The three seemed genuinely shocked at how bad it was on the farm and how the three month presence of war veterans had almost crippled us. They accepted the money I'd given but as I started to walk away they called out: 'what about your car, we need your car to transport people to the rallies at the weekend.' It had gone too far and I flatly refused. They eventually left but said they'd come back with a driver to collect my car later in the week.

On Wednesday they came back for my truck, again I said no. On Thursday they were waiting for me at the store, by then I was a nervous wreck. After a week of awful nightmares and jumping at every creak in the roof, we disabled and hid my truck and at 7am on Friday morning left the farm with passports, title deeds and my enormous pile of emails and videos which are the documented evidence of this nightmare. We had decided it was better not to be on the farm while these rallies were going on so that we wouldn't be forced into a situation we couldn't control, or a confrontation we couldn't avoid. Later we learnt that some of our workers had been coerced into attending the rally on Friday. They were forced to buy Zanu PF membership cards and told that if the MDC won the elections: 'the war is started.'

We came back to the farm on Sunday midday to find everyone still here but Jane, the storekeeper, was in a very bad way, She is absolutely terrified of something but just keeps saying she fell off her bicycle. Jane's mouth is enormously swollen with a long deep cut beneath her nostrils. Her upper lip is swathed in plaster and blood soaked bandage, her face is lacerated, plasma is seeping onto her cheek and she is limping and holding her back. The nurses at the local clinic were unable or unwilling to treat Jane today so a visit to a private GP is top of the list tomorrow.

The terrible week ended when the government published a list of 804 farms that are to be compulsorily acquired. We are not on the list but as I write, our farm is full of strange people. Over a hundred are gathered in the field below our house, others are walking across the lands. Its eighteen days to go before the election.

IN THE NEWS

~*9th June 2000* The United Nations says it will no longer take part in the monitoring of the forthcoming elections in Zimbabwe. The UN says Harare have tried to force it to accept a lesser role in monitoring the poll.

11 June 2000. This is MY Farm

Jane is still not saying what happened to her over the weekend but by all accounts it sounds as if she was scorched with a hot steel bar – the victim of a political beating. I took her to my GP and saw the full extent of the damage. From the base of her nostrils to the top of her lip there is just a huge mush of flesh and I have never seen anyone sit as bravely and quietly in the doctor's chair as Jane did. I had hoped that the doctor would be able to stitch or clip the wound together but it was impossible on a wound of that size and depth, there was just no skin onto which she could stitch and it simply has to be left open and cleaned daily while the layers of flesh and skin rebuild themselves.

For the first three days of the week we have watched with mounting alarm as dozens and then hundreds of people have gathered daily in the field below our house. The people are farm workers and villagers from neighbouring areas and have been frog marched into our fields daily to be 're educated.' They are forced to renew their Zanu PF membership cards and buy 'data forms' and then they are lectured to by war veterans. They sit from 10 am to 3.30 pm, no food or drink, in the rain, mist and wind and are not allowed to leave until the rent-a-mob leaders are finished. On Thursday midday a group of seven invaders made their way up the fields to our back gate, they shouted and whistled, refusing to go away until they had seen me. With everyone unloading four tonnes of winter stock feed at our dairy, I had no option but to go and talk to them because they were threatening to smash the gates down. When I arrived at the gate one man stepped forward and started shouting at me immediately:

'This is my farm, this is my fields, this is my cows and this is my house,' he shouted, foam bubbling at the edges of his mouth. I knew immediately that he was either very drunk or drugged and that there would be no reasoning with him. I just said very calmly to each statement: Oh! When he'd run out of things to claim ownership of, I asked him what it was that he wanted.

'You bring your workers NOW,' he screamed, he wanted them in the field for a meeting. When I told him that they were unloading cattle feed from the National Foods truck, he went mad and launched into another shouting session:

'National Foods is for Africans, we are Africans; you are whites, you f**** off our land, you f**** off back to Britain.' Then he repeated his 'this is my farm speech.' By now I was getting more than a little tired of the rhetoric but he suddenly decided to take it a step further.

'This is my house,' he yelled, 'you get out now, by 4pm, you get out.'

Then I asked him what his name was and that totally pushed him over the edge. 'My name, my farm, my house,' he screamed hysterically, repeating all the rhetoric again. Then he stepped right up to the gate and started shaking it. He opened his jacket and I could see the butt of a revolver in his inside pocket.

'I could drop you right now,' he said. 'You see my gun, I can take you now,' and then he ranted on about his shooting prowess. He had completely lost control so I just quietly said I would go and call the workers to come to his meeting.

I turned my back on the gate and walked away just waiting for the click and the bang. As soon as I rounded the corner to the house I ran. By the time I got to where the workers were I was a hysterical, gibbering idiot but managed to tell everyone what had happened and they ran to their homes to check on the safety of their families.

The seven invaders had already been to the workers homes and had dragged everyone out including a seven month pregnant woman and two children under five. Jane was marched out of the store and everyone was forced to go and sit in the field for the rest of the day. I phoned the farmers union and the police, begged someone to come out and put a stop to this.

Amazingly the police arrived in twenty minutes. They came to the house and got a description from me of the man with the gun and then went down to the field. We heard later that the police told the war vets that if anyone came to the house again, or threatened us, or demanded anything, they would be arrested. The police ordered the leader of the war vets to do a physical search for the gun, which was apparently done (why the police didn't do it themselves, I don't know) but nothing was found. Later the five policemen came back to the house to reassure us. One was the Chief Inspector in charge of rural affairs and he gave me his home phone number saying I should call him day or night if we needed help.

IN THE NEWS

~*17th June 2000* 'Even if we put a baboon in Chivi [electoral constituency] if you are Zanu PF you vote for that baboon,' Vice President Simon Muzenda said at a rally in Chivi.

18 June 2000. Empty Buses

As the intimidation and violence climbed to fever pitch on our farm these past few weeks, I had become increasingly sceptical about going to vote. After what they did to Jane and my encounter with the gun-man last week however, I am now determined to go to the polls. We have all gone through far too much and been stripped of our belongings, human rights, pride and dignity, to sit back now. I've got angrier and angrier all week as people asked me when we're leaving, it seems as if three quarters of the white population of Marondera are going away before the elections to escape the violence.

The laugh of the week came as the two blue and white Presidential helicopters flew very low over our house. 'Oh there goes Mr Mugabe,' I said to one of my farm workers as we both instinctively took cover under a big tree. He laughed and said apparently the President hardly ever actually goes in the helicopter himself; he uses it as a decoy and travels in an ambulance. The last and best laugh came on Saturday from Jane. She said three empty buses had arrived outside the store to collect people for a major Presidential rally being held in Harare. The buses waited and waited and eventually headed back to Harare completely empty; everyone's had enough of being dragged off to rallies.

IN THE NEWS

~24th/25th June 2000 Voting takes place in Parliamentary elections.

26 June 2000. Hand Clapping and Back Slapping

On Friday, the Herald newspaper finally published the list of polling stations and we were shocked to find that our nearest voting station had been changed from a permanent centre into a mobile one and was only to operate for five hours on

Saturday morning. This was a serious blow as we estimate at least eight to ten thousand people are in its catchment area and the chances of processing that many people in the allotted five hours would be a near impossibility. Then we discovered that the constituency boundaries had changed and half of our farm workers were now registered in Marondera West and the other half in Seke. We worked out who had to go where and the transport logistics and set out shortly after 6.30 am and were eighth in line; by the time we left twenty minutes later, there were well over 300 people in the line and more streaming in from all directions.

As always there was cause for amusement on the way to the polls.

The half of our workers who were registered in the Marondera West Constituency categorically stated that they did not want to be seen with us and that they would get public transport to the polling station. Well of course there wasn't any public transport because we've had no fuel in Marondera all week so on the eight kilometre journey to the polling station we passed two of our workers. They looked the other way as we slowed down, so we drove on. A bit further down the road, another two. It was a cold, cold morning and one of them flagged us down. Suddenly they all ran and climbed in the back of the truck! When we arrived at the polling station, they all scrambled out of the truck and pretended they didn't know us. We stood behind each other in the line, not looking or speaking to each other so I played along with the game that wasn't fooling anyone! On Sunday morning I got up at the crack of dawn and took Jane to another polling station far from here where she could vote away from the watchful eyes of the war veterans. Jane came back smiling and singing and there was much hand clapping and back slapping. What a feeling to know we've had a say in our future.

IN THE NEWS

~*End June 2000* Parliamentary election results are announced: 62 seats to Zanu PF (Mugabe); 57 seats to MDC (Tsvangirai); 1 seat to Zanu Ndonga (Sithole) A further 30 parliamentary seats are allocated by President Mugabe (all of which will go to Zanu PF).

3 July 2000. Lobbying for Food

The MDC won an amazing 57 seats in parliament out of a possible 120. This comes after four months of extreme intimidation during which at least thirty two people have been murdered, six thousand have had to flee their homes and many hundreds have been beaten and raped.

Right up to the last minute the war veterans on our farm kept up the pressure. On the very day after polling, the squatters were saying to our workers: 'we are waiting to hear the results on our radio. As soon as we hear MDC have won in Marondera West, we are coming to kill you.' The MDC did not win in our constituency. So, while we thought, hoped and prayed that no one had been listening to, or believing the rhetoric, they obviously had and now it's history. To our new MPs the message is please don't forget the continuing plight of those of us trying to keep the food on your tables; the moment you take your seats in Parliament, start lobbying for food.

Are you serious? Red carpet arrest

'A Gwanda businessman is arrested and fined for stepping on a red carpet laid out for President Mugabe. The businessman is fined $100 after being charged with contravening a section of the Miscellaneous Offences Act.' (The Zimbabwe Independent)

9 July 2000.   The Rape of the Land

For the first time in four months, we went down to the fields below our house where the war veterans have lived for the past sixteen weeks. For the moment they have gone and taken the tent and all their things with them. Our workers have started on the mammoth task of re-erecting the first of many fences destroyed by the squatters. We looked at what the war vets have done to our land. Everywhere there is litter: plastic bags, Vaseline bottles, cigarette boxes, shards of asbestos, beer cans and paper. I got angrier and angrier as I saw the unspeakable mess they had left in the field. In the big tree under which their tent had been, a big, wide square has been carved deeply into the bark. JAR i has left his initials engraved into the wood. I ripped the Zanu PF political poster off another tree on our boundary fence and we closed the gate the squatters had 'liberated.'

We inspected two of their huts and were shocked at how many trees have been cut down to construct these crude structures. One house is about four metres by four metres and the walls are made entirely of poles, each one almost touching the next one. Inside the hut was a huge pile of poles, another of firewood and another of sheets of tin. Outside were three newly dug vegetable beds planted with sweet potatoes. We just looked but did nothing although the temptation to drop a match was enormous.

Next we went down to our little dam and that was even more shocking. Once densely enclosed with trees, the surrounds are now sparse and a cold wind blew through the protected haven where our cattle used to drink. The dam wall has been broken and water gushes out, with no sign that our liberators had even attempted to repair the breech and save the water; great farmers they would be. The entire surface area of the dam is covered with thick, suffocating red Azolla weed. (a proclaimed noxious weed) Floating and bloated in the water was a dead animal; at that sight I couldn't bear to see any more and left the men trying to retrieve the carcase. Later I heard it was an adult male reedbuck with a bullet hole through its shoulder. I am outraged at how these people, supposedly land hungry peasants, desperate to be farmers, have raped our land this past four months. Breaking down fences, burning poles and droppers, defacing trees, littering the fields, felling literally hundreds of trees, leaving exposed pit toilets, a dead animal left to foul the water, my God, my God.

Welcome diversion. Bird brick layers

A pair of wire-tailed Swallows is building their mud nest in the corner of a small alcove wall along the side of the farmhouse again. There's a short roof overhang there which they seem to like and it's protected from wind and rain. They are really striking little birds with red caps and forked tails and it's a real delight to watch their amazing construction skills. Flying off one at a time they return with little balls of mud in their beaks which they spit out and then seem to regurgitate saliva on it to make it stick. The little avian bricklayers have worked for days, adding layers of mud plaster to their nest until it's big and strong enough to hold them and their babies. It has often looked like quite a precarious operation with tails pressed up again the wall and no ledge or other support to actually stop the nest from sliding down to the ground.

Because the nest is so near the roof it's not easy to see at first but the mud splashes all down the wall are a dead give-away to its location. The swallows don't seem to mind being watched and it's hard to imagine building your whole house out of little mud balls and saliva.

IN THE NEWS

~*15th July 2000* Vice President Joseph Msika announces that war veterans should immediately get off farms which are not on the list of properties which have been fast-tracked for acquisition.

16 July 2000. Deja-vu

Last Sunday Police shot teargas into a 40,000 strong crowd of fans at a football match. Thirteen people were trampled to death and the country is up in arms at the reaction of police. Two days later the Minister of Home Affairs, Dumiso Dabengwa, resigned, saying he was old and tired and that the tragedy at the football match had nothing to do with it. President Mugabe accused the MDC of being responsible for the tragedy saying they had taunted Police by showing the open palm symbol of the MDC party.

On Thursday farmers were told that Mr Mugabe had put onto 'Fast Track' his programme of land re distribution. The CFU sent urgent messages to all farmers tb brace for trouble in the coming days. War vet leader Chenjerai Hunzvi appeared on TV shortly after Vice President Msika's announcement that war vets should get off un-listed farms. Hunzvi said that his comrades will not get off any properties regardless of if they are designated or not. The squatters are saying they don't want to move, they like the farms they've chosen and aren't going to listen to anyone anymore. One squatter was quoted in the press as saying: 'We are the government now.'

On our farm on Tuesday, Edward and seventy others cut through our newly repaired boundary fence and invaded the field again. A very depressing sense of deja-vu creeps in; this must be the third or fourth time a senior Minister has told war veterans to get off farms and Hunzvi has said they won't. I've lost count of how many times Edward and his mates have taken over our farm.

IN THE NEWS

~*21st July 2000* The Ministry of Finance reveals that six weeks after it was introduced the Millennium Budget revised expenditure upwards from $99 billion to $142 billion.

~*25th July 2000* Air France Concorde Flight 4590 crashes into a hotel after take-off from Paris killing all 109 people on board and four in the hotel on the ground.

~26th July 2000 Investment in Zimbabwe shrinks by 80% from January to May.

~26th July 2000 Paraffin prices rise by 130% and petrol increases by 20%

29 July 2000. Loaves and Fishes

Farmers countrywide have agreed to embark on a three day shut down. So far this does not have the open approval or blessing of our union, the CFU, who refuse to be seen as the ringleaders. For three days we will not be sending any produce to market: milk, meat, eggs, veggies, fruit, tobacco, flowers. Our workers, on full pay, will stay at home as will we. The Trade Unions have called for a similar national shutdown and the joint effect may finally impress upon our government that now it is enough. By the end of next week Hitler Hunzvi (as he calls himself) will have to put some of his acclaimed strong religious beliefs to work and re-enact the loaves and fishes.

Last Sunday a new group of squatters and war vets gathered at our gate, hoisted the flag and formed the 'Watershed Road Land Acquisition committee.' They elected a Chairman, Secretary and Treasurer and swore in members, each paying $2 to belong. The members were told that the shacks and huts on our farm should be made more permanent and tilling of the land should commence. On Monday Edward, not to be undermined, sent us a message telling us to open our fences as all the people he had sold plots to would be moving in with their cows, goats, chickens, children, pots pans, blankets and belongings.

We headed straight to Marondera Police Station. Unfortunately the really good Member in Charge (Rural) has been sent on urgent leave so we had to settle with a Sergeant. He wrote down everything, including the fact that our farm is not designated, is not on the government's acquisition list and that we have never been told by government to give up our property. The Sergeant went off to discuss this with his superiors while we waited and waited. Eventually he came back and said how sorry he was, how terrible it all is, how he's only human, how dreadful this was for the country. At one point he leant over the desk, looked me in the eye, patted my arm and said: 'but we are very sorry we cannot do anything; we have not yet had a directive from the superiors.'

On Wednesday about eighty people gathered. It was a bitterly cold day with a howling wind. I had wrapped another half dozen layers of rusty barbed wire around our boundary gate into the field and so the invaders sat down outside the gate, had a three hour meeting on the side of the road and then left. They returned the next day, cut the wire and took over the field again.

On Friday, getting home from a long diesel queue, I found a letter from a completely new crowd of war vets – not belonging to Edwards group, Netty's bunch or Satan's lot. Ten of them had climbed through the fence, surveyed the property, decided that the area from our little dam downwards was suitable and claimed it. Their letter read: 'We have decided to come and share the land with you. We are not taking almost everything. Thank you. War Veterans Henry Mugere, Francisca Muneta and G Kokwana.' This situation is completely out of control, farming is untenable and we are financially finished.

IN THE NEWS

~*1st August 2000* The Reserve Bank devalues the Zimbabwe dollar by 32%.

12 August 2000. Ethnic cleansing

The war vets and squatters are back living permanently on our property, driving vehicles across the fields, felling the timber, stripping the bark and piling up big heaps of prime gum poles. We are absolutely helpless and I find it hard to describe the feelings that churn in my gut as I see trees that I planted with my own hands, pruned, weeded and protected all these years, being cut down by war vets and I can do nothing but watch.

Last Saturday a big crowd of people gathered in our fields and waited for the arrival of the Zanu PF MP for Marondera. The MP had apparently sent word that he would be sharing out our farm. People sat for hours until finally a messenger came to say that the MP wasn't coming, he had rolled his brand new government Pajero five times a few kilometres away and was dead.

Three days after the death of our MP, the youngster who pulled a gun on me some weeks ago, moved onto our neighbours land, started felling the trees on their 300 acre plot and building himself a hut in their cattle paddock. Until now largely untouched by the war vets, our neighbours in their seventies have now to endure the rape of their land for the third time. They lost everything in the Mau in Kenya, lost everything again in Nyanga in the 1970s during the bush war and now it starts all over again. We all begin to feel like the Jews who were stripped of their human rights, property rights and then their lives in Nazi Germany. Ethnic cleansing, such a strange term, how terrifying to be the victims of it.

Welcome diversion. Curly chickens and an uninvited guest

One of my curly chickens, actually called frizzle bantams, has been sitting on a nest of a dozen eggs for over three weeks. Whenever I go too close she hisses, clacks her beak and gives me her best, throaty chicken growl which, even coming from a little curly bantam is more of a gargle than a growl but is still pretty intimidating. Whenever I've tried to get a hand underneath her to have a look at the eggs, she puffs out her golden orange feathers, looks very menacing and then bites: quick and sharp snaps. Her behaviour is enough to scare people away but not the large python I discovered has moved in underneath her. When the curly hen stood up in the nest to re-arrange her skirts I managed to peep in and saw that only one egg was left but also that an uninvited guest had moved in. A long black forked tongue came flicking out in my direction and then, ever so slowly, the brown and black patterned coils of the large snake moved around underneath the nesting box. Despite my best attempts to persuade either the curly hen or the slithery python to move out, both of them hunkered down even tighter. The little golden bantam puffed out her neck feathers and flicked the white membrane over her eye in what I could swear was defiant contempt.

Separated by just a thin wooden plank, the grey green snake coils grew tighter, neither bird nor reptile were going anywhere. By the next morning, the last egg and the snake had disappeared and Mrs Curly Chicken sat in the sun having a long dust bath and preening her long neglected coiffure.

IN THE NEWS

~*15th August 2000* Economists say the presence of Zimbabwe's 11,000 soldiers in the DRC is estimated to be costing $1.5 billion a month.

~*17th August 2000* Zimbabwe has less than five days of fuel stocks on hand with no immediate prospects for fresh supplies.

21 August 2000. Burning Next Year's Food

Our little neighbourhood has collapsed this last fortnight. First a neighbour left, just walked out; then we made the decision to be off by mid-October; the farmers next door decided likewise, as did others four kilometres away. The owner of the thriving little butchery over the road says they will have to close too. The neighbourhood has crumbled and with it has gone everyone's products: tobacco and maize from one farm; beef and eggs from another; our beef, lamb, milk and timber, the butchery's meat, another's milk, cheese, butter, chickens and maize.

In this area everyone we know of is at the point of closing down. The worst thing of all is our workers. We only have seven people working for us but they all have wives and children and unemployed dependants so probably at least 40 people depend on us for survival. When I called them together on Tuesday to tell them we would have to leave our farm soon, I broke down in front of them. I cried for our loss, for their loss, for their children destined to stay in dusty villages not able to afford to go to school anymore. One by one I asked them where they would go, what they would do. All gave the same answer: 'we don't know.' These men are all farm workers, their chances of getting jobs in agriculture now are absolutely zero. Even worse, their chances of being given land in the governments resettlement of landless peasants is also zero. Every day this week we've seen TV coverage of people being given plots on farms. 220 workers and their families and dependants (possibly up to 700 people) thrown out while 52 people are resettled in their place.

What kind of madness is this?

With the death of our neighbourhood go the vast sums we pay in rates to the Rural Council every year for the upkeep of the roads. With our demise go the fortunes we pay to the telephone and electricity companies; the endless levies and charges we pay to the employment council, the standards development fund, the agricultural research boards, the NSSA workers' pensions and insurance funds. For us alone this amounts to a figure in excess of $100 000 a year. And then there's the $1.5 million we spend every year on stock feed, it will be a big loss of income for them too. If someone can tell me that these amounts will be realised from the people squatting on our farm, then I'm OK with it as I know the economy and country will survive but, as we say in our house, pigs might fly.

All week people have been wandering around our farm, cutting trees and erecting their huts. On Wednesday, in broad daylight, six men with a pack of hunting dogs marauded through our lands, through my paddock full of sheep, rousting out the last wild creatures that have managed to hide until now: guinea fowl, steenbok, hares. These men are cocky, arrogant people who should be locked up but they know no one dares touch them. They finished their little hunt by parading with yapping, half-starved dogs, right along the security fence that surrounds our house, calling out, taunting me, shouting and laughing as I stood helplessly watching.

On Friday afternoon a great cloud of yellow smoke rose up from the fields. The squatters have started burning the farm in preparation for planting. The fire got away from them and a man ran out from our fields into the road, waved down a neighbour and begged that he call the fire brigade. We watched our farm, their farm, burning; they want to be farmers so let them get on with it. It's an awful thing to say and to think, but enough is enough. They are burning the fields that would have fed 200 cattle for eight months, burning next year's food.

IN THE NEWS

~25th August 2000 Reserve Bank devalues the currency by 2%, with the Zimbabwe dollar trading at between 50–53 to the US dollar.

~1st Sept 2000: Fuel prices rise: Paraffin doubles; Diesel increases by 54% and petrol by 40%.

4 September 2000. Bubbles in the Blood

Since I last wrote Mr T Maingehama has also claimed ownership of our farm and erected his signboard outside our gate. For the last two Saturdays over a hundred people have gathered in the fields below our house addressed by a large man in a blue Mercedes (reg no 642 276A); he too is an invader as he is trespassing and holding public meetings on private property. Every day fifty to sixty head of communal cattle are pushed onto our fields to graze.

On Saturday night a group of men slaughtered one of our oxen in the paddock immediately in front of our house. From the bubbles in the pools of blood on the grass, it seems the ox was stabbed in the lungs. The blood trail indicated that the poor animal was then walked down to our little dam, undoubtedly gasping for its dying breaths, before being finished off and cut up. The meat was carried across our fields to an open space where the squatters blue tent used to be. There, from the signs in the dust and the fur on the fence wire, the carcass was loaded into a vehicle and taken off. The stock thieves left behind the head, guts and hooves. I phoned the police at 8 in the morning; they arrived ten hours later, in the dark, at 6pm on Sunday night. Any chance of tracking or catching the bastards who slaughtered a $15,000 dollar animal was gone. The police didn't even look around but asked if they could have the ox's head (to eat) which they proceeded to load into the police vehicle.

On the 31st of August I called together the farm workers, paid them and told them all that I was very sorry but I was now having to formally give them all a months' notice. They didn't look at me and I could hardly bear to look at them. I feel like such a traitor and can't bear to think what's going to happen to them and their families.

IN THE NEWS

~*15th Sept 2000* The Summer Olympics begin in Sydney, Australia. Zimbabwe has 16 competitors, 11 men and 5 women, taking part in 5 sports.

17 September 2000. Tawanda

As a result of the slaughter of the ox, we have bought all our cattle into the small dairy next to the house and I wake up every morning to look out on the remnants of our lives. The sun rises directly outside my study window and at this time of year is a great red ball, so spectacular that, even after ten years, I still sit and stare at it in wonder every morning. I can hardly believe that in thirteen days' time this part of my life will be over. I'm filled with a huge sense of relief that we're getting out of this alive but so, so sad that what we thought was the security of our old age and a legacy for our son, is gone. My Mum is staying with me at the moment and this week she asked me if it was OK to walk down to her favourite grove of Musasa trees on the farm. I had to say no, not on her own. With that knowledge in mind I know that we have made the right decision to leave the farm.

Going out to meet the workers early this morning, carrying the buckets for milking, I was greeted by a beaming Isaya. The proud father announced that his wife had last night given birth to their third child, a son, who they are going to call Tawanda, it means: 'we are plenty.' Tawanda is our hope, our future. God help him.

IN THE NEWS

~*4th October 2000* Armed police raid Capital Radio studios in Harare, confiscate equipment, dismantle aerials and search shareholders homes.

~*5th October 2000* Serbian President Slobodan Milosevic leaves office after widespread demonstrations.

~*6th October 2000* Government gazettes new broadcasting regulations using Presidential Powers requiring 75% of all programming to be of Zimbabwean content.

8 October 2000. Siya

Our last week on the farm was very, very tearful but interspersed with bouts of great anger. Five days before we moved out, our resident twenty two year old war vet, Wonder, set a fire in the field near one of our big gum plantations. By the time we discovered it, it was out of control and sweeping through the fields. We finally managed to stop one side of it that was approaching the house and at seven in the evening left it to burn. In the midst of the chaos a man appeared behind me out of the smoke and the darkness.

'Can I help you,' I asked politely.

'Siya,' he said quietly. ('leave')

Twice in that last week on the farm I accepted journalists into the house, determined that this story would be told. It didn't matter which country they were from: Sudan, Nigeria, South Africa or Britain, all were totally shocked at what was going on; shocked that we had put up with eight months of harassment, intimidation and lawlessness; shocked that the police continued to do nothing; shocked that we had no recourse to the law and had been stripped of our human, legal and constitutional rights. I told our story and will continue to do so; the world must know what this has been about. I feel an abiding sense of guilt that we have let the side down by leaving the farm but know that I could not have taken much more; a breakdown was dangerously close. We can only pray that the people of Zimbabwe will find courage as those of Yugoslavia have just done.

IN THE NEWS

~17th October 2000 Bread riots break out in Harare after a 30% price rise.

~6th November 2000 University of Zimbabwe students demonstrate in support of striking lecturers. Riot police fired tear-gas around the campus including in the hostels and UZ Clinic. Students are forced off the campus and the institution closes the next morning.

~10th November 2000 The Supreme Court signs an Order by Consent declaring Fast-Track Resettlement unlawful. The

Commissioner of Police is ordered to remove all squatters from farms that have been 'fast-tracked.'

~*21st November 2000* High Court Judge Chidyuasiku issues a Provisional Order preventing implementation of the Supreme Court Order to remove fast-tracked squatters.

~*23rd November 2000* Leading pharmaceutical company, Johnson and Johnson, relocate their manufacturing division to South Africa owing to continuing economic instability.

~*30th November 2000* The CZI (Confederation of Zimbabwe Industries) announce that 23% of local manufacturing companies are disinvesting from Zimbabwe due to economic decline.

~*5th December 2000* The state withdraws all charges against the war veteran suspected of murdering Macheke farmer David Stevens. According to the Public Prosecutor, charges are withdrawn owing to lack of evidence.

On the lighter side. The Mousetrap

A mouse looked through the crack in the wall to see the farmer and his wife open a package. What food might this contain? the mouse wondered. He was devastated to discover it was a mousetrap. Retreating to the farmyard, the mouse spread the warning: 'There's a mousetrap in the house!'

The chicken clucked and scratched, raised her head and said: 'Mr Mouse, I can tell this is a grave concern to you, but it is of no consequence to me. I cannot be bothered by it.'

The mouse turned to the pig and told him: 'There's a mousetrap in the house!'

The pig sympathized, but said: 'I am so very sorry, Mr Mouse, but there is nothing I can do about it but pray. Be assured you are in my prayers.'

The mouse turned to the cow and said: 'there's a mousetrap in the house!' The cow said: 'Wow, Mr Mouse, I'm sorry for you, but it's no skin off my nose.'

So the mouse returned to the house, head down and dejected, to face the farmers mousetrap alone. That very night a sound was heard throughout the house – like the sound of a mousetrap catching its prey. The farmer's wife rushed to see what was caught. In the darkness, she did not see it was a venomous snake whose tail the trap had caught. The snake bit the farmer's wife. The farmer rushed her to the hospital, and she returned home with a fever.

Everyone knows you treat a fever with fresh chicken soup, so the farmer took his hatchet to the farmyard for the soup's main ingredient. But his wife's sickness continued, so friends and neighbours came to sit with her around the clock. To feed them, the farmer butchered the pig.

The farmer's wife did not get well; she died.

So many people came for her funeral, the farmer had the cow slaughtered to provide enough meat for all of them. The mouse looked upon it all from his crack in the wall with great sadness. The next time you hear someone is facing a problem and think it doesn't concern you, remember: when one of us is threatened, we are all at risk. (Source unknown)

Part Two 2001

IN THE NEWS

~*16th January 2001* DRC President Laurent Kabila is assassinated.

~*20th January 2001* George W Bush is elected President of the USA.

~*28th January 2001* Daily News printing presses are bombed.

~*22nd February 2001* Resident foreign journalists Mercedes Sayagues and Joseph Winter are declared prohibited immigrants and ordered to leave Zimbabwe.

~*8th March 2001* Pro Zanu PF judge, Godfrey Chidyausiku is appointed Acting Chief Justice of the Supreme Court.

~*19th March 2001* Zimbabwe Republic Police promote 300 war veterans to ranks of Sergeant and Assistant Inspector.

~*22nd March 2001* Exiled Ethiopian dictator Mengistu Haile Mariam and his family are given permanent resident status in Zimbabwe.

~*10th April 2001* War veteran Joseph Chinotimba declares himself president of the Zimbabwe Congress of Trade Unions.

Dear Family and Friends

28 April 2001. Grass Hat

A year ago a war veteran covered a hard hat with grass, invaded farms, evicted owners, terrorized workers, abducted reporters and shot a woman. This man is employed as a security guard by the Harare municipality. A fortnight ago this man proclaimed himself the head of the massive Zimbabwe Congress of Trade Unions and has launched a major campaign of terror in Harare this week. Mr Grass Hat raided one of the top hospitals in Harare, the Avenues Clinic, then the Dental Centre, Macsteel and Meikles Department Store Group under the guise of championing the cause of aggrieved ex-employees.

When Mr Grass Hat raided a German NGO in Harare it put Zimbabwe back on the world news. Mr Grass Hat was joined by war vet leader Chenjerai Hunzvi who said war veterans would start raiding foreign missions and embassies, 'to deal once and for all with foreign embassies who are funding the MDC. We will be visiting them soon to express our displeasure and to warn them to stop interfering with our internal matters. No one can stop us in our second phase.' Foreign nationals and local businessmen in Harare are getting a small taste of what many hundreds of farmers have endured for fourteen months.

IN THE NEWS
~28th April 2001 Minister of Youth, Border Gezi, dies in a car crash. *~10th May 2001* The British Council closes its Library and Information Department offices in Harare for safety reasons.

~11th May 2001 Eighteen Air Force of Zimbabwe planes are out of service including three Lynx helicopters, two Alouette helicopters, two Hind helicopter gunships, four British-made Hawk fighter planes, an AB412 helicopter and two Cassa 212 transporters.

13 May 2001. Robbing Hood
This weekend sees mayoral elections in Masvingo and it has been a violence filled campaign which has left dozens of people beaten. Tuesday's Daily News had a front page picture of a man with human bite marks all over his back, he had been attacked by war veterans.

War veterans raided the huge Danish factory which makes sweets and chewing gum in Harare. Top employees were threatened and some members of management went into hiding. The Danish Prime Minister, Mr Rasmussen, immediately made a protest to the Zimbabwe government. The behaviour of war veterans was 'unacceptable,' he said, immediately suspending all production in the factory and laying off one hundred and fifty Zimbabwean workers.

After last week's attack by war veterans on the Canadian NGO, CARE, and the abduction of a Canadian national to Zanu PF party offices for interrogation, the Canadians have reacted in protest by announcing the suspension of all new development aid to Zimbabwe. In another devastating blow a German charity organization also closed its doors this week. Kinderdorf, an NGO caring for destitute children, was threatened by war veterans and immediately ceased all operations.

With winter already here we can only pray that Mr Grass Hat, Zimbabwe's 'Robbing Hood,' will give some of the money he's extorted to the hundreds of street children sleeping on cardboard boxes, to help them fill their bellies and keep warm in the next few months.

IN THE NEWS

~*25th May 2001* US Secretary of State Colin Powell announces that the debts of 19 African countries have been cancelled; Zimbabwe is not included.

~*26th May 2001* Defence Minister Moven Mahachi dies in a car crash near Nyanga; five other people in the car at the time only sustain minor injuries.

~*31st May 2001* The CFU withdraws all litigation against the government and announces the formation of the Zimbabwe Joint Resettlement Initiative with Z$1 billion offered in aid for resettled people.

2 June 2001. Widespread Whisperings

News of the death of Defence Minister Moven Mahachi in a car crash has sent an already suspicious, superstitious country into turmoil. A series of news bulletins kept reporting the accident in different ways and placing the offending vehicle in different positions. To add to the widespread whisperings, the

Speaker of the House publicly stated that there was no question of foul play having been involved in the Minister's demise. (The statement made people even more suspicious.) Minister Mahachi was declared a National Hero. Our President, visibly shaken, took the opportunity of Mahachi's funeral to swipe at the world. He said how sad it was that Mahachi had not been able to see the land re-distribution in Zimbabwe through to the end. A programme that had seen: 'innumerable hostile obstacles and had been hindered by an unwarranted British campaign.'

In the space of one month, two top Zimbabwean ministers have been killed in car accidents (Border Gezi and Moven Mahachi), a third (Nkosana Moyo) resigned his post and left the country. Now the war veterans' leader, Chenjerai Hitler Hunzvi has been hospitalized, apparently with cerebral malaria. The fate of Hunzvi is still not clear. When whisperings became roars by the end of last week, Hunzvi was suddenly seen on state TV, apparently OK. The next day he was admitted to a top Harare hospital and we have heard no more.

Last year's election results from Marondera East were challenged in the High Court in Harare this week. The Judge had ordered the Registrar General to present all 12 ballot boxes to the court but on Monday only five boxes arrived. Asked where the rest of the ballot boxes were, the lackeys from the Registrar's Office were ordered to drive to Marondera immediately and collect the other seven ballot boxes. All week the nonsense has been going on and there has still not been a satisfactory answer as to why ballots from a neighbouring constituency (headed by none other than war vet leader MP Hunzvi) were found in the Marondera boxes. Eventually everything was re-counted and cross checked and unsurprisingly the results were still in favour of Minister Sekeramayi (Zanu PF) by a margin of only 25 votes.

IN THE NEWS

~*4th June 2001* It is announced that war veteran leader Chenjerai 'Hitler' Hunzvi has died of cerebral malaria.

~*12th June 2001* Fuel prices increase: petrol 74%; diesel 67%; paraffin 69%. Fuel prices have tripled since January 2000.

16 June 2001. I'm as black as he is

Police arrived on Blackfordby Farm on the outskirts of Harare not to assist the legal owner of the property but to arrest him and the farm workers and to protect the illegal squatters and war veterans. After workers on the farm had attacked some of the squatters, the farm owner and thirty workers were arrested. One farm worker, 32-year-old Zondiwa Dumukani, was beaten to death by war veterans with a golf club after being accused of trying to run away from a political meeting on the farm. Witnesses positively identified the four war veterans who beat Zondiwa to death; one of the attackers was a Form three student from a nearby high school.

On a farm in another district, war veterans grabbed the farm manager, surrounded him with hay bales and then set the hay alight; the man is alive but, like so many thousands of others, he will never forget. On another property the farmer was told that if he did not vacate his home he would: 'have his legs beaten until he fell.' On another, the farmer was visited by army men and interrogated: 'which land are you going to give us, we want milk, give us meat,' they said.

On a farm in Chegutu where one hundred people are employed to tend tobacco and soya beans, there was an invasion by eighty people led by four policemen and the District Administrator. The farmer was given seven days to get off his land and out of his house; the farmer did not wait the seven days, he fled immediately. This farm is owned and run by a black Zimbabwean, Philemon Matibe. Mr Matibe was not too scared to speak to the press. He has engaged a lawyer to sue invaders for unlawful occupation and he said to reporters: 'Mugabe says he is taking land from the whites and giving it to blacks. I'm as black as he is. Now he is taking land from some blacks and giving it to the blacks who support him. I've lost everything overnight. Everything I worked for all my life has disappeared.'

The 'Protection from Eviction Bill' was gazetted this week. The Bill prevents squatters and war veterans from being evicted from private property. The Bill also forbids any Court from trying to enforce previously granted eviction orders.

IN THE NEWS

~27th June 2001 Two Roman Catholic Church farms in Gweru are listed for government seizure. The farms are registered to the Bishop of the Diocese of Gweru.

30 June 2001. Statistics don't bleed

The government announced on Wednesday that 180 foreign owned farms had been de-listed. The owners of these farms are signatories to BIPPA (Bilateral Investment Protection Agreements) and will not have their farms compulsorily acquired. A government spokesman said: 'This will help us show the world that we do not break agreements that we would have undertaken to adhere to and that we respect the rule of law.' (sic) What an outrage, allowing foreigners to retain their farms but not third or fourth generation Zimbabweans.

Yesterday's newspaper listed 2,030 properties for seizure, some were repeat listings but there were 1,020 new farms to be compulsorily acquired. The lists ran to 18 broadsheet newspaper pages. Imagine seeing your name in a newspaper with a notice telling you that the government is taking your land, your home, your job, your life's work – just taking it. They might pay you for the house but, very sorry, haven't got any money to pay you for it right now. A friend said this week: 'statistics don't bleed.' These farm acquisition lists may be a statistic for some people for others it's our lives.

IN THE NEWS

~4th/5th July 2001 85% of businesses and workers heed the Zimbabwe Congress of Trade Union's call for a two day national stay-away.

~*6th July 2001* New Chief Justice Chidyausiku says previous Supreme Court rulings against the government's land reform programme were incorrect; four judges in the Supreme Court disagree with the judgment.

~*6th July 2001* Legislation is gazetted barring dual nationality in Zimbabwe.

7 July 2001. Can you hear the drums?

A grandfather phoned me to see if there was anything I could do to help his son, daughter in law and three grandchildren under 10 years old who had been barricaded into their farmhouse by two dozen war veterans. Gates had been smashed down, fires lit on the lawn, dogs cowed into submission and through the night the mob sang, drummed and pelted the roof of the house with rocks to try and chase the family out.

Can you imagine the sheer terror of this? Of being barricaded in your own home, hearing the tremendous noise of things falling on your roof, smelling the smoke of fires right outside your bedroom window, listening to the cries of your young children and being able to do absolutely nothing? Can you imagine your relief when the police do finally arrive and then your despair when less than five minutes later they leave, saying they can do nothing because it is political and will return sometime tomorrow? This is an abomination; the war veterans on our farms are out of control and above the law.

As I write this letter there is another abomination going on a few kilometres from here. A man who has already been assaulted before and had his face on every newspaper around the world, is being held hostage on his own farm. There are more than 60 war veterans involved, people who are being inspired by a man in a grass hat. Less than a year ago the man in the grass hat was employed as a security guard by the Harare municipality, now he wears a three piece suit, drives a brand new Cherokee Jeep and lives in a mansion in an affluent Harare suburb.

Close your eyes for a minute. Can you hear the drums, the rocks hitting the roof, the children crying, can you smell the smoke?

IN THE NEWS

~11th July 2001 Minister of Lands Agriculture and Rural Resettlement, Dr Joseph Made, dismisses the entire board of directors of the Grain Marketing Board (GMB) saying this was necessary to allow his ministry greater control in the operations of the parastatal.

14 July 2001. They came at night

The Marondera farmer who was being held in his own home by armed war veterans last week finally got out on Sunday afternoon. His name is Iain Kay and this was the third very close encounter he has had with war veterans. His wife Kerry later told how farm workers were beaten by war vets in front of the police, how farmers from three districts were on standby to help, how a Priest risked his life to go and pray at the gate of the besieged property, how a woman and her son who work for the Kays did not run away but hid in a linen cupboard while armed men roamed the house. A 'kangaroo court' which eventually led to Iain's release, told the Kays they have 30 days to get off their property and out of their home.

Both Iain and Kerry are determined not to compromise their principles and beliefs. Their faith, courage and patriotism is an inspiration to us all.

Evidence is presently being given in the High Court in Harare by the widow of an MDC man who was murdered last year. These extracts are not for the feint-hearted, they are not sensationalized, they are the truth about what our government has done and condoned under the guise of land redistribution.

Extracts from the Daily News, quoting the horror encountered by the widow of Fainos Zhou at the hands of war veterans:

'They came to my home at night. One of them used a knife to tear apart my petticoat. He forced an iron rod into my private parts. He ordered me to stop crying. They urinated into a container and forced me to drink it. They threatened to force me to eat their stool if I refused.' When Mrs. Zhou was finally able to get away, she and her family searched for her husband Fainos for three days, when she found him he was dead: 'He had wounds all over his body as if he had been assaulted with a hot iron bar.'

Welcome diversion. Tapping on the windows

I find the continual knocking on the windows to be quite unnerving in view of everything that's going on in the country recently. The regular tapping on the window stops every time I approach and starts again a few minutes later. It's not the squeaky, teeth-jarring scraping of a tree branch but more of an insistent, urgent tapping. When I can't bear the not-knowing anymore I retreat to a doorway and stand very still, peeping round the corner. I don't have to wait long. A ground-scraper Thrush hops up onto the windowsill, tips its head to one side and then the other and then starts tapping. Eight or ten repetitions at a time the bird knocks on the window with its beak, keeping it up for over ten minutes. As soon as I step into view the bird takes fright and flies away but doesn't go far. While I watch from the window the Thrush seems to be waiting for me to go away. It puts its head down, runs a few quick steps on the lawn and then looks up, flicks its wing and waits. At first I assumed the knocking on the window was some sort of territorial or breeding behaviour; the bird seeing itself in the window and attacking the challenger that is its own reflection. When I got a closer look however, I can see that the Thrush has a distinct yellow gape flange on its beak indicating that it's still a youngster. How it doesn't do some damage to itself with the continual banging against the window is a mystery but as soon as I go out of view the ground-scraper Thrush with its black earrings and speckled chest returns and starts knocking all over again.

IN THE NEWS

~*18th July 2001* The government bans private trade in maize and wheat, declaring them to be 'strategic commodities.'

21 July 2001. Asking for another five months

Horrors engulfed the Odzi farming area this week. A farmer ran over and killed a land invader on the road near his farm. Apparently both sides of the road were crowded with squatters, there was an approaching petrol tanker and the man ran out into the road in front of the farmer's vehicle. The farmer, Phillip Bezuidenhout, said because there were so many squatters around he felt he shouldn't stop so he went to the nearest police station, reported the incident and was taken into police custody. The war veterans and squatters immediately said it had been a deliberate, cold blooded murder and went on the rampage. They broke into Mr Bezuidenhout's home, looted valuables and trashed the house. Reinforcement war veterans arrived from Harare, went to two neighbouring farms, broke in and looted them too.

War veterans' leaders announced that all whites within a twenty kilometre radius should vacate their properties within 24 hours or would have to bear the consequences. Neither the police nor Mr Bezuidenhout's lawyer were allowed to go and collect statements or evidence; a police spokesman said they had been warned to keep away by the war veterans. The leaders of the war veterans' made increasingly inflammatory statements with each passing day, ordering all farmers on designated properties all over the country to vacate, threatening retribution. Many farmers in the Odzi area evacuated their properties after reports of gangs of men in trucks driving around the area threatening retribution. When Mr Bezuidenhout appeared in the Mutare Magistrates Court, he was alone, his lawyer had been warned by police to stay away as the war veterans were incensed that a black man was representing a white farmer. Police said they could not guarantee the safety of the lawyer and so the farmer, in handcuffs and leg irons, appeared alone.

The incident has raised numerous questions, uppermost being the identity of the squatter. Looking at his newly acquired piece of land that had been allocated to him by war veterans, the squatter was a 31-yearold accountant, a Finance Manager with the Mutare Board and Paper Company. The 'settler farmer,' as he is being called by the state press, was not a landless peasant and was too young to have been a war veteran; he was gainfully employed, earning a better than average salary and living in a city. Why had he been allocated a piece of land?

Last year our Supreme Court ordered the government to stop acquiring land for resettlement by the 1st of July 2001. The Supreme Court also ordered the government to come up with a workable land reform plan and re-establish law and order on farms. This has not happened. This week the government submitted papers to the Supreme Court applying for an interdict to the ruling. The government has requested an extension of the date to stop grabbing land from the 1st of July to the 30th of November 2001. The government wants to keep on grabbing land for another five months.

IN THE NEWS

~26th July 2001 Government suspends the accreditation of BBC journalists working in the country. Information minister, Jonathan Moyo, accuses the BBC of 'deliberate distortions.'

28 July 2001. Locked in a container

A man was in his farmhouse with his 78-year-old mother last Saturday when a mob of youngsters arrived and told him he had thirty minutes to get out of his house or they would kill him. The man refused and called the police but while he was waiting for them, the mob broke down his fence and camped out all over his garden. They lit fires, sang, shouted, drummed and beat tins. When the police arrived, unbelievably they told the rabble they could stay in the garden but they must retract the death threat. The man and his elderly mother were held prisoners in their own home from Saturday lunch time until Thursday evening. The mob outside took turns to keep the noise going: all day and all night, banging on doors, rattling windows. The tactic was simply to wear the farmer down until he walked out of his own home. It is now crystal clear that this is not about land, it is simply a case of we want what you've got.

In another farm siege situation in Marondera, a mob rampaged through the workers' village destroying property, beating people and then burning what was left. In a heart-breaking account, a 52-year-old woman working on the farm said: 'I was told not to remove anything from the house. So I just watched helplessly as the war veterans burnt down my three huts, including everything that was inside.'

Farmers are not alone in this insanity. By-elections are being held this weekend in Bindura and MDC leader Morgan Tsvangirai's convoy of vehicles was attacked by youths as it approached the town for a political rally. A number of shots were fired, one vehicle was burnt and press pictures showed men dripping blood after having been assaulted by stone throwing thugs. The Bindura police refused to provide an escort for Mr Tsvangirai, even after the attack.

A human rights organization in Zimbabwe this week released partial court testimony given by Philip Marufu in Mount Darwin, a victim of last year's political violence.

'Marufu was abducted by Zanu PF supporters before the elections. He was kept in a container, which is a long iron box without windows that ships use to carry cargo. He was kept in the container all day, which was locked from the outside. It had no toilet. His 12-year-old son was abducted by the same perpetrators a week later and was locked in the same container with his father. He witnessed his father being beaten, verbally abused, threatened, kicked and hit with hard objects. The boy also received verbal abuse and threats from the perpetrators. He said the perpetrators bought their girlfriends to the container and had sexual intercourse with them while he and his father tried to sleep.'

Welcome diversion. Tail-light night visitor

Repeated high pitched screams in the middle of the night woke me. As soon as I was sure it wasn't coming from Richie's room I sat listening to what was an unexpected noise in an urban area. There was a thump as something jumped onto the roof, followed by thuds, rustles, creaks and bumps from a night visitor running overhead. The next morning the leftovers and wrappings from the midnight feast lay in the sand. Still damp and slightly sticky pink pips from an unknown fruit had been dropped from the branch of a nearby tree.

Little chips of tough avocado pear skins littered the ground and clearly visible teeth marks were scratched into the skin of a half-eaten avocado. I still didn't know who my night visitor was but had a pretty good idea which I confirmed a few nights later.

At about eight in the evening the screaming started in the distance and not long afterwards came the thumps and bumps on the roof. It was very cold and dark outside, there was no moon and the stars were spectacularly bright thanks to the lack of light pollution due to yet another electricity cut. Sweeping the torch beam slowly around the garden, the avocado tree revealed the bright, tail-light eyes and small rounded ears of the night visitor. The small primate covered in beige fur with an extraordinarily long, fluffed out tail, sat perfectly still with its arms around a branch of the avocado tree. The Night Ape's eyes were bright orange in the torch light and for a minute or two it stared straight at me before slowly climbing up the branch and out of sight. In the nights that followed the Pookie came back frequently, using its lofty track from trees and walls to roofs and fruit trees, never needing to ever set foot on the ground.

IN THE NEWS

~30th July 2001 Government awards $1 billion in unbudgeted funds to war veterans in a 25% increment of their tax free monthly gratuities, backdated to January 2001. Prior to the increment each of the 55,000 war veterans was earning $5,500 per month.

~*1st August 2001* Michael Gillespie, who has been a High Court judge for the past five years, tenders his resignation to President Mugabe.

~*2nd August 2001* The Zimbabwe Democracy and Economic Recovery Bill, which imposes some sanctions on individuals in Zimbabwe, is passed by the United States Senate.

4 August 2001. Burning plastic

The Zimbabwe Human Rights NGO Forum has released a report on human rights abuses committed prior to last year's election. It gives personal statements, names, places and the most horrific details of torture, murder and rape. It tells of torture centres and re-education camps, of locked rooms with barred windows. It names both the victims and the perpetrators and many of the latter are men now sitting in our Parliament As I sit here on this beautiful spring morning in Zimbabwe, I cannot believe the horrors that have gone on, and are still going on in the name of land re-distribution. The 77 cases reported in the document are not of whites or of farmers but of ordinary men and women who have dared to stand up for democracy, dared to suggest that they no longer want to be ruled by a one party state.

One of the reports read: '3rd June 2000: They made us lie down. They took ropes and tied our hands and legs and they started assaulting us. They were beating us with sjamboks. At around 7.00pm, they took us to their base at Texas farm. They made a fire and began assaulting us using fire. First it was my friend BM. They tied plastic around his hands and legs and then lit it. Next it was my turn. They beat me first. Then they used all the same tactics, wrapping my legs, hands and private parts and lighting the plastics. They also lit some plastic and then dropped it on us as it melted. They were taking hot ashes and spreading them on my body. I have burns all over my back, front, buttocks, private parts, thighs and legs.'

This is just one statement from 46 pages. Others tell of horrific sexual abuses, of the use of electricity, water, whips, batons, bicycle chains and iron bars to inflict beatings on people suspected of not supporting Zanu PF. The people committing these crimes are not in prison, they are still out there, still being paid to kill and maim us. If you are white and speak out you are called a racist and a colonialist but regardless of the name-calling, these abominations are being committed by black people against black, white and brown people.

This week particularly I have questioned my place and my role in this country but then I turn in my chair and look at the collage of family photos that hangs on my wall. My mother, father and stepfather all fought for freedom and democracy in Zimbabwe twenty years ago. They gave me these feelings of patriotism, these beliefs in right and wrong, they taught me to stand up for what is right. As I write, three children are lying on the carpet watching cartoons, one is white, two are black. It starts there: racial harmony, goodness and honesty, morals and principles all start there. They do not notice that their skins have different hues, they are children together and every Zimbabwean owes it to them to fight this evil.

IN THE NEWS

~10th August 2001 A red $500 bank note is issued and becomes known as the 'Ferrari' due to its rapid acceleration out of the pocket due to soaring inflation currently at 76%.

11 August 2001. Baying for blood

All hell has broken loose. Last Friday night war veterans cut telephone lines and broke into the Kwekwe farmhouse of 76-year-old widower Ken Corbett. They attacked him with an axe. Mr Corbett suffered severe brain damage and died. On Monday, a group of forty war veterans stormed the homestead of a Chinhoyi farmer. When they attempted to break the door down to get inside, the farmer, Mr Barklay, called for help from neighbours and police on the farm radio. A group of farmers arrived to help, pushing their way through the mob. A tussle ensued between farmers and thugs resulting in minor injuries on both sides. The police arrived and ordered all the farmers to go and report the incident at the station. Seventeen did so and were all arrested. None of the war veterans were arrested or detained.

The following morning another group of farmers went to the Police station to ascertain the condition of their colleagues; they too were arrested. (23 now in custody) A 76-year-old doctor, his son and three of the farmers' wives went to the police station to offer medical support and blankets to the incarcerated men. The doctor was attacked at the police station gate, in front of uniformed police officers, by thugs wielding a bicycle chain. The doctor's glasses were smashed and he sustained severe internal and external damage to his eye. Police in the Charge Office refused to accept a Report of Assault and refused to provide a Medical Report Form. The Charge Office then filled up with thugs and two of the farmers wives were pushed and shoved. When the women decided their lives were in danger and fled the Charge Office they found that the tyres on their vehicles had been deflated; they managed to get to safety in Chinhoyi town.

Later that day mobs of thugs went on the rampage through Chinhoyi town, targeting white people. There were more than a dozen incidents including: a 72-year-old woman assaulted whilst standing in a queue in the post office; a 45-year-old man chased down the street, kicked, beaten, punched and stabbed: he needed twenty stitches. A 50-year-old man was beaten and whipped with sticks and truncheons. A woman in her forties was punched in the face as she left the police station where she had been completing a vehicle registration formality.

The 23 farmers appeared in the Chinhoyi Magistrates Court on Wednesday on charges of public violence. One farmer collapsed in the dock and was taken to hospital, another was discharged but further proceedings were adjourned as mobs chanted outside and the Magistrate remanded the remaining 21 men in custody. On Thursday the 21 farmers again appeared in court, they were denied bail and remanded in custody. A senior Police spokesman said: 'There is no enough manpower to secure their safety.' (sic)

On Thursday violence spread to farms in Chinhoyi and other areas. A farmer, his wife, their teenage daughter and nine month old baby were barricaded into the farmhouse by thugs.

Seven hours later this farmer and 19 others in the area fled their properties. Thugs proceeded to break into a number of these homes and loaded up furniture and personal belongings. Official estimates say as many as 10,000 farm workers and their dependants have been displaced because of the lootings and evacuations. On Friday violence and looting spread to neighbouring farming areas of Mhangura and Doma and a number of farmers have evacuated their properties fearing for their own safety.

On Friday, the 21 Chinhoyi farmers appeared in front of the Magistrate again. They were again remanded in custody until the 24th of August. Today is a public holiday known as Heroes Day when liberation war heroes are honoured.

IN THE NEWS

~*17th August 2001* Following a SADC summit in Malawi, Swaziland's King Mswati III says: 'We have already appointed three heads of state to deal with Mugabe on the land grab issue. We felt that what our colleague is doing was beyond the premises of democracy, and he has to be stopped.'

18 August 2001. The Litany bird

I sat outside last night watching the most beautiful African sunset. The sun was a huge red ball, the sky a kaleidoscope of beige and orange, purple and grey. A V formation of birds flew overhead and the nightjar started calling for its mate, a call which for so many of us is synonymous with Africa. The nightjar is called the Litany Bird and its call is: 'Good Lord Deliver Us,' particularly apt in Zimbabwe.

I tried, just for a few precious minutes, not to think about the 21 farmers (now with shaven heads) still in prison; I tried not to think about the looted and destroyed homes on 53 farms in Chinhoyi, Doma and Mhangura. I tried not to think about four top journalists who have been arrested for reporting on the farm lootings and face charges of sedition; I tried not to think about the 8,000 farm workers left homeless and destitute after last weekend's insanity, or of the 2,200 farm workers near me who are now living in tobacco barns and workshops after being evicted from their homes by war veterans. Just for a few minutes I let the peace and breathtaking beauty of an African sunset revive me and sweep away the despair that has become a part of our lives.

In his speech on Heroes Day President Mugabe did not condemn the violence or order the police to enforce the law. Instead he said land reform would continue at a faster pace. He said that war veterans and 'settlers' on farms 'would not be provoked.' As the President spoke hundreds of people were on the rampage in the countryside. Eyewitness reports told of farm workers being pulled out of their homes, beaten with thorn encrusted branches and ordered to load their employers' belongings onto stolen tractors and trailers. In what can only be described as a frenzied orgy, homes have been completely trashed, lives destroyed and even pets whipped so severely that they have had to be put to sleep. Eyewitnesses told of electronic equipment being thrown in swimming pools, ceilings chopped down, door and window frames smashed out of walls. One heart-breaking letter from a woman returning to her trashed home said all that remained of her life was a photograph of her father-in – law, a serviette ring and the pellet ridden corpse of her cat.

As I write 21 farmers are still in jail. Their passports have been taken away and requests for bail have been twice postponed. The 21 men are being treated like convicted criminals before their case has even been heard. 12 of the 21 farmers are in prison because they went to the Police station to find out about their colleagues. Three policemen who allowed blankets to be given to the farmers in prison cells have been suspended and 'disciplined.'

The CFU in Harare published details of support for affected farmers and their workers. This consists of financial help for farmers and their workers, assistance with school fees and provision of basics such as blankets, pots and pans and food. The CFU have teams of social workers, psychologists, counsellors and lawyers on hand as well as offers of accommodation for displaced people and animals.

IN THE NEWS

~*20th August 2001* South African Airways stops accepting payments in Zimbabwean dollars saying it has accumulated Z$1 billion which it has been unable to repatriate to South Africa. Passengers are now expected to pay for tickets in foreign currency.

~*22nd August 2001* Twenty thousand farm workers and their families are evicted from their homes in Wedza by war veterans and are camped out by the side of the road.

Are you serious? Please come back to prison

'Zimbabwean police appealed on Monday to 16 serious criminals who were mistakenly released from custody to return to jail and finish serving their sentences 'for the good of society'. The 16 felons were erroneously freed on August 11, two days after President Robert Mugabe granted amnesty to 3,000 of the country's 22,500 convicted inmates in a bid to reduce overcrowding in prisons. The 16 inmates freed mistakenly from Karoi Prison, were serving lengthy terms for housebreaking and theft. 'The error was only discovered five days later,' said police spokesperson Andrew Phiri, who appealed to the criminals 'to be honest and return to prison where they belong, for the good of society.' (AP)

25 August 2001. Selective Justice

Farmers countrywide continue to watch helplessly as huge swathes of grazing land have been deliberately burnt as war veterans resort to desperate tactics to chase people off their land. In every direction the sky is filled with smoke. On almost every road the verges are ash filled and the fields beyond are blackened. There is very little grazing left and livestock farmers are desperate. Foot and Mouth disease broke out on six properties this week. All livestock movement has since been restricted, all beef exports cancelled and this has dealt another crippling blow to our economy. Agriculture Minister Joseph Made announced the disease had broken out saying domestic cattle had probably come into contact with buffalo. He did not acknowledge that for eighteen months war veterans have destroyed fences, prevented patrols and driven livestock onto private property with absolutely no regard for disease control.

Speaking to a veterinary inspector recently he told me the situation was desperate. He has been unable to do his job for almost two years. When he arrives on a farm to inspect livestock, war veterans throw stones at his vehicle, chase him away and hurl abuse at him, saying he is not wanted as he is a 'sell out.' This man, an educated professional, employed by the government told me that he has been unable to go to his rural home for over a year as he and his family have been threatened by war veterans.

People calling themselves war veterans went on the rampage in the little town around the world famous Victoria Falls this week. They raided shops and supermarkets before closing the border post down for an hour. When the Vic Falls Zanu PF Mayor protested he too became a victim. War veterans stormed his premises, broke up a meeting, frog marched him and four others through the town, lashing at them with sticks and kicking them as they walked. Last weekend war veterans broke up a gathering of 3,000 Methodist women and chased them away from their church. War veterans stormed a mining auction this week, broke up proceedings and chanted: 'down with whites, down with the MDC, down with Agribank, down with AFC.'

Everyone in Zimbabwe has become a victim, few have escaped the attentions of these past liberators; it becomes more and more apparent that all control is lost. The 21 farmers from Chinhoyi were finally granted outrageously high bail of $100,000 each and released; they have had their passports seized and been banned by the Court from going back to their homes.

IN THE NEWS

~28th August 2001 War veteran Joseph Chinotimba threatens to close the Financial Gazette, Daily News and Zimbabwe Independent for writing negative stories about war veterans and President Mugabe.

1 September 2001. Blood Money

There is a litany of horror taking place all over Zimbabwe. Foot and Mouth disease has spread to Beitbridge and there are now ten infected properties. Despite repeated appeals by veterinary officials and attempts to control the movement of livestock, this highly contagious disease means nothing to the people calling themselves war veterans. An eyewitness on a farm outside Bulawayo described how war veterans moved cattle from a village onto a cattle ranch and instructed the farmer to remove his 1,000 head of cattle saying it was now their farm. When the owner refused, the war veterans herded the farmer's cattle onto the road, demanding the animals be taken away. When the owner said there were veterinary controls preventing livestock movement, the war veterans said 'none of those stupid factors' concerned them. With this mentality the disease is sure to spread and destroy the beef industry as well as killing the animals which rural peasants depend on for milk, to plough their fields and feed their families. Meanwhile government officials continue to make statements blaming whites for deliberating starting the disease by forcibly herding buffalo into cattle farms in order to destroy the country.

On another farm near Bulawayo a war veteran arrived in a red Jaguar and informed the owner that he was taking over the farm and that all workers and equipment should be removed by the weekend or he would burn them out. On a safari property war veterans arrive at the weekends in luxury four wheel drive vehicles and shoot sable; on another property 22 giraffe have died in snares and on a huge ostrich farm the owner and his workers have been evicted, the birds are dying of neglect and there is absolutely nothing that can be done; the police will not attend saying: 'It is political.'

On a farm in Norton a military truck arrived with armed, uniformed men who assaulted workers with whips and sticks and when they got tired, forced the farm foreman to continue the beatings. Last year's Tobacco Grower of the Year had his tobacco seed bed pipes destroyed, hydrants sabotaged and was ordered to stop his tractors and halt production. As a result he has had to lay off his workers. On a farm in Selous last year's Cattleman of the Year has been ordered to remove all his cattle from his farm and war veterans have moved their cattle and goats into his fields. On farms in Marondera, Wedza and Raffingora farm workers are being rounded up after dark and forced to attend all night political re-education meetings where they are made to sing, chant, march, shout slogans and denounce opposition political parties. Farm workers evicted by war veterans from their homes in Wedza remain in hiding in the bush and are absolutely destitute. Official estimates are that as many as 70,000 farmers, workers and their dependants have been evicted from their homes in the past fortnight.

Villagers and families in Epworth, Mount Darwin and Muzarabani have been evicted from their rural homes, accused of being supporters of opposition political parties. They have lost their grain, goats, chickens, clothes and belongings and had their homes burnt to the ground. They have been beaten, kicked, whipped and warned not to speak out. Earlier this week two young men sat in a Zimbabwean prison accused of political violence. One was an epileptic but his jailers refused him access to his medication. His friend in the same cell begged the guards for help, his friend was having repeated seizures; the guards said, 'monitor him, we will see in the morning.' The fits escalated and the man died, watched by his friend. The guards did not come and the man lay next to the corpse of his friend until the next morning.

This week details emerged of a deal between the governments of Zimbabwe and the Congo. Thirty three million hectares of indigenous trees are to be felled in one of Africa's biggest rain forests in the DRC and sold in Asia and France. Zimbabwe will share the profits as compensation for participation in the war in the DRC. The environment will be destroyed to compensate our dead Zimbabwean soldiers. Will the relatives of these dead youngsters see a single dollar of this blood money?

IN THE NEWS

~*7th September 2001* The Abuja agreement is signed in Nigeria. It states there will be 'no further occupation of farms' and 'on undesignated farms, occupiers will be moved to legally acquired land.' The Abuja Agreement says there is 'a commitment to restore the rule of law to the process of land reform.'

~*11th September 2001* 2,996 people are killed after hijacked planes are crashed into the World Trade Centre's Twin Towers in New York, the Pentagon in Virginia and in rural Pennsylvania.

22 September 2001. Mock funeral

In the last few days three truckloads of war veterans and youths arrived on Bita Farm in Wedza. Two men fell off the back of one of the vehicles and died when they were run over by another truck. The farm owner, 70-year-old John Bibby, had heard the vehicles approaching and he and his wife locked themselves into the farmhouse. The first John Bibby knew of the deaths was when war veterans and police arrived at the gate and told Mr Bibby to accompany them to the farm workers' village. Mr Bibby did so and then he and seventeen of his workers were arrested and taken into police custody. Mr Bibby was charged on two counts of murder by a Marondera magistrate. When journalists from the Daily News went to Bita Farm, three reporters and a cameraman were attacked by war veterans with poles and chains. They ran for their lives, hid in the bush and were only rescued eight hours later. Whilst the journalists were being brutally attacked, the Assistant Commissioner of Police agreed that he was actually on the property at the time but said: 'I don't have any comment on that issue. I think they are confusing me with someone else.' Part of Bita Farm falls in the Chikomba parliamentary constituency where a by-election is being held this weekend to fill the seat left vacant after the death of Chenjerai Hunzvi.

On a farm south of Harare this week, a couple were barricaded into their home by war veterans. No one has been allowed in or out the farm which has not been listed for government seizure. The farmer's wife described how two boxes in the shape of coffins were placed outside the house and decorated with flowers in the shape of crosses. 'They had a mock funeral for us today and they say the boxes are for my husband and myself.'

On a farm in Karoi an American tourist was attacked and beaten by war veterans. A newspaper report from the same area read: 'The Karoi officer in charge for the CIO is now the proud owner of the farmhouse and a plot at Nyamambizi farm which was left by Sven Johnson who abandoned it at the peak of the farm invasions last year.'

All these incidents have taken place since the Abuja Agreement was reached in Nigeria. Minister of Agriculture, Dr Joseph Made said: 'Commercial farmers are on a blitz to undermine the Abuja Agreement by saying all kinds of lies.'

Welcome diversion. Blue headed monster

It seems like days since the blue-headed monster's been able to come down from the tree.

Day after day it sits on the trunk of the Musasa, nodding its head, every move watched intently by the dogs who sit patiently waiting for the chance to get it. He's a very handsome creature, particularly at this time of year and his head seems to be getting bluer by the day. This particular blue headed tree Agama seems to patrol a territory of about twenty metres, running across the ground between two big trees and that's when the dogs try and get him. He's got a spreading, bulging belly, orange tail, greenish yellow spots down his back and long, thin, clawed toes. But it's his head which is the showpiece. Distinctly triangular shaped, the Agama's head is a deep, sky blue with puffed out spiked blue cheeks. He's not awfully swift on the ground but puts up a real fight if he gets cornered, hissing and huffing and displaying a wide open mouth which is bright orange inside. Apparently he can give a nasty bite too but I'm not going to put that to the test.

After a few scorchingly hot days I put a little pottery bowl on the ground at the base of the Musasa tree intending it for the little birds and couldn't believe it when the Agama came nodding down the tree and stopped at the bowl. With no dogs in sight the Agama stood up on its back legs, gripped the edge of the bowl with its front feet. Using its tail to support its body weight, the Agama bent over and drank from the bowl. I ran for my camera, sure it would have gone by the time I returned but it was still there and stayed for another ten minutes, while the dogs snored at my feet and I took pictures out the window.

IN THE NEWS

~*22nd Sept 2001* A week into legal and constitutional arguments against the government over land seizures, the CFU halts proceedings in the Supreme Court saying they wish to engage in dialogue with the government.

~*25th September 2001* The IMF cuts off Zimbabwe, saying it is ineligible for loans because it fell into arrears in February and owes the IMF US$53 million.

29 September 2001. Who is fooling who?

Since the Abuja Agreement the CFU say 900 farms are unable to operate. In Chinhoyi dogs have been poisoned and war veterans are demanding rent from farm workers. In Karoi, police refused to sign affidavits from a local clinic stating that farm workers had been beaten by war veterans. In Norton army personnel forced farm workers to extinguish a bush fire using their bare hands and feet. In Marondera farm workers have been forced out of their homes. In Beatrice army trucks are loading and removing gum poles from a farm and an Arabian stallion was shot with a bow and arrow and died. In Somabhula cattle were driven onto a railway line, three were killed by a train and a fourth so badly injured it had to be destroyed. It seems that as long as police do not officially acknowledge the crimes then they are not in fact happening. Who is fooling who?

The Zimbabwe Independent reported this week that war veterans are calling for a 300% increase in their monthly pensions and demanding that they be given seed maize, fertilizer and Title Deeds for the farms they have invaded. The demands raise the burning issue of Title Deeds and future land ownership. Will these seized farms be in the same category as communal land where no individuals have Title Deeds? It's a situation where borrowing can't be undertaken because there is no collateral and improvements are minimal due to insecurity of tenure.

IN THE NEWS

~3rd October 2001 The Supreme Court with three newly appointed judges makes an interim ruling allowing the government to carry on seizing white farms. Chief Justice Chidyausiku says the court had overturned a ruling by his predecessor Chief Justice Gubbay who resigned in March after being threatened with violence by Zanu PF supporters.

~7th October 2001 The USA invades Afghanistan with participation from other nations.

7 October 2001. You may not grow food

For two days I've been travelling around meeting farmers and listening to stories that defy all reason. I cannot believe some of the things that I've seen out on those bumpy, dusty roads that lead to the farms where all our food is grown. About twenty metres from one farmers' garden gate is the war vets camp. A few rough branches have been hacked off nearby trees; tall, scraggly thatching grass has been leant up against them and in this hovel the squatters live, making their statement to the farmer that they have claimed his land. In another collapsing lean-to is a bush latrine and sitting around are half a dozen surly, grimy, bored looking individuals.

These people are the only law on this farm. They decide which fields the farmer can plough and plant and where he can graze his cattle. The road leading to the farmlands is covered in tyre tracks because every night vehicles drive in and out, loaded with men, snares and spotlights. Every night they drive around this private property hunting animals that have survived the fires. Every night the farmer lies in bed, hears the vehicles, sees the dust swirling in sweeping spotlights but he can do nothing. In the land are the ploughed and ridged tobacco fields which the occupiers said the farmer could plant. One day after he started planting the tobacco seedlings, they changed their minds, erected a crude hut on the newly turned red soil and said the farmer couldn't plant any more.

On another farm a young couple show me into their sparsely furnished farmhouse. For months they have lived with the bare minimum of their possessions in case they are suddenly evicted; in case squatters become looters. They describe how their home was recently assessed by two young government valuators. These men arrived with two of the farm squatters saying they had come to value the house so that compensation could be paid when the farmers are evicted. The owners would not let the two squatters in, only the government valuators. They measured the outside perimeter of the house and counted door and window frames. They asked which rooms had ceramic tiles on the walls, how many fitted cupboards, geysers, toilets and baths there were. They did not measure the length or height of the perimeter security fence and gates. They did not measure or record burglar bars, electrical sockets, mains boards, pelmets, curtain rails, ceilings or taps. They did not look at the roof or its timbers, did not record guttering, wiring, plumbing, underground piping. How deep is the swimming pool, they asked? They did not look at the tiles, paving or filters. When they left, the valuators did not give the farmer a copy of their notes which they had recorded on a scrap of paper. That night the two valuators slept in a house with the war veterans who are squatting on the farm.

Everywhere in the area there is fire, smoke and ash. Beautiful flocks of Boer goats pick through blackened fields looking for a blade of green grass. Cattle are desperately thin, every rib visible and they stand huddled in small, dusty paddocks because war veterans will not let farmers put the animals out to graze. A call comes in on the radio, a fire has been started in hay bales meant to support starving cattle. In a few minutes Z$400,000 of feed is reduced to ash and blows away in the wind. Everywhere there are war veterans' huts, not being lived in, not surrounded by ploughed fields; they just stand derelict, a statement to Zimbabwe: this is our land and you may not grow food on it.

Are you serious? Sex immobilizers

'A Zimbabwean healer came up with the idea of using a technique which involves magically 'locking' women and immobilizing men, to bar them from having extra-marital sex, alongside condoms and abstinence, because the latter only have a limited impact on stemming the spread of AIDS in Zimbabwe. Chikede's proposed technique uses traditional herbs to cast a spell which can be administered by a healer even in the absence of the subject. It has become popularly known in Zimbabwe as the 'central locking system,' or 'immobilizer.' When applied, the spell is supposed to ensure that one cannot have sex outside marriage.' (The Herald)

13 October 2001. Plunged over the edge

Night after night America bombs Afghanistan in its fight against world terrorism and while it does so Zimbabwe's terror increases while no one is watching. The only difference is that our terror is not being inflicted by men in bunkers but by our own government.

This week the economy was plunged over the edge when the government announced price controls on a dozen basic commodities and slashed their prices, in some cases by as much as 50%. The affected products include bread, sugar, flour, milk, maize meal, cooking oil, margarine, salt and meat. Government said they had introduced the controls because consumers could no longer afford these basics. They did not address the root cause of the problem which is farm invasions and war veterans. Ironically, it was war veterans who demanded the price cuts, threatening unspecified action if they were not implemented.

In local supermarkets the shelves holding controlled products emptied rapidly. In Mvuma, Karoi, Murehwa and Kadoma war veterans ordered shopkeepers to put their prices down. Retailers who were not prepared to sell their stocks at less than they paid for them closed their doors but then riot police moved in and forced them to open. The Master Bakers Association did not bake any bread at all, refusing to sell their product at a loss. Newspaper headlines yesterday summarized the chaos: 'Shops forced to close over prices.' 'No Bread.' 'Controls trigger shortages.' 'Police step in to quell demonstrations.'

IN THE NEWS

~*17th October 2001* Bakers are losing $ 1.8 million a day and the CZI President says: 'It's not possible to produce bread at $52 and sell it at $48.'

~*October 2001* Inflation rises to 97% during the month.

3 November 2001. Children are being raped

This week a US Court ruled that Zanu PF was liable for murdering and torturing political opponents in the run up to last year's parliamentary elections. In his ruling Judge Marrero said: 'The prevailing trend teaches that the day comes to pass when those who violate their public trust are called upon, in this world, to render account for the wrongs they inflict on innocents.' Two of the five Zimbabweans who initiated the case spoke after the ruling. One said: 'This decision lets Mugabe and his henchmen know that the civilized world will not allow their political terror to go unpunished.' The other said: 'at least I can tell my children I did everything in my power.'

Meanwhile in Kadoma and Gweru teachers and students are being forced to attend Zanu PF rallies and chant political slogans. One teacher said of the perpetrators: 'They are armed and the police are doing nothing. There are no normal lessons going on in Vutika secondary school.' Seven schools have been closed and scores of teachers have fled. Assistant police Commissioner Bvuidzijena declined to comment saying he was busy.

Finance Minister Makoni in his budget presentation said that 75% of the population is living in abject poverty. He said the economy was set to shrink by a further 7.3% in the coming year and called the situation 'perilous.' Minister Makoni said there was a 'shortage of teaching and learning materials... high levels of emigration which are robbing the country of badly needed skilled personnel ...revenue sources such as taxes are declining ... substantial deterioration in the balance of payments and a build-up of external payment arrears.' Makoni said the country's economy had a negative growth rate in all sectors except mining, finance and insurance. The next day we laughed at the Budget Supplement in the Herald, thinking the printers had inserted the graphs upside down. Then we realized, the graphs weren't upside down, they were showing our negative growth.

IN THE NEWS

~9th November 2001 Daily News founder Geoff Nyarota and editor in chief Wilf Mbanga are arrested and charged with fraud and violating investment laws.

10 November 2001. Burned on the soles of their feet

As I write this letter all the presenters on ZBC's Radio One are saying goodbye to their listeners. The government has declared that Radio One, the only easy listening and news station will close down next Thursday and be changed into a sports channel. This is almost the final step in our government's programme of silencing the media.

This week I am haunted by the photographs of a 27-year-old man's feet. He had been accused of supporting the MDC and burned on the soles of his feet with heated iron bars by men calling themselves war veterans. This man is one of dozens to have been tortured in the same way; the wounds are massive, purple and suppurating; the look on the man's face is of pure agony. The perpetrators have been identified and are known to the police who have not made any arrests.

Forty marauding war veterans went on the rampage through three farms just outside Marondera one evening this week. Farm workers, their wives and children were ordered by war veterans to vacate their homes. When they did not come out, the veterans' smashed all the windows, broke down the doors and pulled people out screaming and kicking. They chased everyone out, ordering them to leave. Anyone who could not run fast enough was beaten by men with sticks, knobkerries, chains and stones. A five year old child could not run fast enough and was whipped across his face by men with sticks. The attackers are known to the local police, none have been arrested, they all reside in shacks on invaded farms in the area. The child's forehead, cheek and upper lip are swollen and lacerated. Seeping wounds ooze under his nose, his upper lip is enormously swollen. In his mother's arms, this five year old boy in his little blue and green checked shirt, dried blood caked on the collar, could be your son or mine. His eyes show fear and exhaustion, confusion and pain.

If I didn't know better I would say the look in the child's eyes is the same look I have seen a dozen times this week in the eyes of all the people I have spoken to: a look of despair and resignation. A look I saw on a nurse's face who has not had disposable gloves to wear at work for over two months. A look I saw on a newly redundant businessman's face; on the face of a man who was approached by a terrified farm worker who had only eaten roots and insects for four days and was hiding in the bush with his family after being evicted from his home by war veterans. It is the look I saw on the face of a middle aged farmer who had been ordered to vacate his home by war veterans and he was trying to decide what to do with a lifetime's work and possessions.

IN THE NEWS

~15th November 2001 Inflation rises to 97.9% during the month.

17 November 2001. Bruised and terrified

According to the WFP, the UN and Oxfam, one million Zimbabweans will be in urgent need of food aid within the next month. Our government, having acknowledged the crisis, has banned all foreign aid agencies from distributing humanitarian food aid. Our Minister of Information said: 'We will not allow strangers to roam around our country interfering.' He said foreign aid agencies were: 'planning to smuggle election monitors into Zimbabwe using the guise of food aid to de-campaign the present government.'

To compound this imminent crisis is the devastating announcement this week that, using the Presidential Powers Act, the Land Acquisition Act has again been amended. Farmers who have been served with a Section 8 letter informing them of the seizure of their land, have been told to immediately cease all farming operations and have 90 days to get off their farms and out of their homes. The starvation we face now will be compounded a hundred fold in 2002 and 2003.

The CFU have described the amendment as 'potentially devastating' and have estimated that 85% of farmers are affected. In a telephone interview with South African television this week, our Minister of Agriculture, Dr Joseph Made clarified the position on the payment of compensation to farmers evicted from their properties. Again he said that it was up to the British to pay for the land. He said that the Zimbabwe government would pay for 'improvements' (buildings, fencing, dams, etc) but could only afford to pay 25% now and the balance over 5 years. Worse though, Dr Made has now classified the payment as being only for improvements that were 'required' or 'relevant.' Asked by the interviewer what a farmer should do if the government did not find a specific improvement to be 'relevant,' Dr Made said the farmer should 'dismantle and remove it.'

While farmers were trying to decide what to do next, the country witnessed burning, looting and beating in Bulawayo. An abducted war veteran was found murdered. Two terrified young men stood in front of a ZBC TV camera and 'confessed' but there was a huge wave of arrests. As I write more than sixteen people are in police cells, all are active members of the MDC, one is an MP. Many have been denied their rights to legal counsel, held for more than 48 hours without being charged and all have been denied bail.

War veterans across the country have denounced the murder of their compatriot and police have stood by and watched as government supporters have burnt down houses, looted property and beaten people. Images this morning showed a man who had been whipped on his arms, hands, back, legs and feet. The look in the man's eyes is of utter desperation, he has no one to turn to for help. Neither has a Magistrate in Gokwe who this week convicted two government supporters to eight months in prison after finding them guilty of robbery. That night the Magistrate was attacked by a mob in his home. His windows were smashed, furniture trashed and he fled, bruised and terrified, into the night. The Magistrate is unable to return to either his home or workplace and is in hiding.

IN THE NEWS

~20 Nov 2001 Agriculture Minister Joseph Made announces maximum sizes for commercial farms and says that any farm which exceed the limit will be sub-divided into smaller plots. In arable areas no property can exceed 250 hectares and in ranching areas 2,000 hectares.

24 November 2001. Look after Mummy's special friend

This week it was announced that a 1997 Supreme Court Ruling which allowed freedom of movement was to be overthrown. The carrying of ID cards is about to be mandatory again and

Justice Minister Chinamasa said this was being done to: 'combat criminal and terrorist activities.' The government then went on to name newspapers they say are: 'distorting the facts and assisting terrorists': The Times (UK), Independent (UK), The Star (South Africa) and the Zimbabwe Independent.

My nine year old son goes off to camp on Monday and is so excited that he is beside himself. He has promised me that he will keep saying his prayers at night and won't forget to say: 'and please look after Mummy's special friend Simon in Bulawayo.' (Simon is one of the many innocents in jail for the murder of the war veteran) I am glad that there is still some normality in parts of our lives because after four days with no petrol or diesel, no sugar or fresh milk in Marondera, life's everyday events become that much more precious – and as always teach me not to take anything for granted anymore.

IN THE NEWS

~*28th November 2001* Zanu PF owes the City of Harare over $20 million in unpaid rates and water bills incurred at its headquarters and the former head offices at 88 Robert Mugabe Road.

Are you serious? Stealing traffic lights

'Police in Harare have recovered $300,000 worth of traffic lights stolen around the city recently. The lights were recovered after police on patrol became suspicious when they saw a truck being loaded with goods in a bush near King George Road in Avondale last week. On seeing the police the group sped away but police gave chase. When the suspects realised that police were gaining ground they stopped their truck and took to their heels. One suspect was arrested and the lights recovered. Thieves steal the lights and strip aluminium components, which they sell as scrap metal. Avondale police officer-in-charge, Assistant Inspector Robert Dondo said theft of traffic lights, street nameplates and even road reflectors had increased in Harare.' (The Herald)

1 December 2001. Stripped of our dignity

Last Sunday night, just before 7.30pm, a farmer was ambushed and shot twenty metres from his home in Macheke. Alan Bradley, his wife and their two young children were coming home from a day out. It was dark, Anthea was driving, one child sat on Alan's lap in the front passenger seat, the other lay dozing on the back seat. A barricade of branches had been spread across the road. Anthea slowed and stopped; Alan got out of the car to move the branches when they saw at least one armed man. Alan scrambled back into the car and as he did so shots were fired through the drivers' window. The window shattered and collapsed over Anthea. Alan was shot in his upper arm, his chest peppered with shrapnel, four broken ribs and his lung pierced. The two young children witnessed the entire horror but were not physically hurt and Anthea managed to drive her family to safety where they were met on the road by other farmers and an ambulance which had been dispatched from Marondera. All week Alan has been in a critical condition but as of last night was breathing on his own and stable.

Later in the week a crisis unfolded at the retirement home in Marondera. Nurses at Borradaile Trust Frail Care centre went on strike, assisted by war veterans and set up a barricade at the entrance gate. The thought of men and women in their 90s, unable to feed or wash themselves and stripped of their dignity appalled me so I went to see if I could volunteer to help. I was met at the entrance gate by about fifty men. They had tied placards onto the boom and I immediately knew this was not simply nurses striking for money – it too had become a political platform. Some of the signs read: 'Close it, we can run it better.' 'Give us what belongs to us.' 'Close it down we'll make a college.' One placard which really exposed the truth said: 'We are tired of burning grass, hospital next.'

A man approached my car and I politely asked to be let in, he refused, glared at me and told me to read the signs. I told him I had read the signs but would still like to go in. After a short, aggressive lecture the man, wearing dirty overalls and a large floppy hat, let me in. I drove past the nurses, ten of them, sitting quietly under a tree in the shade. They did not glare and shake their fists at me as the men at the gate had done, in fact, they looked embarrassed and would not meet my eyes. Later I learned that this was just one of a number of similar 'assisted strikes;' retirement homes in Harare, Bulawayo and Masvingo were also affected.

To end on a cheerful follow up note: my son got back from camp where there are elephants, rhinos and maybe war vets. He'd had a wonderful time; the highlights were rock paintings and lots of animals. What animals did you see I asked – rabbits and frogs he said!

IN THE NEWS

~7th December 2001 Amnesty International say police and security forces in Zimbabwe are waging a campaign of violence and intimidation against judges, journalists and opposition leaders in advance of presidential elections.

8 December 2001. Foaming at the mouth

The world has suddenly started speaking out about Zimbabwe. South African President Mbeki said: 'In a situation in which people are beaten up so that they don't act according to their political convictions, there can't be free elections.' The Congress of South African Trade Unions, (Cosatu) said: 'We should be doing more than sending a memorandum. We should be mobilizing workers to defend democracy.' New Zealand's Foreign Minister Goff, calling for Zimbabwe's expulsion from the Commonwealth said: 'Mr Mugabe appears ready to do anything to stay in power including destroying his country.'

But the most damning indictment came when America voted 396– 11 in favour of the Zimbabwe Democracy Bill. This Bill asks President Mugabe to do five things: 'Get your soldiers out of the Congo; return to the 1998 world backed plan for land reform; allow freedom of the press; restore law and order; and allow election observers into the country to ensure a free and fair election.' If Zimbabwe agrees to these five issues, the Americans will release US$20 million for land reform: US$6 million for election monitoring and additional amounts for humanitarian and food aid. Failure to meet the criteria will result in targeted sanctions which will: 'impose travel restrictions on President Mugabe and his associates; block aid and debt relief; freeze Zanu PF assets abroad and freeze new investment into Zimbabwe.'

This combined international attack on our government has left our propaganda peddlers foaming at the mouth. All week the state controlled radio, television and newspaper have lambasted the world. It seems that sanctions against Rhodesia and apartheid South Africa were good but against Zimbabwe they are bad.

While all this was going on President Mugabe made no comment but spoke to teenage boys graduating from the government's Youth Brigade. He said: 'We realised that we had beaten the snake (whites) but left out the head. What is left is to finish off the head (the MDC).' President Mugabe said that the Youth Service would now be mandatory for anyone applying for work in government departments or entering Zimbabwean universities.

Lastly this week came the news that the Supreme Court ruled that law and order had been restored on our farms and that the government had come up with a satisfactory land redistribution exercise. The newly appointed Chief Justice of the Supreme Court, Godfrey Chidyuasiku, had been asked to recuse himself from the hearing on the grounds of political bias but he refused. The request had followed a question in Parliament where Justice Minister Patrick Chinamasa was asked to explain why $1million had been allocated to furnishing Justice Chidyuausiku's new government house.

IN THE NEWS

~14th December 2001 MDC President Morgan Tsvangirai's house is raided and he is arrested for being in possession of walkie-talkie radios without a licence. The radios have a range of 50 metres, do not need a licence and can be bought in supermarkets.

15 December 2001. Smeared under the foreskin

This week six foreign ministers from SADC were in Zimbabwe and after two days in a Harare hotel said they 'welcomed the improved atmosphere of calm and stability' and were 'gratified to learn that violence on farms had reduced significantly.' Their spokeswoman was Malawian foreign minister Lilian Patel and although she spoke with apparent conviction, her words make no sense at all in view of recent statements condemning events in Zimbabwe from her own President and others in the region.

A calm and stable situation was certainly not the case for 29-year-old Augustus Chacha who was kidnapped from Gonye Village in Gokwe in front of his wife and five children last weekend. Augustus was the MDC youth organiser in the area. His body was found floating in Gonye Dam two days later. In another incident the newly elected MDC mayor of Chegutu, Francis Dhlakama, was forced out of his office on his first day at work. 50 war veterans, chanting and singing pro-government songs ordered him out and although police were present, they did nothing to assist the Mayor elect who left to avoid violence.

The November report on political violence has just been released by the Zimbabwe Human Rights Forum and reports on 6 deaths/executions: 8 kidnappings, 81 cases of property damage and 115 cases of torture/rape. The Forum defines torture as: 'severe pain and suffering, intentionally inflicted, with a purpose, by a State official or acting with the acquiescence of the State.' The 25 page report makes for horrific reading. It tells of people having their heads forced into antbear holes, having their mouths filled with sand, being beaten by gangs armed with chains, sticks, knobkerries and rubber hoses. It tells of highly irritant plant powders known as 'huriri or uriri' (Buffalo Bean) being soaked into people's clothes, stuffed into their anuses and smeared under the penile foreskin.

Welcome diversion. Oozing butter

A bang on the gate, a smiling, friendly face from the village and a green plastic carrier bag heavy with fresh picked maize. These are the first cobs from the crop: young, firm, plump. The tough outer leaves squeak as I peel them back and snap them off at the base. With each layer the leaves get softer, paler, thinner. I stop when there are two or three leaves left and I can see the fat white kernels underneath. Gently I pull and wiggle at the silk until most of it comes loose without disturbing those last, almost transparent leaves. Straight into a pot of fast boiling salted water and the cob is done in just a few minutes. Peeling away the leaves and picking the last of the silk from between the lines of fat, shining kernels, my mouth is watering. The butter melts as I run the knife along the cob, dripping onto my fingers. A shake of salt, a few turns of the black pepper mill and a flood of memories return: childhood, boarding school, farming. I can't stop the child in me from eating in straight lines along the cob, starting with the big fat pips, savouring every bite as the seeds get softer, sweeter and smaller as they near the tip. Everything else in life is turmoil, sadness and confusion but this hasn't changed, this taste of that first green mealie: soft, sweet, oozing butter, chin dripping, finger licking.

IN THE NEWS

~19th Dec 2001 Inflation rises to 112% during the month.

22 December 2001. Hold on just a little bit longer

On Tuesday, a 24-year-old farm manager, Duncan Cook, was attacked in the fields of the farm where he works. He was slashed across the right side of his forehead with a machete by a government official. The photograph of this man, barely out of school, deathly pale, lying in blood-saturated bedding with a massive line of stitches from his right ear to his eyebrow has left us in deep shock.

On the same day, the Daily News reported that two children died of starvation in Hwange on a farm where people have been resettled. A relative of the deceased children said: 'There is no maize meal in the shops. More people will die, especially children, because we are going for days without food.' Shop owners in the area confirmed that they have stopped selling maize meal because they are making serious losses due to the price controls on the staple food.

While people are now literally starving to death, our President and 7,618 delegates held their annual Zanu PF congress in the Victoria Falls. The Zimbabwe Independent estimates the cost of the transport and accommodation alone to have been $440 million.

Newly resettled farmers this week told the Financial Gazette that they were having to sell the fertilizer and seed maize they had been given by the government under the fast track land re-distribution scheme. One settler said: 'What will I be living on until next year? If I manage to sell some of the fertilizer to make a living and send my three children to school then I do not see anything wrong with that.' Zimbabwe's new farmers simply do not have the resources to grow the food needed to support 13 million people.

All week we have been absolutely bombarded by state owned radio and TV telling us that this has been the best Christmas for 100 years because Zimbabweans have been given back their land and are expecting 'bumper harvests.' I went away for a few days, travelled a couple of hundred kilometres and saw for myself the state of the crops on Zimbabwe's farms. What is most striking is that we have gone backwards in time. From tractors and pivot irrigation we have gone to oxen pulling hand ploughs in little squares which may produce enough food for one family for three or four months. Our prime growing season is going to waste while our Agriculture Minister is sitting in Harare saying that we are in for a bumper harvest.

This has not been the best Christmas in 100 years for four people who were murdered in political violence this week.

Trymore Midzi, (24) was brutally assaulted in Bindura by men wielding machetes. He died in hospital. Titus Nheya, (56) was stabbed to death in Karoi. Milton Chambati, (45) was attacked by a mob of fifty, stabbed in the back and then beheaded in Magunge. Laban Chiweta, (24) was beaten to death by armed riot police near Bindura.

As the laws close in on us, every word becomes harder and more dangerous to write or say. This week a new radio station began broadcasting to Zimbabwe from London. SW 1 Radio Africa at 6145 kHz on the 49 metre band is telling us the truth every night from 6–9pm. The tears spilled as I listened to their first broadcast and the closing message, sung by and for Zimbabweans was: 'Hold on, just a little bit longer.'

Part Three 2001

Dear Family and Friends

5 January 2002. Bleak but blatantly obvious

Less than three years ago Zimbabwe was a major regional exporter of food but in January 2002 we are begging international donors for US$100 million of urgent food aid. This is needed to feed the estimated two million Zimbabweans who experts say will face starvation within the next three weeks. After almost two years of the most extreme policies, harassment, intimidation and murder of our country's farmers and workers, we have now run out of food. There are no maize reserves left and 95% of our commercial farms have been gazetted for state seizure. The Zimbabwe government this week began publishing the names of people who have been allocated plots of land on the seized commercial farms. So far 5,000 names had been listed and less than twenty of the beneficiaries have been given large scale plots. Most have been given barely enough land on which to support themselves let alone grow a surplus to feed our population of 13 million. Included in these first lists of people whom we are told are 'landless peasants' are the Mayor of the City of Chitungwiza; the Deputy Minister of Transport; the MPs of Mutoko, Buhera and Hurungwe. Also benefiting are a number of journalists from the state run Herald newspaper including the Deputy Editor, Business Editor, Features Editor and Health Reporter.

I stood dumfounded in a Marondera supermarket yesterday morning looking at a bag of four apples priced at $320. I couldn't afford them so instead bought an $80 weekly newspaper whose front page story is of the latest government pay rises. All Zimbabwe's uniformed forces have been awarded a 100% pay rise effective from the 1st of January. This includes police, army, air force, prison service workers and war veterans (the latter now fall under the Ministry of Defence).

Stringing a few other facts together paints a bleak but blatantly obvious picture of a government willing to do anything to stay in power. Presidential elections are due in 8–10 weeks' time; citizenship laws have been changed; 300,000 farm workers are about to be jobless and destitute; electoral and media laws are about to be changed; five Judges have left the benches in the last eight months; 100,000 people have been displaced internally because of violence; ninety people have been murdered for their political beliefs. It is an abysmal situation and we are completely powerless to do anything about it.

IN THE NEWS

~*11th January 2002* The General Laws Amendment Bill is passed; it bans independent election monitors and denies voting rights to millions of citizens abroad. The Public Order and Security bill is passed; it criminalizes criticism of the President and gives the government sweeping new security powers. Both Bills are passed by a majority of 62 votes to 49.

12 January 2002. The dustbin of my nightmares

The dates for Presidential elections have been announced and we will go to the polls in 56 days' time on the 9th and 10th of March. On Tuesday, the General Amendments Bill was defeated in Parliament when only 22 ruling party MPs were in the house. On Thursday, the Bill was re-introduced even though by law it cannot be heard again in the same session of Parliament. MPs debated until 4.15am and then it and the Public Order and Security Bill were passed. Public gatherings and political rallies are now restricted as is the distribution of election pamphlets, the displaying of election posters and the presentation of voter education material, even that produced by Churches. It is illegal to go on strike and police may shoot demonstrators. It is an offence to criticize the President, Government or Police. It is an offence to leave your home without personal identification documents and the Bill also allows for arbitrary search and seizure.

Zimbabweans remember some of these regulations in place during the Smith government. One aspect of arbitrary search and seizure in the 1970s was called Cordon and Search. A street was sealed top and bottom by police, their dogs and armoured cars. A whistle was blown and everyone had to stop walking and stand still. Police systematically searched everyone in the street, looked in bags and parcels and you had to raise your arms and stand with legs slightly apart as your body was frisked – and God help you if you ran. The memories send chills down my spine, I thought they were consigned to the dustbin of my nightmares.

IN THE NEWS

~12th January 2002 The EU gives Zimbabwe a week to declare in writing that it will accept international observers and news media during the March presidential elections.

19 January 2002. Men in single file

I woke up this morning to the sight of men walking past my house in single file, many carrying sticks. At first a dozen men, then fifty and then well over a hundred. It bought back a lot of memories for me and a lot of fear too. We all know what to do now and the gates, doors, windows and curtains are closed The political rallies have started and the atmosphere everywhere is very frightening and very tense.

The new school year started this week and in between sewing on name tapes and covering books I opened one of my son's new exercise books. I read his first piece of work. His teacher had told the class to write a prayer about anything that they needed help with. My nine year old son had written: '

Dear God, please help Zimbabwe. All of us don't like what is going on now so will you please help Zimbabwe and my family and all my friends and teachers. Armen.'

This situation in Zimbabwe has touched us all and I am lucky that my son is still able to go to school. Last week it was reported by GAPWUZ (The Agricultural Workers Union) that at least 10,000 children will not be going back to school this term because their schools, situated on farms, have either closed down or are un-staffed because the teachers are too scared to work there. The education of a huge number of

Zimbabweans is under threat and the recent 300% rise in the fees at Zimbabwe's Open University will have far reaching implications for the future. Meanwhile it was reported in the South African Sunday Times that thirteen Zimbabwean government ministers, the Speaker of the House of Parliament and a provincial governor have their children studying in schools and universities in Switzerland, the UK, America and South Africa. Our schools and universities are obviously not good enough for our leaders' children.

IN THE NEWS

~*1st February 2002* The Access to Information and Protection of Privacy Bill curbing media freedom is passed through parliament. Founding Zanu PF member Eddison Zvobgo says twenty clauses are unconstitutional. He calls the Bill: 'ill-conceived, dangerous and a calculated and determined assault on our liberties.'

~*9th February 2002* Foreign Minister Stan Mudenge says only election observers from nine of the fifteen EU countries will be admitted, and that they should form part of a joint mission led by the African, Caribbean and Pacific group of countries.

9 February 2002. Electrodes under the fingernails

The stage is set. Presidential candidates are nominated. The laws are now all passed; our hands are tied, voices silenced and movements curtailed. There are now 36 days to go until the elections.

This weekend the government officially began their campaign to retain the Presidency. The rallies have started and before the guest speakers arrive, youths go in to prepare the groundwork. Election campaigns start door to door, not with badges, smiles and kisses for the baby but with demands: show your party card, give us money, food, a cow to slaughter, milk, firewood, eggs, chicken. Refusing the demands is not an option. Across the country people are being forced to give whatever is demanded of them and then ordered to attend the rally or face the consequences.

132 people have been killed in political violence in Zimbabwe since March 2000, 15 of those people died last month in what is being called Bloody January. One brief excerpt from the January ZHR i Political Violence Report reads as follows: 'They demanded to know the names of the people in the MDC party structures... then he was tortured by being squeezed with great pressure around his diaphragm and then had electrodes from the battery of the car attached to his inner thigh and under his fingernails and was given electric shocks. They beat him on the head and legs with sticks and then forced him to swallow a herbal mixture that caused severe diarrhoea. TK subsequently died.'

Welcome diversion. Multi-storey mushrooms

A towering red mud city sprang up almost overnight in my small storeroom. Made of soft damp red soil, at first it was just a line along the wall, rising from a crack between the wall and the floor. By the second morning it was calf high and then knee high and then it was covered with what looked like eggs or little white beads. By the third morning it had turned into a magical miniature city. The little white beads from the day before had opened and were in fact tiny white mushrooms which had erupted from the mud in clusters and layers, spreading in distinct circles like lights in a multi storey high rise building at night. By the next morning, the mushrooms had increased and there were many hundreds, even thousands of them. Their thin delicate stalks had grown longer and their heads had opened slightly to reveal pale pinkish gills topped with a little pointed cap. The mushroom layers rose eight storeys high on the red mud castle and then, as suddenly as they had arrived, when I looked on the fifth morning they had all collapsed and died leaving a rather smelly, slimy, muddy mess to clear away.

IN THE NEWS

~*12th February 2002* The trial of former President of Yugoslavia, Slobodan Milosevic begins at the UN war crimes tribunal in The Hague.

~*13th February 2002* Sir Garfield Todd, former Prime Minister of Southern Rhodesia and recognised supporter of the liberation struggle is removed from the voters roll, told he is no longer a citizen.

16 February 2002. Threaten and bluster

Some election observers have begun arriving in the country but our Minister of Foreign Affairs refused to accredit any from Sweden, Finland, The Netherlands, Germany, Denmark and the UK. This pettiness is insulting to countries whose people and governments have poured hundreds of millions of US dollars into Zimbabwe in the last two decades. Up until two years ago, when land invasions began, the people of these six countries were building schools, hospitals, clinics and dams here. They were donating drugs, caring for AIDS victims and looking after street children. They were sinking boreholes and setting up irrigation schemes, constructing bridges and giving us their expertise in the form of doctors, nurses and teachers. For two decades we took their money with both hands, now our government uses those same hands to slap them in the face and tell them they are not welcome to observe our elections. We are ashamed and these sentiments are not representative of the people of Zimbabwe, only of our leaders.

Meanwhile the EU does nothing but threaten and bluster as the absurdities grow. Disbelief came at the weekend when an interdenominational church service in Bulawayo ended in the arrest of eleven people. The service was one of a regular series planned to take the form of a walking procession from church to church in the Bulawayo suburb of Hillside, with services held in each church. After receiving a letter from the local police forbidding a march on the grounds that they couldn't guarantee the walkers' safety, Rev Noel Scott of the Anglican Church, suggested the procession take place in cars rather than on foot.

This was done, and at each service a police presence was observed. After the final service, the police arrested Reverend Scott under the new Public Order and Security Act. When other clergy who were present went to the police charge office, knelt on the floor and prayed, they were arrested for disturbing the peace.

IN THE NEWS

~*16th February 2002* Pierre Schori, the head of a team of thirty EU election observers is refused accreditation and told to leave Zimbabwe.

~*19th February 2002* The EU withdraws all its election observers from Zimbabwe and imposes 'smart sanctions' on President Robert Mugabe and his senior aides. An arms embargo, travel ban and assets freeze, target Mr Mugabe and 19 senior ministers, army and police commanders and their families.

~*22nd February 2002* The US imposes a travel ban on Robert Mugabe and senior aides.

23 February 2002. The sound of terror

On a clear, star-filled evening this week all semblance of peace and normalcy was shattered in a quiet residential Marondera neighbourhood. The first hint of something being amiss came from dogs barking in all directions. It was angry, excited barking and nothing could quieten the dogs – they could hear the sound of approaching terror. Some neighbours reported hearing windows being broken, others heard whistling. No one went outside their gates to see what was going on, no one does anymore because it isn't safe to do so. A house belonging to a senior member of the opposition MDC had been targeted and was being looted of television, radio, videos, clothing, a bicycle and computer. There were people in the house at the time including a young child who hid under a bed and managed to escape the notice of the looters.

Shortly before 9pm there were a series of explosions and I watched in absolute horror as a house within sight of my own burnt uncontrollably, spitting sparks into the darkness, lighting up the night with a huge orange blaze. The noise for the next two hours was terrifying as windows exploded, roof timbers collapsed, asbestos cracked and shattered. Later came the sound of two or three blasts from a hooter and whistling from all directions. The Fire Brigade did not come and the neighbourhood was powerless to help or act as a home was looted and burned while a child hid under the bed.

IN THE NEWS

~23rd February 2002 200 Zanu PF supporters assault South African election observers who were meeting MDC officials in Kwekwe. Four MDC members are hospitalized.

~25th February 2002 MDC's Morgan Tsvangirai, Welshman Ncube and Renson Gasela are charged with treason.

2 March 2002. Lot 39

I sat in my car outside a small Marondera shop this Friday morning and cried. Four pick-up trucks filled with shaven headed youngsters had passed me carrying flags and waving their fists to demonstrate their allegiance to Zanu PF. On the corner a few metres away a dozen armed police reservists stood watching and almost every car I saw had government number plates. An opposition rally was being held in Marondera and most ordinary shoppers had stayed at home. I tried for the fifth time this week to buy maize meal, sugar, cooking oil or margarine but there was none so instead I bought a dozen eggs for $150, 1kg of rice for $290 and a copy of the state owned Herald newspaper. I cried as I read in the newspaper that my farm has been listed for seizure by the government. For me it is exactly two years ago, to the day since this hell started. Now I read in the Herald that in terms of the Land Acquisition Act, 'the President intends to acquire compulsorily the land described in the Schedule for resettlement purposes.'

Exactly seven days before the election I am told that the President intends to seize my farm – which President, the outgoing or incoming? Along with thousands of other Zimbabweans I will now start the fight for my legal and constitutional rights to own a piece of land in the country of my birth. A piece of land which was bought legally in 1990 backed by a Zimbabwe Government Certificate of No Interest. A piece of land which, according to the government, is now number 65 of Lot 39.

Are you serious? The sympathy vote

'In 1979 Nitaro Ito, a candidate for Japan's House of Representatives, died in an attempt to gain sympathy during his election campaign. Having persuaded one of his employees to punch him in the face, Ito then stabbed himself in the leg. Unfortunately, he hit an artery and bled to death before any aid could be given.' (Wikipedia)

IN THE NEWS

~2nd March 2002 Supreme Court judge Ahmed Ebrahim resigns days after he rejected new electoral legislation saying amendments had been enacted illegally in January.

9 March 2002. Touching forearms

I have just got home after standing 4 hours and 10 minutes in a queue to vote. I was number 152 in the line and estimate at least 5,000 stood behind me. Reports coming in from other centres also tell of huge queues but enormous determination. Apathy is not going to be a factor in this election, the crowds were happy and cheerful, in fact I don't think I've heard so much laughter for two years. Blacks and whites stood together and laughed together; many did not shake hands but touched forearms so as not to risk being marked with voting ink. Gone for a few hours was the fear that has become a part of our lives. There were many familiar faces in the queue including men who have invaded farms, youths who have stood around on street corners waving their fists and hundreds of ordinary, decent peace loving people who have spent most of the last week standing in queues for sugar and maize meal. I saw at least a dozen people wearing bandages and with black eyes – they too were determined to cast their vote.

There were a few angry outbursts as groups of young shaven headed men tried to push into the queue but were chased off by people determined not to be intimidated anymore. On one occasion a very young policeman got fed up with a group of arrogant queue jumpers and sent them packing to the delight of us all.

Putting a cross on a ballot paper this morning is the most enormous achievement after a week of the outrageous last minute changes by the government to electoral procedures. Voter's rolls were not available for inspection; thousands of internal observers were denied accreditation; lists of polling stations were only announced two days before elections; urban polling stations were reduced by 40%; previously permanent stations were changed into mobile centres. Reports of intimidation, harassment and violence have continued up until the last moment and dozens of internal opposition observers have been beaten and bloodied but the people appear to be showing that they are determined to have their say in the future.

IN THE NEWS

~March 2002 Inflation rises to 113% during the month.

13 March 2002. So many questions

78-year-old President Mugabe, in power for 22 years has just won a fifth term in office and will rule us for another 6 years. President Mugabe will be 84 years old when his term expires. The final count was Mugabe:

1,685,212; Tsvangirai: 1,258,401.

There are so many questions and very few answers. Why has the army been put on high alert? How will the people of Zimbabwe react? How will the government restore law and order? Will the Police now start arresting criminals who rape, beat, burn, torture and throw petrol bombs? Will the judiciary now start convicting murderers? What will happen to an inflation rate already over 110%? How will the government stop a massive exodus of skilled people? What will be done to reduce the 60% unemployment rate? What will the government do to stop run-away corruption? Where will the government get foreign currency from to buy medicines and petrol? What will election observers say about the process?

The most important question is where is the food going to come from? How will Zanu PF, who have cut themselves off from the world, now find the food for 13 million people? There is no basic food to buy in the shops and almost no food in the ground. Will our government again stop farmers from growing food? Will it really continue with their plan to seize every farm in the country and give the land to people who have neither the means nor the expertise to grow food on a large scale?

IN THE NEWS

~14th March 2002 Amnesty International express deep concern over the safety of 1,400 people detained by police during last weekend's presidential election. Most of those detained were polling agents of the MDC.

17 March 2002. Humility

Darlington, a young farm security guard was murdered in Marondera on Friday and his employer was beaten with wooden pick handles on his buttocks after being accused of having helped MDC polling agents during last weekend's elections. Little is known about Darlington and although all attempts were made to save his life, the young man died on his way to Marondera hospital.

It took a visit to see his employer at the hospital and the sight of massive black and purple bruising on a man's buttocks, to put things back into perspective for me. A young man with a wife and two infant daughters cannot lie on his back, he cannot sit down and is barely able to walk. He is not broken though and we talked, laughed and cried together. This man can still hear the thud of wood on his backside, he can feel the excruciating agony, the sound of his own voice begging them to stop is still in his head, but he knows that Darlington, moments away from death, must have said something that saved his employer's life.

Across the country reports are pouring in of ruling party youths engaged in witch hunts, searching out people suspected of being MDC supporters, beating them, evicting them from their homes and burning their possessions. Two people had died before the weekend even began and there are reports of many farmers being given 6 hours to get out of their homes.

While this horror unfolded Mr Mugabe prepared to be sworn in, the ceremony broadcast live on ZBC TV. A President whose entire election campaign has been an incessant slamming of everything western and colonial, stood under a marquee on the lawn of State House. He was bedecked with medals as were his security forces in their white gloves and the country's chiefs in their red and purple robes and spotless pith helmets.

The ceremony could not have been more colonial if it had been held on the lawn of Buckingham Palace. Mr Mugabe again swore to: 'be faithful and true to Zimbabwe and to observe the laws of Zimbabwe, so help me God.' Minister of Information Jonathan Moyo was the Master of Ceremonies and the official guests of honour included Joseph Kabila who is not even an elected president.

In his speech President Mugabe was the statesman. He called for unity of purpose, for brotherhood and sisterhood. He called on Zimbabweans to come together and 'work jointly to reconstruct our economy.' He talked of rebuilding the economy, increasing jobs, improved health care, vast agricultural outputs and greatly improved fiscal policies. President Mugabe said not one word about law and order in Zimbabwe but instead spoke of his 'personal joy and sense of humility' at having been re-elected President. My humility came from sitting with a man whose buttocks are black and blue, who was not ashamed to let me see his tears. For the moment, the only hope we have is hope itself. Slowly we are coming to terms with what has happened and bracing ourselves for what lies ahead. People are starving and beaten but they are not broken.

IN THE NEWS

~20th March 2002 Zimbabwe is suspended from the Councils of the Commonwealth.

23 March 2002. Their silence is frightening

The picture on the front page of this week's Zimbabwe Independent is gruesome and shocking. It is of murdered farmer Terry Ford, lying in a pool of blood, his body covered from top to bottom in wounds and bruises. Terry, trying to escape from his farm which had been over-run by a mob, had been caught, tied to a tree, bludgeoned and then shot. Terry's family was brave enough to allow the world's cameras in to expose this horror but his murder is only one of seven that have taken place in the last ten days. This letter is dedicated to the lives, loves and in memory of seven men who have been murdered by government supporters in the last ten days: Terry Ford, Ernest Gatsi (MDC activist – beaten to death), Tafi Gwaze (MDC Polling agent – abducted, tortured and beaten to death), Laurence Kuheya (MDC activist), Funny Mahuni (MDC supporter), Owen Manyara (MDC activist – beaten to death) and Darlington Vikaveka (Farm security guard – beaten to death). In addition, scores of people have been beaten, a dozen farms have been looted or trashed and an estimated 1,200 MDC polling agents are on the run as they are being hounded by government supporter's intent on hunting down anyone who dared to differ in our recent elections.

Throughout two years of hell I have never seen so many distraught people: women sitting in a restaurant, holding hands, crying and praying aloud; middle aged men shaking and speechless, with only the clothes on their backs, having been evicted from their homes by juvenile mobs; a third hand message from an old man to his son: 'don't come home it is not safe, they are still looking for you;' an exhausted and bruised husband and wife standing at a petrol station telling me how they have been beaten and are on the run, they don't know where to go but they cannot stay in our little town anymore. The violence this past ten days has been horrific and stunned us all into terrified silence.

Across the country reports continue to pour in, detailing lawlessness and violence. The government's silence on this awful situation makes a complete mockery of President Mugabe's inauguration speech calling for unity, brother and sister hood and rebuilding. Their silence on food security is even more frightening. There is still no maize to buy, no cooking oil, sugar or milk. Land preparation for winter wheat has not commenced; paprika has been trashed in the fields by youths; 13,000 litres of milk were destroyed by men who tipped stock feed into the bulk tanks; irrigation equipment has been trashed and yesterday more than 300 properties were listed for government seizure in the newspaper. It is beyond belief and almost defies words.

The only comfort is that world pressure is mounting. We have been suspended from the Commonwealth Council for a year. Denmark has closed its embassy in Harare and suspended all development aid and Switzerland has imposed travel and financial bans on President Mugabe and other top government officials.

IN THE NEWS

~*26th March 2002* The MDC publish a 200 page document detailing rigging of the Presidential election including:

185,961 missing votes in 48 constituencies; an extra 246,445 votes in 72 constituencies; unusually high voter turnouts in ruling party strongholds and a decline in voting in urban opposition strongholds.

30 March 2002. Stand up and be counted

This week Agriculture Minister Joseph Made said that commercial farmers being evicted from their properties could not take their moveable assets, such as tractors and irrigation equipment with them. He said the Government was considering introducing a Statutory Instrument to stop farmers from removing their farm implements when they are evicted from their land. I quote: 'These agricultural assets must be left on the acquired farms for use by new commercial farmers. We are stopping forthwith the exportation of agricultural machinery and equipment. No asset of an agricultural nature should be moved off the commercial farms.' Grabbing the farms and now the equipment; how can this be?

People everywhere are so tired of it all; tired of being beaten and chased out of their homes; tired of tending the wounds on the backs of their husbands and sons; tired of standing for hours at a time to buy sugar, oil and maize meal. People are tired of the lies, hatred and violence and they are hungry. People are tired of worrying where the money will come from to buy a loaf of bread, particularly this week when it was announced the price of yeast went up by 142%. People are tired of hearing that government youths have gone on the rampage and this week prevented 600 tonnes of sweet potatoes from being irrigated. I do not know of a single household where there is not a story of horror waiting to be told: a husband beaten up, a son abducted, a friend tortured, a relation in hiding, an uncle in prison. People are tired of government ministers making speeches filled with hatred and anger such as the words spoken this week by the female Deputy Minister of Youth, Gender, and Employment creation: 'Zanu PF will not continue to sell maize to MDC supporters because they oppose us Anyone who continues to support MDC should be beaten.' People who have chosen to stay silent must stand up and be counted now or think of ways of telling their children why there is no supper tonight or breakfast tomorrow.

IN THE NEWS

~*30th March 2002* The US adds Anglican Bishop of Harare, Nolbert Kunonga and Zimbabwe's richest businessman, John Bredenkamp, to its list of people targeted by sanctions and travel bans.

~*4th April 2002* The US government prepares to deliver the first consignment of a 34,430 tonne contribution of maize meal to help feed Zimbabweans facing food shortages.

13 April 2002. Wandering around aimlessly

Exactly one month after Presidential elections in Zimbabwe, Registrar General Tobaiwa Mudede held a Press Conference and announced new election results this week. In his 'new figures' Mudede has found a further 4,002 votes for the MDC. Reporters who were demanding explanations for a number of conflicting figures and totals, saw Mr Mudede get very annoyed and finally lose his cool altogether. 'Get Out!' he shouted at the Daily News chief reporter, 'call the boys' he said to his officials.

The MDC had just filed papers with the High Court challenging the results of the presidential elections. The challenge runs to 138 pages and Mr Mudede is one of the respondents. The MDC say the elections were not free or fair; they cite violence, murder, intimidation and rigging. They pinpoint militia and terror bases set up throughout the country, ballot boxes which had been opened at the bottom, court rulings which were ignored and they say the figures announced on ZBC by Mr Mudede had been doctored.

Yesterday Agriculture Minister Dr Joseph Made also held a press conference which he said was needed to 'give direction in order to complete land reform.' Minister Made said that 'white commercial farmers must stand warned that government will not tolerate interference of the operations of newly settled farmers.' He said civil servants within his own ministry who had been working hand in hand with farmers would be 'dealt with.'

Andrew Ndlovu, the secretary for projects in the War Veterans' Association has also been ordering white farmers off their land. War veterans have been delivering letters from Mr Ndlovu to farmers telling them they must be off by the end of the month. Ndlovu said: 'We have so far issued ultimatums to more than 800 farmers. The farmers have to vacate their farms regardless of whether their farms have been listed for acquisition by the government or not.' Ndlovu said that farmers should 'go and get compensation from Britain and if they [farmers] refuse to go peacefully, we will remove them violently.'

Neither Andrew Ndlovu nor Dr Made explained why armed riot police this week forcibly evicted 80 people who had settled on a seized farm just outside Marondera. The farm is apparently wanted by the Minister of Defence, Dr Sekeremayi. 80 people, 20 of whom were women with babies on their backs, gathered outside our Governor's office and demanded an explanation. Finally the Marondera DA ı explained the situation by telling settlers who had been on that farm since March 2000: 'that was random occupation. This is now land reorganization.' Women with babies on their backs have nowhere to go and neither do white farmers who sit with huge truckloads of furniture in car parks and wander around aimlessly.

IN THE NEWS

~*17th April 2002* The US government imposes an arms embargo on Zimbabwe. Saying it is in response to: 'Zimbabwe's subversion of the democratic process, which culminated in a fatally-flawed presidential election in March.'

20 April 2002. They all took turns to rape me

The Zimbabwe Women Lawyer's Association has begun gathering evidence to help release women being held and sexually abused in camps run by government youths. Horrific tales are surfacing of women and girls being abducted, gang raped and used day after day by young men in these camps.

A 55-year-old woman from Murombedzi, told how she was forced to attend a rally and gang raped when she tried to leave. 'I did not do anything wrong. For these youths to do this to someone old enough to be their mother is unthinkable. They all took turns to rape me.' Another woman from Rushinga said: 'How can you be a legitimate leader to me when you got that position by raping me, beating me up, burning my property, scarring my son's back, taking over my home and taking away my dignity.'

This week there have been renewed attempts by our government to silence journalists. Under the guise of either the Public Order and Security Act (POSA) or the newly passed Access to Information Bill, Daily News owner and editor-in-chief, Geoff Nyarota was arrested along with his chief reporter Pedzisai Ruhenya. The Zimbabwe Independent's Editor, Iden Wetherell and senior correspondent Dumisani Muleya were also picked up and charged.

IN THE NEWS

~21st April 2002 A customized, armoured Mercedes Benz S600 LV AMG (Pullman) arrives in the country for President Mugabe. In the same consignment are two Mercedes Benz S320 saloons for Mugabe's two vice presidents and 19 presidential escort trucks. The total value of the vehicles is estimated at over US$250 million.

~25th April 2002 President Mugabe grants amnesty to 4,998 prisoners. Justice minister Patrick Chinamasa says Zimbabwe's prisons can accommodate 16,000 inmates but currently hold 22,500 people.

27 April 2002. A man called Wind

Last Saturday morning a war veteran named Wind, accompanied by a bunch of young men, arrived on my old neighbour's farm and gave him two days to get out saying it was now their farm. All the men, women and children living and working on the farm were also evicted. Wind said that all the cattle and laying hens belonged to him and were not to be moved. He ordered that all agricultural equipment be left behind including a tractor, plough, borehole motors, feed tins, water pipes, wheelbarrows, drums of fuel and tools. The police were informed but did not come saying it was 'political.'

I went out to the farm to help my neighbours pack. Driving towards the farmhouse gate I was met by Wind. He was wearing orange overalls with a brown leather belt; a big hat and he had a large Zimbabwe flag on a thin pole stuck in his back pocket. At his side was a scrawny dog and a number of youths were hanging around, many with shaven heads and wearing dark sunglasses. A friendly face was waiting for me at the gate and I drove in rapidly before Wind and his mates could get in.

There were no friendly, barking dogs to meet me as usual; they had been put to sleep the evening before: a realistic but grim and heart-breaking decision. Inside the house was utter chaos. The contents of a 22-year life on this farm were strewn everywhere. Boxes and crates were filled, curtains taken down, pictures removed from walls, furniture standing outside on the lawn. Everything was done in haste and all under the watchful gaze of Wind and his men who patrolled up and down the driveway, leant against the gate, climbed trees and stared. When the removal truck was loaded, we sat on the front step of the little porch and looked for one last time out on Micky and Myrtle's farm. We shared a cup of coffee out of the only things not packed – a cracked plastic cup and a chipped china mug without a handle.

There was so much to say but nothing we could say. For me there were a million memories of happy days spent here: lunch parties, fat cattle at the feed tins, burning firebreaks together under the pine trees, glossy starlings at the bird bath, cornering a night ape which had been stealing eggs. For the owners there were just silent tears. For them this is the end. They are too old to start again anywhere else. They had invested their life in this farm which is not even forced to just walk out and let a bunch of thugs move into their home. There is no money, no compensation, nothing: just get out or else. When we were ready to leave Wind was waiting at the gate. Bored thugs leant against the fence and trees down the driveway and we all thanked God we had got out alive. There had been no time to harvest vegetables or fruit in the garden; paw paws and bananas drooped from the trees; no time to dig up treasured plants from the flower beds.

The immediate results of Wind's actions on this and another nearby farm this weekend are that 63 people are now homeless, 28 adults and 35 children. Because of these evictions, Zimbabwe is immediately deprived of 110 dozen eggs, 1,500 litres of milk and 1,000 kgs of beef a week.

Are you serious? Man dies in Kachasu drinking competition

'An illicit kachasu drinking competition ended tragically on Independence Day when a 25-year-old Harare man died after taking too much of the drink. Mr Moses Luka Mwata of New Tafara drank eight bottles (250ml each) of the illicit brew in a bid to win a $500 bet.' (The Herald)

IN THE NEWS

~2nd May 2002 The Guardian's Harare correspondent, Andrew Meldrum, is arrested in Harare. The 51-year-old American journalist, a permanent resident in Zimbabwe, is accused of 'abusing journalistic privilege and publishing false news.'

4 May 2002. 'You People'

Towards the end of the week I finally managed to get in to see a senior local government official to advise him that three unknown men (calling themselves war veterans) were now living in my seized farmhouse and had broken the borehole. The war vets kept sending me messages saying that because I was still the owner of the farm I should pay for the borehole motor to be repaired as they could not survive without water. I explained politely to the local government official that as the government had never served me with any acquisition papers I was extremely worried about my assets which I had not received any compensation for.

The official got extremely angry with me, gave me a long lecture about the history of Zimbabwe and said the reason the country was now in this state was due to: 'you people who have made concerted efforts to demonize Zimbabwe and tell lies to the world.' The senior official was extremely offensive and told me to go to another government department, fill in forms to have my property valued and then hand over my Title Deeds. I am of course not prepared to give my Title Deeds to anyone before compensation is agreed and paid.

When I left the official's office he and the CIO agent who had been present during the entire meeting, stood watching me from the window. I turned back and looked at them, trying to stand tall, something which is becoming increasingly difficult.

IN THE NEWS

~*May 2002* Inflation rises to 122% during the month.

18 May 2002. Pretenders and imposters

Last weekend police arrived at two venues on the outskirts of Harare and loaded 270 displaced farm workers and their families onto trucks. These men, women and children had been evicted from farms in Marondera and Wedza by war veterans who have taken over properties in the area. The farm workers and their families have no homes to go to, no jobs and no money. They were being housed in tents and provided with blankets and food by the Zimbabwe Farm Community Development Trust. These men, women and children were not causing a disturbance but police loaded them onto trucks and got them out of sight. They were taken back to the same invaded farms they had been evicted from in Marondera where they were met with a hostile reception by war veterans who had moved into their houses. Latest reports are that many of the farm workers and their families have now fled into the bush. It is winter, night temperatures drop to 2 degrees centigrade in Marondera; what will become of 270 men, women and children hiding in the bush without food, shelter or warmth.

These 270 people are not alone in their plight. The Minister of Home Affairs, John Nkomo, this week announced that any person who settled on a farm after the 31st Mach 2001 will be removed. Over 12,000 people who have been occupying farms in the Masvingo province have now been removed from what they thought were their new homes by police this week. Interviewed on ZBC TV last night, Minister Nkomo was asked to explain what was going on. The Minister said police were: 'removing all pretenders and imposters who arrived on farms after the 31st of March 2001.' He said that people being evicted were: 'non deserving applicants who should move out to where they came from and apply [for land] through the relevant levels.'

Asked to comment on the humanitarian aspect of this massive removal of settlers from farms in Masvingo. Nkomo said: 'pity the humanitarian point of view, what about the humanitarian point of view of the government.' Asked if the removal of what the Minister called 'imposters and pretenders' was going smoothly, Nkomo replied: 'there is some resistance here and there.'

The commonest sight in Zimbabwe these days is of trucks full of people and belongings: farm owners, farm workers and now settlers – all being evicted and moved around like pawns on a chess board.

Welcome diversion. Owl skirts

Almost every night a spotted eagle owl comes to my front garden. I always hear it before I see it. 'Who, hoo, hooo,' it calls repeatedly in a deep, haunting tone. It usually appears at about dusk and sits on top of the streetlight that doesn't work or the electricity pole, both of which provide a good view over a couple of gardens and nearby vlei. There was murder early one evening when the owl swept across the garden in a silent glide and disappeared into the branches of a big gum tree. A few minutes later the owl reappeared, flying low over the garden with a chick hanging in its talons. Two birds followed the raptor, mobbing it fearlessly, one from below and one above. The little birds dived and pecked repeatedly at the owl but to no avail; the predator wasn't giving back its prey and by then the chick was surely dead anyway.

The owl often returns to the garden later at night when it's inky black and the sky is heavy with stars. It sits on the wobbly perch I've put up on the lawn and seems to have learnt that it's safest to sit in the middle of the rickety plank and not at the ends where there's a real danger of collapse. Waking up long before dawn I saw the owl standing on the top step of the swimming pool with its wing and tail feathers in the water. For ten minutes it didn't move before finally hopping out looking bedraggled and requiring prolonged shaking and preening before its skirts were dry enough to enable lift off.

25 May 2002. Land to the people – which people?

Lists of the new owners of Zimbabwe's seized and previously most productive commercial farms have been made public. The list so far has 187 names and it is shocking. The new owners of Zimbabwe's commercial farms are not farmers at all. They are not graduates from our agricultural schools and colleges; not young men and women who are ready to toil under the baking African sun tending crops and livestock.

The new owners of Zimbabwe's farms include the following people: Vice Presidents Muzenda and Msika; the Ministers of Transport, Industry, State, Energy, Defence, Higher Education and Youth. The Deputy Ministers of Health, Employment Creation, Justice and Local Government. The Mayor of Bindura and ex-Mayor of Chitungwiza, six MPs, five Permanent Secretaries, four Governors, four District Administrators and two Provincial Administrators.

From our armed and security forces, farm beneficiaries are the Commissioner of Police, his deputy and the ZRP official spokesman. The Head of the Prisons service, the chief Prison officer and his deputy, two retired army generals, six brigadiers, a colonel, major and wing commander. From our judiciary, farm beneficiaries named include the Chief Justice of the Supreme Court, three lawyers, one attorney and one retired Judge. From the state owned TV, farm beneficiaries include ZBC Chief Correspondent Reuben Barwe, Anchorman Supa Mandiwanzira and Head of Sports Admire Taderera. The VIP beneficiaries have got farms ranging in size from 300 to 1,200 hectares which include the houses, infrastructure and equipment. Landless peasants have also been given land but only in the form of little plots of less than 20 hectares with no house or infrastructure, no Title Deeds and no equipment.

The list of Zimbabwe's new commercial farmers is a Who's Who in Zanu PF. It is a list of the people who have been at the forefront of what Zanu PF calls Zimbabwe's Third Chimurenga. Our government got back into power on the promise of land to the people and now we can see exactly which people they were talking about.

IN THE NEWS

~*31st May 2002* Junior Minister of Information Jonathan Moyo orders⅃ Joy TV to stop broadcasting. Joy TV was the only independent television station in the country.

1 June 2002. Begging bowls

The UN World Food Programme and the FAO say six million Zimbabweans in both urban and rural areas need emergency food aid. They say that even after pledged aid has been given and government food imports have been made, the country will still have a shortfall of 1.5 million tonnes of cereals. The statement acknowledged that two years of farm invasions have compounded this massive food shortage and said that unless international food assistance was given urgently: 'there will be a serious famine and loss of life in the coming months.'

The UN also spoke of the effects of drought saying Zimbabwe had just experienced the longest dry spell in 20 years. What they did not say was that most of Zimbabwe's dams are full because the water has not been used to irrigate crops and there are almost no crops in the ground. In fact, as anyone that has lived in Zimbabwe will know, the dam percentages in all the provinces are very good for the time of year. (Masvingo 91%, Matabeleland 79%, Mashonaland 89%, Midlands 88% and Manicaland 100% full).

This week agriculture minister Dr Joseph Made said that any white farmer who did not put a crop of wheat into the ground would have his farm listed for seizure. I'm not sure where the Minister has been these last two years because he has already listed 95% of Zimbabwe's farms for government seizure. There are now only thought to be 308 farms in the entire country not listed for state seizure. Neither Dr Made nor any of his officials are prepared to offer any written guarantees to a farmer that he will be able to grow, reap and sell his wheat before the government moves in and takes the farm over. We have become like Somalia and Ethiopia and are holding out our begging bowls to the world.

IN THE NEWS

~*15th June 2002* The IMF announces a declaration of non-cooperation on Zimbabwe's overdue financial obligations and suspends technical assistance to the country.

15 June 2002. Goose liver pate

Grocery shoppers in our country have a strange disease. We walk around supermarkets with empty baskets and trolleys; pick things up, look at the prices, turn them over and then put them back on the shelves. We spend entire mornings standing shivering in lines waiting patiently for our turn to buy one small bag of sugar and then, when we have the little plastic packet in our hands, we glow with delight and scurry home to show our families how lucky we've been. While we do this President Mugabe and his entourage have been staying in a luxury hotel in Italy where one room costs the equivalent of Z$480,000 per night, the same as 8,000 loaves of bread in Zimbabwe. The Presidential party are attending the UN Summit on reducing world hunger where journalists reported that lunch on one day was goose liver pate, followed by lobster, Italian ices for desert and all washed down with the finest Italian wines.

Are you serious? The King who ate himself to death

'Adolf Frederick, the King of Sweden, died of digestion problems on 12 February 1771 after having consumed a meal of lobster, caviar, sauerkraut, smoked herring and champagne, topped off with 14 servings of his favourite dessert: hetvägg served in a bowl of hot milk. He is thus remembered by Swedish schoolchildren as 'the king who ate himself to death.'' (Wikipedia)

IN THE NEWS

~*16th June 2002* Officials in Zimbabwe claim that British High Commissioner, Brian Donnelly, has been placed under 24 hour police surveillance after allegations that he is coordinating efforts to overthrow Robert Mugabe.

23 June 2002. Human excrement encrusting their feet

On Monday morning 51% of Zimbabwe's commercial farmers will be confined to their homesteads and forbidden to continue operating. If they attempt to keep producing food they face two years in prison, a fine of $20,000 or both. 2,443 farmers have Section 8 letters of Compulsory Acquisition and from Monday have 45 days in which to pay off their workers, pack their belongings and get out of their houses. This is a sickening irony in a country where almost seven million people are facing starvation and need international food aid.

Officials estimate that by the end of the year, when the remainder of Zimbabwe's farmers with Acquisition Notices have been evicted, two million people will be homeless and jobless. ZBC TV interviewed a man described as a Zanu PF strategist and this incredibly young Brigadier General gave his opinions on the coming eviction of farmers and their workers. 'We should not give these people even two days to get out. We want our land; we should move in with our security forces and just take it. What is the law for, we should just take it.'

To really appreciate the enormity of the tragedy in Zimbabwe, I paid a passing visit to our farm just outside of Marondera this week. I am unable to go onto my own farm anymore, denied entry by the war veterans, but had been told that upwards of 500 people have been dumped there and that two people died there last week. What I saw was beyond all comprehension and I am still struggling to come to terms with the reality of it.

Our farm is being used by the government as a dumping ground for squatters who have been evicted from other farms which have been claimed by senior government officials.

There were at least 500 people on my farm but they aren't squatting all over the 1,000 acre property, the majority are camped out in less than 5 acres on the driveway, in the house and garden, in and around the tobacco barns, workshops, bulk feed rooms and in the dairy.

The homestead area is littered with plastic and tin shacks and approximately 200 children, barefoot and in raggedy clothes play amongst goats, chickens and ducks. Only three pit latrines have been dug in the area and locals say that the smell of human faeces is permanent and nauseating. They say you cannot walk in amongst the squatters because the ground is a swamp of human and animal excrement. The new group of war veterans who took over control of the farm six weeks ago burnt out the borehole so there is no water and fears of cholera grow. Never did I imagine that children would run through our timber plantations with human excrement encrusting their feet.

IN THE NEWS

~28th June 2002 Twenty seven child deaths due to malnutrition-related diseases are recorded at Binga hospital between January and June 2002. Donor organizations left the area after war veterans demanded priority in food distribution be given to Zanu PF supporters.

~30th June 2002 President Mugabe warns food companies he will 'take over their enterprises' if products are not sold at prices set by his government.

30 June 2002. Fishing worms and firewood

I went on a four hour journey through what used to be one of the most productive farming areas of the country this week and now there are just miles and miles of nothing to see. Most of the road signs have gone, the tin stolen to be made into pots and pans. In all the little towns along the road, the sales yards are crammed full of second hand farm equipment waiting to be auctioned, but there are no buyers. Signs of neglect and squalor are visible in all the towns: potholes, litter, shanty flea markets, beggars and street kids. The fields which at this time of the year should be bursting with crops of irrigated wheat and winter vegetables are deserted, brown and weed filled. Boundary roadside fences have disappeared and everywhere indigenous trees are being chopped down and sold as firewood. There were few stretches of the road where there was not a wildfire burning.

Zimbabwe's new farmers are concentrated in camps near the roadside and are living in primitive conditions. Their houses are tatty little shacks covered with thatching grass or old plastic, their complexes are surrounded by felled trees and the men sit around in groups near the edge of the road. There was no sign of any production at all and small herds of cattle look painfully thin. On a four hour journey through Zimbabwe's prime agricultural land, the only things on the side of the road available to buy were fishing worms and firewood. One man had half a dozen pockets of sweet potatoes to sell but at $100 a kg, he didn't have many takers. The price of a single egg on my own farm in 2000 was $1, today that same egg costs $23.

At the end of a long and tiring day I got home to the news that yet another friend had been forced off her farm. Given two hours' notice to vacate her house, she lived through that day of hell which has now become commonplace in Zimbabwe. Within months they will leave the country of their birth because they are farmers and know no other way to earn their living. They will have to go somewhere where they are allowed to grow food.

On the lighter side. Going fishing?

Sign on the roadside: 'Fishing wemps and slerms for sale.'

IN THE NEWS

~*1st July 2002* Bread is unavailable countrywide as bakers run out of flour and salt. The State owned Grain Marketing Board (the only permitted traders in maize and wheat) has reduced wheat allocations to millers from 7,200 to 4,000 tonnes a week.

~*1st July 2002* The International Criminal Court is established to prosecute individuals for genocide, crimes against humanity and war crimes.

~*12th July 2002* Britain freezes £76,000 in assets belonging to Zanu PF.

13 July 2002. Goodness and Godliness

A farmer came to visit this week and told me how the people who say they have been allocated his farm arrived at his farmhouse last weekend in a green Landover. The five men demanded to move into the farmer's small guest cottage. The farmer, his frail wife, their almost blind son and his wife and two young children were completely powerless to stop this obscenity. They stood and watched as the five men went into the guest cottage, removed all the furniture and dumped it outside on the lawn. The five men removed the farmer's lock from the front door of the cottage and put on their own padlock. With beds and tables, chairs and bookcases lying on the grass in the farmer's garden, the five men left having claimed another man's home and life.

This story is being repeated on farms all over the country but this particular incident has horrified me because I know the man who came in the green Landover. I know his wife and son and I know that he is an educated, middle class man who already has his own farm. I know that he is not a landless peasant but has allowed himself to be consumed by the greed which is sweeping our country.

When the farmer who visited me was leaving, he said he had one more thing to tell me. This man, moments away from losing everything he's worked all his life for, said he had visited my farm on the outskirts of Marondera this week. He'd heard that 500 people had been dumped there and were literally starving to death and so he took them a 50 kilogram bag of maize because he couldn't bear the thought of children starving. He asked me if I blamed him for helping the people who have taken over my farm. I do not, I thank God for this farmer's decency, goodness and godliness.

IN THE NEWS

~*15th July 2002* Guardian journalist Andrew Meldrum is acquitted on charges of publishing falsehoods but Immigration officials order his deportation from Zimbabwe.

~*21st July 2002* MDC Spokesman and MP Learnmore Jongwe hands himself over to police on Sunday and confesses to the fatal stabbing of his wife.

~*23rd July 2002* The EU imposes a travel ban and asset freeze on 52 more members of the Zimbabwean ruling party, including Grace Mugabe.

3 August 2002. Last handshakes

Four people sat around my kitchen table this week; they had come to say goodbye to each other. They were a white farmer and his wife and their two black employees. The white farmer had been evicted from his home of 23 years by a bunch of thugs claiming to represent the government. The farmer had not received any notification of compulsory land acquisition from the government but was powerless to protect himself, his wife, their employees, livestock, equipment or property. The farmer lost everything he had worked his entire life for: his land, house, fencing, timber plantations, borehole and motor, farm buildings, cottage, dam, cattle race and dip tank. He lost his tractor, plough, fuel and tools. He lost 2,000 laying hens, their feed and all the equipment in the runs. Worst of all he lost his retirement and pension, his security and peace of mind. Everything was taken by a mob of men who arrived at the gate and just took over. The farmer and his wife are leaving the country, they know only farming.

Across the table from the farmer sat the last two workers. Both men had worked for the farmer for two decades, both are married with a number of children and both knew that this was the last goodbye. The older of the two men, Sekuru, doesn't know exactly how old he is.

His eyesight is not too good anymore and most of his teeth are gone. Sekuru's wife is blind, diabetic and asthmatic and it took almost his entire monthly wage on the farm to buy her medicines. These two men have also lost everything to the bunch of thugs that came to the farm gate. They have lost their jobs, homes and income. They have lost the ability to buy food and medicines and pay school fees for their children. They have lost the eggs, chickens, meat, vegetables and fruit that the farmer regularly gave them. They have lost the ability to provide for their families.

The eyes of all the people around my kitchen table were filled with tears as the farmer and his wife paid off their last two workers. They had shared so much and I could hardly bear to watch their last handshakes or listen to their final good-byes. It is an image that will stay in my memory forever. This scene is about to be played out on 3,000 other Zimbabwean farms with at least a quarter of a million people having to say goodbye.

IN THE NEWS

~7th August 2002 The EU announces a £23 million emergency food aid package for Zimbabwe despite political differences with Robert Mugabe and Zanu PF.

24 August 2002. Standing together

Over 200 commercial farmers were arrested this week for attempting to grow food for a starving nation. Amongst them was a 63-year-old man who has had prostate and renal cancer, suffers from a liver disease, chronic bronchitis and has recurrent sepsis in his eye socket. Despite written medical evidence and appeals for mercy against his detention, the farmer was held in custody.

Five farmers in another area handed themselves over to police in solidarity with their colleagues. One man, off his farm for over a month, telephoned the police to report that his centre pivot irrigation equipment had been stolen. The police told the farmer to come to the station to make an official statement and when he got there he was arrested. In another area a 70-year-old woman was arrested in place of her son who wasn't there.

This month a 63-year-old MDC MP was re-arrested in Bulawayo. Fletcher Dulini Ncube is a diabetic and during his last stay in prison in late 2001 was denied sufficient medication and had to have one of his eyes surgically removed on the 9th of August. On the 10th of August, with bandages over his eye socket, Fletcher was re-arrested and detained by police. Intense lobbying got him removed to hospital where he was shackled in leg irons and guarded day and night by 5 men for two weeks until finally being released on bail.

The real Zimbabweans are standing together as never before and showing their true patriotism. In my own hometown black and white people have joined hands to feed people who have been dumped on the side of the road. They are too scared to let me tell their amazing story or of the condition of the 200 children they are keeping alive but their story too is one of bravery and incredible unity. Farmers, opposition politicians and ordinary men and women are showing the world that our crisis is not about land or race, it's only about political power.

Welcome diversion. Green lights at night

Closing windows and curtains at about 5.45 pm before it was even really dark, I saw a bright light shining in a far corner of the garden. After two years of war vets and lawlessness I thought someone was in the garden, crouched down smoking a cigarette. The light had a sort of neon greenness about it and the longer I looked the more I realised it couldn't possibly be a person and I was being paranoid. Going outside to investigate, the closer I got, the light still didn't move. In the sand under the hedge in a dry barren little place covered with termites and ant holes there was a small pale worm about two centimetres long. Creamy white at one end, orange at the other, the neon light shone from the white end. I had a glow worm in my garden, something I'd never seen close up before. Taking photographs wasn't very successful because the camera's flash blinded the glow worm's light and if I shone my torch on the insect for more than a minute, its light went out. Later I discovered that glow worms are actually classed as beetles and the female's lamp glows at the tip of the abdomen. This intriguing little creature eats slugs and snails and every evening I've taken to looking for her. She's a very welcome visitor helping to control the inundation of snails attracted to my attempts at growing vegetables amongst the flowers in my garden. What a relief to know it's a glow worm in my garden and not a war vet!

IN THE NEWS

~August 2002 Inflation rises to 135% during the month.

7 September 2002. Rewards for dirty deeds

After 29 months of political turmoil and the almost complete cessation of commercial agriculture, small traditionally agro-based towns are falling apart. In Marondera town the commonest sight is of crowds of people waiting for one thing or another. They are waiting for jobs, for food deliveries to supermarkets, for fuel deliveries to filling stations. Outside government offices they are waiting for bits of paper which tell them which piece of seized land they can occupy; whether their application for government project money has been approved; whether their request for free seed, fertilizer or school fees has been accepted or not. Outside the once beautiful Marondera Municipal offices this week, lines of tired and thin women sit with their hungry babies waiting for a piece of paper with a government stamp on it entitling them to queue for maize at the town's grain marketing board.

At the main Marondera hospital there are hundreds of people sitting on the ground in the sun, waiting for a doctor or a nurse, a pain killer or bandage. Around the town litter is everywhere, the roads into the suburbs are mapped with deep potholes, two out of every ten streetlights work and nine out of ten street signs have been stolen.

On the 67km journey from Marondera to Harare the neglect is phenomenal. Almost all the farms have been taken over, the fences are gone or falling down and the fields are deserted, burnt or barren. Travelling this road late on a Sunday afternoon the new owners of the seized farms turn out onto a highway where the road signs have been stolen for the tin and the reflective cats' eyes have been dug out of the tar for their aluminium content. If these people driving home into a glowing red sunset are landless peasants then, as my parents used to say, I'll eat my hat. They are driving $20 million Pajeros and Mercedes, they are Zimbabwe's new weekend and cell-phone farmers who acquired these new properties as rewards for their dirty deeds in political power struggles.

IN THE NEWS

~*14th September 2002* Police arrest a retired white judge who tried to have the Justice Minister detained on contempt of court charges. This is the first time a Judge has been arrested in Zimbabwe.

Are you serious? Magistrate fines himself

'In 1874, Francis Evans Cornish, while acting as a magistrate in Winnipeg, Canada, had to try himself on a charge of being drunk in public. He convicted himself and fined himself five dollars with costs. But then he stated for the record: 'Francis Evans Cornish, taking into consideration past good behaviour, your fine is remitted." (Wikipedia)

14 September 2002. Little white stickers

Many farmers have been forced out of their homes in the past few days. One friend said they were ordered out of their home by a senior politician who has now claimed five farms in the area. The farmer and his family were given 12 hours to pack up and get out. They do not know where to go, have no plans in place but knew that they had to get out or risk being put in prison. They went into a mad flurry of activity and when everything was piled up outside on the lawn Mandy's husband suggested she go around and stick white labels on the boxes and items that were the most important so that they would be easily identifiable when they found somewhere to live. Mandy walked around looking at the contents of her life strewn on the lawn and with the help of Albert, one of her farm workers, stuck little white labels on her most treasured possessions. When she had finished, Albert picked up the roll of stickers and stuck a little white label onto his own chest showing that he wanted to come too and should not be forgotten. Mandy started to cry, she and her family have endured so much in the last 30 months and in her words they have been trashed and looted and are now booted.

The International Crisis Group said this week that Zimbabwe's farm workers are literally falling through the cracks. Official sources estimate that less than 1% of the country's 1.5 million farm workers have been given pieces of land by the government and have become homeless, jobless and destitute and some are resorting to desperate measures as a means of survival. One of these is extortion and it is absolutely tragic to see what is happening in labour offices all over the country.

It was not enough for the Zimbabwe government to seize the land, crops, equipment and then homes of white farmers. They then gazetted legislation ordering that if a farm was seized by the State, farmers would have to pay enormous retrenchment packages to their workers. In hundreds of cases a farm worker who was perhaps earning ten to fifteen thousand dollars a month is walking away with amounts of three quarters of a million Zim dollars. Everyone who ever worked on a farm, even for a month weeding between a line of maize, is climbing on the bandwagon demanding they be paid retrenchment. A friend told me this week about how the relatives of a worker who had died of alcohol abuse four years ago were claiming the retrenchment package. Another told of a worker who, dismissed for theft, tried and convicted, had also arrived demanding a million dollar package. If you dispute the claims you have to go to a 'hearing' at the Labour offices. Here dozens of people wait for many hours in dark, filthy corridors until an exhausted official is finally able to see you. It has turned into a nightmare of plain and simple extortion and is so tragic to see people abandoning pride and dignity because they know there is no law.

One farmer described paying the retrenchment package and watching her elderly and newly jobless, homeless, barely literate employee take a wad of 50 thousand dollars and blow it all in one weekend at the nearby bottle store. There are also hundreds of farmers who literally do not have the money to pay out these huge mandatory retrenchments. The legislation says that in these cases half the amount must be paid on leaving the farm and the balance when the government pays compensation to the farmer. Both farmer and worker know the chances of government compensation ever actually materializing are virtually nil and so there is a stalemate. If the farmer refuses to pay, a mob arrive at the gate, bang tins, light fires, barricade you into your home and demand that you start selling things in order to pay them.

In less than a month the summer crops are due to be in the ground and the men and women who have the experience, expertise and capital to grow this food are not allowed to do so. In an area near here there are only 12 farmers left out of 76 who used to farm in the district. Many of the farm homes have been taken over by politicians and army personnel; greenhouses for export flowers have been dismantled, tobacco seed beds have not been planted, there are no cattle to be seen and the fields stand barren and unprepared. All this for a cause which is neither about land nor race but politics. There is a Zulu saying which warns that: 'The infant who does not cry, will die on the back of its mother.' Zimbabwe is crying but no one hears us.

IN THE NEWS

~18th September 2002 The European Council of Ministers extends to 79 the list of individuals subject to targeted sanctions in order to reflect the recent cabinet reshuffle by President Mugabe.

21 September 2002. Not a single seed to buy

Summer has arrived in Zimbabwe, the days are getting longer, the sun is getting warmer but there's not a single seed to buy just a fortnight or two before the rains begin. On these gorgeous days it's perfect weather for farming and for sport. I sat on the edge of a sports field one evening this week to watch my son playing a friendly hockey game and a stranger came and sat next to me. The stranger was an 11-year-old farmer's son and when I asked him why he wasn't playing, my question opened a flood gate. This boy is one of thousands of Zimbabwean children whose life has been changed forever. His parents have been chased off their farm; the only home the boy has ever known has been taken over and he is struggling to understand it and come to terms with reality.

The boy asked me why these men are doing these things to us; why they are taking our things and want our houses and why the police don't do anything to stop them. He asked me why the people grabbing our farms aren't growing any crops. He wanted to know why some of these new farmers are just breaking everything in the farmhouses, smashing baths and toilets off walls and taking the roofs off the houses. He asked me why President Mugabe doesn't like whites anymore and what we'd done to make him do these awful things to us. He said that his Mum wouldn't answer these questions, had told him he must forget the farm and stop worrying, but the boy just can't.

Now an 11-year-old boy worries about if his Mum and Dad will get jobs in Harare. He says they only know how to do farming and they've both had to go back to school like him to learn other jobs. He said that all his friends are leaving and his best friend had gone to Australia. 'Who's going to be left?' he asked me. 'Why don't our parents want to tell us what's really going to happen?'

I didn't have a lot of answers for an 11-year-old boy sitting next to me on the edge of a hockey pitch. Nor I could answer my own question as to how we will grow enough food for the country this season when there isn't a single seed to buy. When I left the hockey game the boy was playing dinky cars with some other children in the dusty driveway under a spectacular full moon and we waved to each other. He'd gone back to being a child; I hope that one day both he and I will have answers to some of his questions.

IN THE NEWS

~25th September 2002 Registrar-General Tobaiwa Mudede files an urgent application in the High Court seeking an order to destroy ballot papers used in the disputed March presidential election, despite the ongoing legal challenge to President Robert Mugabe's victory.

28 September 2002. Tasting white blood

Forty second in the queue for a loaf of bread, it ran out long before I got to the front so I bought the weekly newspaper instead. On the front page is the story that the government's much talked about crop of irrigated winter maize which is about to be harvested. At best it looks as if the crop, which they said would save the country from starvation, will only yield enough food for the country for one and a half days.

Leaving the supermarket with only food for thought I passed the arrogant groups of youngsters wearing Zanu PF T shirts who've been crowding our town the whole week, ready to harass voters in the weekend's council elections. A man stood at my car window, his hands held as if in prayer: 'please help me with something to eat,' he begged.

Town or country, horrors have become a part of everyday life in Zimbabwe. A woman arrived on a farm this week, accompanied by five men armed with AK rifles, and told the owners to get out as this was now her home. She refused to shake hands with the farmer saying she didn't shake hands with whites and went on to say she: 'hadn't tasted white blood' since 1980. This woman gets away with saying and doing these things not because she is black but because she belongs to Zanu PF and is the wife of the Commander of the Zimbabwe Army. This is the calibre of our new commercial farmers.

Welcome diversion. Lofty hotel bedrooms

Hysterical barking, hair standing up along their backs and with acrobatic leaps, the dogs were making a very determined effort to retrieve some sort of creature from a dense and overgrown area in the garden. A large bird had crash landed in the shrubbery and seemed to be caught. It was thrashing around so much that it was hard to tell what the big black and white bird was at first but once the dogs were out of the way I saw it was an Abdim's Stork, something I was very familiar with from farming days.

They used to always arrive on the farm in large numbers just before the start of the rainy season. A few at first and then more and more until there were dozens and then a few hundred. Standing in the fields or grassland the Abdims had mastered the art of keeping statue – still during the hot, humid days of October and November. Like the farmers, the Abdims were just waiting for the rain and their arrival was a signal: if the rain hadn't started, it was about to.

Standing nearly a metre tall the big glossy black birds have white chests, long legs, pink knees and feet and long grey bills which are perfect for stabbing and picking up rats, insects, frogs, and lizards – anything disturbed by man or machine at the start of the new farming season. Every year on our farm the Abdims would roost in four huge gum trees which towered outside my study window. It had been a daily ritual to watch them checking into their lofty hotel bedrooms at the end of each day. They would soar down, lower their landing gear and then glide into place in the tree. As more birds arrived and the roost got crowded, squabbles broke out everywhere with much wing flapping and re-arrangements until three or four hundred birds had settled down for the night.

The lone Abdim's Stork tangled in the shrubbery of my garden in town was a far cry from the hundreds of birds I used to watch on the farm. It panted and snapped as I tried to give it some water and as twilight came the bird's struggles grew less frantic and sometime in the night it died.

5 October 2002. Electrodes on his ears

The phone starts ringing early in the morning and always the calls are questions. Do you know if there's any petrol? How long is the queue for bread? Any chance of sugar today? Have you heard of anyone getting a maize delivery? The search for food has become a nightmare. Every day the list of things we can no longer get increases and now includes maize meal, sugar, cooking oil, salt, biscuits, potatoes, flour, bread, petrol and diesel. The food that is still available in the shops goes up in price at least once a week. Minibus fares are $100 in the morning and $150 in the evening to go the same distance because the drivers have to buy petrol on the black market.

In Marondera all week there have been massive queues outside every supermarket, grocery shop and kiosk. Everyone is desperate to buy bread and the lines start shortly after dawn. By 8 am the queue is anything from 200 – 400 people strong but most go away empty handed. Zimbabwe has run out of wheat, maize and almost all the other staple foods that we have always taken for granted. Few people can afford the rapidly dwindling supplies of protein and carbohydrates that are still on the shelves. Eggs which were $350 a tray (30 eggs) a year ago are now $1,060. Pasta was $30 a packet last year now it's $360. Two kilos of potatoes cost $80 last year, now if you can find them, they cost $400.

While we all search for something to eat, political insanity has escalated with hundreds of people beaten and homes burnt as council elections were held around the country. Roy Bennett, the Chimanimani MP came across a rural polling station where great piles of maize meal were available for voters to buy at hugely subsidized prices, if they put their X against the name of the Zanu PF candidate. Roy videoed the evidence of food for votes and was then arrested along with his bodyguard and a friend and they were held in police custody for two days. Roy's bodyguard was severely assaulted and Roy was slapped around, kicked and told he was a 'white pig' who should 'go back to Britain' by members of the CIO.

In Harare 18-year-old opposition activist Tom Spicer and four friends were arrested. They were held in police cells on trumped up charges, beaten on the soles of their feet and subjected to extreme violence. Tom was handcuffed, blindfolded and had electrodes attached to his ears where repeated electric shocks were administered. This is the eleventh time Tom Spicer has been arrested.

IN THE NEWS

~*October 2002* Inflation rises to 144% during the month.

12 October 2002. Two little boys

The rains have arrived after five months of clear skies and dry days heralding the rapid approach of the growing season.

With more than half our population starving you would think that there would be a great flurry of activity out on the farms and the government would be working 24 hours a day to get professional farmers planting seeds in the ground. Exactly the opposite is happening as the government's 'Land Task Force' have been touring the country and evicting every commercial farmer they can find. It doesn't seem to matter where the farm is, what is being produced or how desperately the country needs the food being grown on a particular farm, the government wants these professional food providers out.

A farmer who was arrested recently shared his prison cell with four adults and two young boys. The boys, aged twelve and fourteen, had been thrown into prison after stealing a pair of shoes. They had been there for five days already and in that time had not seen a lawyer and had not had any food at all. Also arrested this week were top officials of the teachers union including Raymond Majongwe. Seriously assaulted whilst in custody Majongwe was unable to sit or stand, had suspected broken ribs and internal bleeding.

IN THE NEWS

~*13th October 2002* Sir Garfield Todd, Prime Minister of Southern Rhodesia from 1953–1958 and defender of human rights dies aged 94 in Bulawayo.

~*13th October 2002* Australia imposes sanctions on Zimbabwe's leadership, including travel bans and a freeze on assets.

18 October 2002. No hugs in public Mum

Life in Zimbabwe has a strange duplicity about it: everything seems so normal on the surface and yet so abnormal under the veneer. My ten year old son went on a school camp to Bulawayo and Victoria Falls this week and while I made the preparations and did the packing, it all seemed so normal. A huge list of things had to be crammed into the smallest possible case: sleeping bag, pillow, clothes, toiletries and homemade biscuits. The abnormality started as Richie and I walked to the car with his kit bag. 'I hope we don't meet any war vets Mum.' he said. I made all the right reassuring noises but my heart was in my mouth. I'm not sure if Richie believes me anymore when it comes to these sort of conversations. I've made him so many promises before and every time I've been proved to be lying as war veterans have taken everything we've ever had and there's never been anyone able to help us. I had an anxious four days while Richie was away on his adventures and was looking forward to having him safely back at home on Thursday afternoon. The bus was very late arriving and sitting in the darkening school car park there was nothing to do except try not to worry and just soak in an African night.

The almost full moon rose, the temperature dropped and a million crickets and cicadas began their nocturnal chorus. Bats flitted across the car park and a night jar swooped low in the moonlight, its call of 'Good Lord Deliver Us' bringing goose bumps to my arms as the minutes dragged by and still the bus didn't come. When the children finally dragged themselves off the bus, filthy, exhausted and more than five hours later than promised, I wanted to just fling my arms around my son. He's ten, status is everything and hugs in public are most definitely not allowed.

Life soon got back to normal, the ring of filth around the bath, blaring television and sagging washing line brought normalcy back. When I asked Richie what the best and worst things about his trip were, he said that the train toilet was 'gross' as it empties straight onto the railway lines and the best was climbing the granite rocks of the Matopos, watching the black eagles and seeing the 'olden day' ox carts in the natural history museum.

Abnormality kicked in the next day when we went to do our weekly shopping. No bread, milk, flour, sugar or biscuits and a small packet of chicken pieces costing over $1,000. We joked as we stood in line at the post office, Richie insisting the parcel we were waiting for would be for him. 'How boring,' he said when it was for me and it was yeast so that I can make bread for his school lunches.

Richie and his classmates were so lucky to have had such a wonderful adventure while so many of the country's schools were being plunged into utter chaos. The government say they have fired 627 striking teachers and there were reports of huge senior schools being manned by as few as three staff members.

IN THE NEWS

~22nd October 2002 Former MDC spokesman Learnmore Jongwe (28) awaiting trial for murdering his wife, is found dead in prison under unclear circumstances.

~31st October 2002 A government project to produce 18,000 tonnes of winter maize in Chiredzi fails when only 7,500 tonnes are harvested – enough to feed the country for only one day.

2 November 2002. Vindictive victory

A Short Wave Radio Africa reporter was conducting a telephone interview with a man in Insiza a few days before the parliamentary by-election being held there. Suddenly the man said he had to go; the place was being stormed by government supporters. 'They are coming,' he shouted, leaving his phone on so the world could hear what happens when elections take place in Zimbabwe.

When the results from the remote, dusty, hungry part of Matabeleland South were announced, Zanu PF claimed victory; their candidate got 12,000 votes while the MDC received 5,000 votes. Barely seven months ago in the Presidential election almost these exact same figures were announced but the results were the other way around: MDC 12,000, Zanu PF 5,000. Hard to believe that seventeen thousand people can change their mind in such a short space of time.

In the weeks preceding the by-election 16 MDC supporters and 8 MDC activists were arrested; the MDC parliamentary candidate was stopped by police at a roadblock and refused entry into his constituency. The MDC were denied access to the voters roll and one of their supporters was shot in the back either by the winning Zanu PF candidate or his aide. The UN had stopped distributing emergency food aid in Insiza ten days before the elections saying the food distribution was being manipulated. Government officials had helped themselves to three metric tonnes of maize from an aid organization and gave it out at rallies. They told voters they would only be given the food if Zanu PF won the election. On voting day observers and diplomats confirmed that great piles of maize meal stood outside polling stations.

Once the results had been announced, the winners celebrated wildly and then went on the rampage. To Zanu PF victory is vindictive and eleven MDC polling agents were rounded up, taken away and severely assaulted. The MDC offices in Bulawayo were stoned and several vehicles damaged. Contacted for comment on their win, a Zanu PF official said he was too busy celebrating and told the reporter to: 'call Britain for comment.' Four days after Zanu PF won the by-election in Insiza, 54 farms were listed for government seizure, 40 are located in Insiza.

IN THE NEWS

~7th November 2002 New Zealand increases smart sanctions against Zimbabwe to cover 142 officials of President Mugabe's government and business associates of Zanu PF.

16 November 2002. Brandy man

There's nothing nicer than sitting outside with a cup of tea and watching dawn break. Weaver birds in their magnificent breeding colours flit around the lawn picking up all the Christmas beetles that have hit the lights overnight. Lilac breasted rollers wobble on the telephone lines and every now and again a hammerkop comes down, nodding and bobbing his head as he patrols the garden for insects. Over the wall I wave to my neighbour who is already hard at it. He is in his suit, jacket hanging on a thorn bush, tie flipped over his shoulder, sleeves rolled up, a hoe in his hand. He is weeding between the lines of maize and beans that he's planted on the side of the road.

There are already a lot of people on the road but they're not going to work, they're going to a house a block away whose enterprising owner sells groceries. Known as a 'tuck shop,' you can get more of life's basics here than in the supermarkets. Every morning the line starts at 5am. A hundred or more people wait until 5.30am when the door opens and each person can buy one loaf of bread. By 6am there's nothing left. If you don't go to the tuck shop you have to jostle amongst the 47 trucks and 500 people who wait at the only bakery still operating in our town.

Waiting in a hundred car queue for fuel in town, a woman with a small enamel bowl comes to my car window and tries to persuade me to buy a small plastic tube filled with frozen drink. These frozen coloured drinks used to be called cent-a cools because they cost one cent, now they are just called freezits and are $50 each. I watch as two young men in green uniforms with shining police boots strut up the road carrying black rubber truncheons. No one makes eye contact; these are the notorious graduates from the Border Gezi training camps and everyone calls them 'green bombers.' The pair go up to a man with a pile of wilting cabbage, pick one up, laugh and throw it down. The cabbage rolls onto the road but no-one moves or says anything until the green bombers have gone.

A man wearing blue overalls and a black leather hat caught my attention. He was sitting on a tyre on the road opposite the petrol queue, decanting brandy into a half empty coke bottle. His wife, her face covered in new scars, stood beside him with one bag of fertilizer and two large bags of belongings. A minibus with the name 'Commander' was waved down and the man sat drinking brandy and coke while the woman negotiated a price to go 'to the farms.' The man carried on drinking while the woman carried the two bags and then the 50kg sack of fertilizer to the vehicle. Brandy man is one of Zimbabwe's new farmers and it is in him that we have to put our trust to grow food for a nation.

IN THE NEWS

~*16th November 2002* The Government announces price freezes on a wide range of goods including food, fuel, medicines, electrical appliances, agricultural machinery, fertilizers and school textbooks.

~*18th November 2002* Government publishes new laws making it a crime to gesture rudely or swear at President Mugabe's armed motorcade. The road traffic regulation states that when the presidential motorcade passes you: 'shall not make any gesture or statement within the view or hearing of the state motorcade with the intention of insulting any person travelling with an escort or any member of the escort.'

~22nd November 2002 The final contingent of Zimbabwean troops in the DR ı Congo are due to return home. It is not known how many Zimbabwean troops went to the DRC or how many lost their lives there.

~27th November 2002 The Zimbabwe government refuses to renew the work permit of Agehce France Press (AFP) who have had a regional office in Zimbabwe for 22 years.

30 November 2002. Beyond Tears

I sat on a hard bench in the Harare High Court one morning this week with two of the five farmers who were abducted at gun point from a Zimbabwean police station and tortured in April 2000. There were not many people in the room aside from prison and court officials, an interpreter, four witnesses, one of the accused and a couple of journalists who had all come to hear of the circumstances which led to the horrific murder of commercial farmer David Stevens.

I could not help but look back into my childhood memories as we waited for the judge to come in. My father had worked in this High Court, was called to the Bar here and somewhere there is a photograph of him, gowned and wigged, standing proudly in the courtyard of these same buildings. I could not stop myself from thinking that my Dad would be turning in his grave if he could see the place now. The white walls are filthy, covered with the grimy tide marks of people's heads and hands, there is nowhere for people to sit before they go into court, except on the floor. The windows, doors and ledges are coated in thick, brown dust. The tar which covers the upper walkways is melting and bubbling up in great shiny blobs. Finding a toilet was nearly impossible and the longed for mouthful of water was never realised.

The red-robed, grey-wigged Judge arrived and sat with two Judge Assessors and he, like the rest of us, struggled to hear the proceedings because the microphones had not been switched on. In a little over an hour it was all over. Neither the Prosecutor nor the Defence was ready to proceed with the case even though David Stevens was murdered thirty one months ago. The Judge released the accused man on $5,000 bail and postponed the case for another five months. David Stevens is just one of well over 200 people who have been murdered in political violence in Zimbabwe in the last three years and this is the only case which has got to court so far.

IN THE NEWS

~November 2002 Inflation rises to 175% during the month.

7 December 2002. Three wise men

Two hours after a hot sun had risen in the sky, a glorious red-winged starling called repeatedly and then settled down to sleep in a pine tree outside my study window. The dogs curled up and went to sleep and there was a strong, cold wind in the darkening sky. My ten year old son and I rushed outside with a mirror, a piece of smoke-blackened glass and a sheet of cardboard with a small circular hole punched into it. Everywhere the shadows were suddenly filled with little half-moons. Richie and I stood with our backs to the sun, held the cardboard up and watched the little reflected circle of white light change into a fingernail sliver and then fill with a glorious rainbow of colours on the kitchen wall. For forty seconds Zimbabwe grew dark and completely quiet as the moon passed over the sun in a total solar eclipse.

Another great darkness is engulfing Zimbabwe, but it isn't only going to last for forty seconds. Aerial photographs taken by the Daily News this week reveal the reality of the 3,000 farms seized by the government. These frightening pictures show miniscule, little squares of cultivation in the centre of huge un-used fields which stretch to the horizon.

Preliminary results from the latest census show that our population has dropped to 11.6 million. Over three million Zimbabweans are estimated to be living outside the country and one person dies from AIDS every five minutes in the country. Headlines in the latest Financial Gazette are that at least half of the country's manufacturing, mining and agro-industrial companies will close next week for the Christmas break and will not re-open until March as they simply cannot survive the inflation and overall economic collapse.

Just before schools closed for the December holidays I sat watching Richie's Christmas school play. The children who were playing the Three Wise Men arrived at the nativity on bicycles with rucksacks on their backs. They did not produce gold, frankincense and myrrh. They presented one loaf of bread, one bag of a sugar and a large piece of white paper which read 'One US dollar.' These things are the most precious gifts in Zimbabwe.

IN THE NEWS

~December 2002 Inflation rises to 198% during the month.

14 December 2002. Sacred ibises and a litany of hate

Opposite two of the main banks in my hometown there is a little park where I often used to push my son on the swings when he was a toddler. The swings and see-saw have long since disintegrated and the surrounding fence is a tangle of rusty, patched wire but towering high above the ruin of our once beautiful park the pine trees are still standing. Hundreds of birds have taken over the trees and the branches are crowded with Egrets and Sacred Ibises. The birds are constantly squabbling for the best spots in the branches which are overflowing with nests of sticks and twigs. The pavement and street below are grey with droppings and you have to shout to hear above the noise of many hundreds of fidgeting birds. Normally this natural wonder would attract many spectators but this year we are all too busy looking for fuel and food.

In the midst of enormous suffering of ordinary Zimbabweans, Zanu PF held their annual party congress in Chinhoyi. Three thousand delegates were seated on white plastic chairs under a huge white tent decorated with gold tinsel. Ninety percent of the delegates were wearing clothes (dresses, shirts, trousers and scarves) which had President Mugabe's face printed on the fabric; even Mr Mugabe was wearing a pea green shirt with pictures of himself on it.

In his seventy minute speech Mr Mugabe did not mention 6.8 million starving people; 70% unemployment; 5 kilometre queues for fuel or the fact that there is no bread, milk, maize, sugar, flour or cooking oil to buy. Neither did he comment on the fact that one dozen eggs cost $480 seven days ago and today are $660.

After President Mugabe had finished speaking a little boy was brought up to the microphone. With glazed eyes he shouted out what he said was his poem entitled: 'The Land.' My eyes filled with tears as this boy, the same age as my own son, used words he could not possibly know or understand, including 'repression, arrogantly, colonialism, rebellion and juxtaposition.' In the poem the little boy said Zimbabwe was for Zimbabweans and Africa was for Africans; 'whites are not welcome,' he said. While the child shouted out his litany of hate, President Mugabe was being served tea in delicate white china cups by a waiter, dressed all in white and wearing white cotton gloves. The child finished his recital, stumbling slightly on his last sentence which was: 'Down with Tony Blair and his wife Tsvangirai.' Dear God, what are they doing to the children?

IN THE NEWS

~19th December 2002 The Zimbabwe government's fuel debts are revealed: Tamoil Trading of Libya: US$20m, the Independent Petroleum Group of Kuwait: US$65m; BP SA: US$17.8m; Engen SA: US$12m; Mobil Africa: US$1.1m; Caltex:

US$7.8m; Libya Arab Foreign Bank: US$43m and the government of Botswana: US$4.4m.

21 December 2002. Counting our blessings

Zimbabweans are doing the best we can this Christmas. For most of us there won't be lavish gifts and excesses of alcohol this year. Nor will there be chicken or turkey, rice, ice cream or Christmas pudding. Rather it is a time of quiet contemplation, counting our blessings and giving thanks for what we have got. Many Zimbabweans are fasting by choice, organising prayer vigils and doing whatever they can to help and support their friends and neighbours. We have all learnt to give thanks for the simplest of things like a loaf of bread or a glass of real milk and to take nothing for granted an experience which is cause for both humility and gratitude.

Two days after the most frugal Christmas I can ever remember, I was treated to lunch at a beautiful garden restaurant outside my hometown. The gardens at this time of the year are superb, the lawns thick, lush and impeccably trimmed and the rose bushes crowded with glorious colours. We sat under a towering paperbark Acacia tree and the sky was endlessly blue. Only the faint smell of smoke hinted that perhaps everything was not quite as perfect or normal as it seemed.

We were served by an ever smiling, cheerful waiter who left us until we'd half-finished our gin and tonics before he presented us with the menu. He waited politely as we mulled over the leather bound, gold edged menu which boasted three pages of mouth-watering possibilities, ranging from

Inyanga trout or prawns to gammon or fillet steaks smothered in pepper, mushroom or garlic sauce. It was time to order and although we couldn't afford anything exotic from the menu, we put forward our requests. Sadly, the waiter just shook his head and said he was unable to supply any of the things we asked for. More and more orders were made and turned down so eventually we asked the waiter to tell us exactly which of the fifty odd possibilities on the menu the kitchen could provide. He told us that there was no gas to run their stoves so we could only have what could be cooked on the open fire they had burning outside the kitchen door. Another gin and a long wait before smoky hamburgers arrived reminding me that everything about life in Zimbabwe has a veneer about it. On the surface everything looks so absolutely normal and yet in reality it is falling apart.

On the lighter side. A Christmas recipe
CHRISTMAS CAKE.
Ingredients:
1 cup water
1 tsp baking soda
2 cups dried fruit
1 tsp salt
1 cup brown sugar
lemon juice
4 large eggs
1 bag nuts
1 bottle Vodka
Sample the Vodka to check quality.
Take a large bowl, check the Vodka again.

To be sure it is the highest quality, pour one cup Vodka and drink.

Repeat.

Turn on the electric mixer.

Beat one cup of butter in a large fluffy bowl.

Add one teaspoon of sugar. Beat again.

At this point it is best to make sure the Vodka is shtill OK. Try another cup, just in case.

Turn off the mixerer.

Break 2 leggs and add to the bowl and chuck in the cup of dried fruit.

Pick fruit off floor.

Mix on the turner.

If the fried druit gets stuck in the beaterers, pry it loose with a screwdriver.

Sample the Vodka to check for tonsisticity.

Next, sift two cups of salt. Or something.

Check the Vodka.

Now shift the lemon juice and strain your nuts.

Add one table.

Add a spoon of sugar, or somefink. Whatever you can find.

Greash the oven.

Turn the cake tin 360 degrees and try not to fall over.

Don't forget to beat off the turner.

Finally, throw the bowl through the window, finish the Vodka and kiss the cat.

Fall into bed.

Cherry Mistmas.

Part Four 2003

Dear Family and Friends

4 January 2003. Anyone for cricket?

Two men were arrested on Thursday afternoon for attaching a poster to a tree in Bulawayo. The poster, referring to no food or fuel in the country read: 'Hoot! Enough is Enough.' By the weekend, the men were still in prison, had been denied access to lawyers, refused bail and were not allowed to receive food bought for them by family members. Whilst this was happening I, along with 11 million others living in Zimbabwe, was desperately searching either for food or petrol. There was none of the latter so I spent my Friday morning trudging from shop to shop and after three hours gratefully clutched two loaves of bread I had tracked down for four times the official price. I know I shouldn't buy food on the black market but principles pale into insignificance when you have a hungry child to feed.

This is the face of life in Zimbabwe today and yet the ECB (English Cricket Board) are still debating whether or not it is right to come and play cricket here and are worrying about who will pay them compensation if they don't come. It's absurd that they can talk about compensation for a cricket match when 300,000 farm workers have been made destitute, 4,000 farmers have been evicted from their homes and had their properties grabbed by the state, 200 people have been murdered and not a single one of us has seen justice done or been paid compensation for our losses. 6 million Zimbabweans are facing starvation, 2 million of our citizens have been forced to leave the country, one person dies every 5 minutes from AIDS related malnutrition, inflation is at 175% and there is no food or fuel in the country and yet the world is in an uproar about six cricket matches. Where's the perspective?

A few months ago a friend took a wrong turning near the Harare cricket grounds and pulled into an unmarked driveway nearby to do a U turn. In an instant his car was surrounded by armed men and he was ordered out of his vehicle. Everything was pulled out of the car, he was interrogated at length and then taken behind a wall where he was pushed around, knocked to the ground and kicked in the side of his head. Five hours later he got home, exhausted, in shock and with a ruptured ear drum from being kicked in the head. My friend's crime had been to turn into the driveway opposite State House. The World Cup cricket matches are being played in the grounds next door to State House.

Sports and politics don't mix but when you know that people have been tortured with burning plastic, locked in steel containers and had electrodes attached to their genitals for wanting democratic governance, then cricket doesn't really seem appropriate.

Are you serious? Cricket in Zimbabwe

'Cricket civilizes people and creates good gentlemen. I want everyone to play cricket in Zimbabwe; I want ours to be a nation of gentlemen.' (Robert Mugabe. 1984)

IN THE NEWS

~*2nd January 2003* In a Presidential amnesty 3,600 prisoners are released from prison.

~*8th January 2003* Sixty four men and women are given prison sentences ranging from six months to life while twenty six others are sentenced to death for the murder of President Laurent Kabila in the Democratic Republic of Congo two years ago. Kabila was shot by a teenage bodyguard in his marble palace as he was seeking treatment for an ailment.

18 January 2003. Cows head in a trolley

So many people ask me to describe life in Zimbabwe now and it's hard to know where to start. Every little thing that just sounds like an annoyance has enormous repercussions throughout the country. There are now almost no farmers growing export crops which means no foreign currency. This means there are no spare parts, and very little gas and fuel. No gas might cause huge headaches to restaurants but far worse are the month long backlog of bodies at mortuaries, waiting to be cremated in gas incinerators. The chronic shortage of fuel means there is very little traffic on the roads, including delivery vehicles. Supermarket shelves are getting emptier by the day, there is less and less food to buy. Small towns which always depended on agriculture are collapsing fast. In Marondera this month our only private veterinary surgery closed, our only private dentist has closed, two of our private doctors have announced that they are leaving, one private school headmaster has already left and another leaves before winter.

I went in search of vegetable seeds for my garden. Seeds are not easy to find anymore, mostly because the majority of farmers who grew seed do not exist anymore in Zimbabwe; they too have been casualties of our government's land grab. I finally tracked down some very expensive seeds in a butchery but my shock at their price was overshadowed by the sight in front of me. Sitting in a supermarket trolley was a cow's head: eyes, ears, horns and fur intact. I made a point of expressing my disgust to the owner of the shop who simply shrugged at my complaints of both the sight of the animal's head and the flies around it. We are gripped by a contagious epidemic of moral decline where no one cares, no one complains and everyone just shrugs their shoulders.

With morale at its lowest we had a visit from the South African Minister of Labour who declared that South Africa had a lot to learn from us. I'm not exactly sure what the South African Minister wants to learn from Zimbabwe – how to stay in power or how to destroy a country. How to reduce productive farms to wasteland; how to turn a major exporting economy into a begging, famine ridden one; how to beat, maim, rape, torture and harass a population into submission and subservience. With each passing day Zimbabwe is sinking deeper and deeper into the mire.

Are you serious? Committing crimes on the way home

'At least 10 prisoners released under a Presidential amnesty a fortnight ago have been arrested after going on a housebreaking rampage in the Midlands, stealing property worth millions of dollars. Police spokesman Inspector Oliver Mandipaka said, 'some of them committed crimes on the day of their pardon on their way home.'' (The Herald)

IN THE NEWS

~*20th January 2003* A 36-year-old Harare man is stabbed to death near Lobels Bakeries after being wrestled for the dozen loaves of bread he was carrying.

~*28th January 2003* At a meeting between the CFU and seven cabinet ministers, white farmers who lost their properties are given an assurance that they will be re-allocated land elsewhere.

1 February 2003. 21st Century pioneers

How do you describe the death of a country that was beautiful and thriving only three years ago? Shall I write about the riot police who fired tear gas to disperse a residents meeting called to discuss the water crisis in Harare? Or about five international Lutheran church workers who were deported after being accused of being journalists in disguise, or two American journalists who were detained by police for 7 hours after they took photographs of a grain marketing depot. Perhaps I should write about the announcement by the

American State Department advising their nationals not to travel to Zimbabwe because of security concerns.

While the big picture unravels, the littlest of things have become critically important to everyday life. A petrol delivery where the queue is only a two hour long line gives you the chance to catch up on reading and just sit and watch people. The things you see in petrol queues today were never seen three years ago. White and black people stand and talk together, taking turns to push each other's cars forward. Everyone watches for line jumpers and in these queues more is being done to improve race relations in Zimbabwe than has been done in the past 22 years.

Petrol and food are the two things uniting Zimbabweans. In the main Marondera supermarket today there were 42 empty shelves. The list of things not available grows longer every day: bread, flour, milk, cereals, biscuits, pasta, margarine, dog food, sugar, salt, maize meal, washing powder. This week we heard that Colgate Palmolive is closing its factory and relocating to South Africa. They are the biggest manufacturers of detergent, soap and toothpaste in the country. Circle cement, the biggest producer in the country have also announced that they have ceased their operations and are closing down. As these huge companies close, we don't just lose the products, machinery and expertise, we lose the professionalism that has been decades in the making and we lose just another little piece of Zimbabwe's identity.

This government have taken our country decades back in time. Tractors and combine harvesters have been replaced with ox carts and hand ploughs. Bread and maize meal have been replaced with porridge made from wild nuts and berries. Women's sanitary towels and tampons have been replaced with toilet paper by those who can afford it and rags and leaves by those who cannot. This government and its policies have stripped our men of jobs and resources, our women of pride and dignity and our children of education. The school fees are unaffordable, the children are fainting in the classrooms and the dropout rates are escalating. We have become 21st century pioneers and scavengers, living like animals in the most modern of worlds.

On the lighter side. The definition of cricket

You have two sides, one out in the field and one in. Each man that's in the side that's in goes out, and when he's out he comes in and the next man goes in until he's out. When they are all out, the side that's out comes in and the side that's been in goes out and tries to get those coming in, out. Sometimes you get men still in and not out. When a man goes out to go in, the men who are out trying to get him out, and when he is out he goes in and the next man in goes out and goes in. There are two men called umpires who stay out all the time and they decide when the men who are in are out. When both sides have been in and all the men have been out, and both sides have been out twice after all the men have been in, including those who are not out, that is the end of the game. (Source unknown)

8 February 2003. No deck chairs or umbrellas

The World Cup cricket is coming to Zimbabwe after all and there was a half-page advert in the state controlled Herald today telling us which roads will be closed along with a list of 'ground rules' for spectators. The following things will not be allowed into the grounds:

No cold drinks of any type, regardless of the container it is in.

No banners or flags which are supported on a stick.

No trumpets, drums or musical instruments.

No deck chairs, umbrellas or gazebos.

'Banners and flags may only include wording which is: tasteful, non offensive, non-vulgar, non-political, non-racial, non-discriminatory and non-sexual.'

To people outside this may sound utterly ludicrous but to us who live here it has a tragic undercurrent. The world will watch cricket being played in Zimbabwe while some of us will be remembering the life of a very brave young man who has just died.

Edison Mukwasi aged 29 died in a Harare hospital this week. Edison was an ordinary man working on a construction site in Harare when he became the MDC's youth chairman for Harare. His nightmare began in January 2001 during the Bikita West by-election. Edison and 12 others were picked up by police, tortured for four days whilst in detention and then dumped in the Gonarezhou National Park. According to Edison's mother, her son's lungs and liver were perforated during the torture. In November 2002 Edison and others were arrested by police at a cricket match in Harare and allegedly tortured again whilst in police custody. He was accused of public disorder but was later released without being charged. Two months later Edison died; he is survived by his wife Gladys and their two week old daughter Nyasha.

Zimbabwe mourns the death of Edison Mukwasi and also of at least 50 others who died when two trains collided last weekend in Dete. The scenes of the mangled, melted carriages were horrific. A female reporter on ZBC TV said: 'body parts are going to be pulled out in order for the corpses to be identified.' The lack of sensitivity and compassion is overwhelming.

IN THE NEWS

Inflation rises to 220% during February.

15 February 2003. Laughter in the wind

A friend phoned early one morning this week; she was leaving for the airport. Linda and her family are emigrating. We did not talk for long, neither of us wanted to actually say the word 'goodbye' because we both knew we would cry. Instead the words were the usual ridiculous ones which say nothing but mean everything. Linda and her family are farmers. For three years they have waited for permission to grow food on their own farm but it hasn't happened and they have no other option but to leave. Farming is all they know. Their farm, house, business, assets and land have been taken over by a government heavyweight. They have left behind their home, lives, friends and forty years of service in providing food for their country. They have received no compensation for the seizure of their assets, were not allowed back to say goodbye and their memories remain only as laughter in the wind.

When I lived through the hell of an invaded farm and the incessant harassment and humiliation from the mob of men who took over our lives, the only thing that kept me sane every day was to watch the sunrise. It's three years ago now but I can still see that view in my mind. The peach tree covered with pink blossoms outside my study window. The weaver bird's nests hanging and swinging gently in the breeze, the magnificent dawn chorus and then the eerie silence as the spectacular red ball of sun appeared over the horizon. That view has gone forever now but it's been replaced by another which I look to every morning to try and find peace and courage to face another day. Over the African bush the dawn mist hangs low in a distant field, francolins call noisily as they patrol the grassland and a crested barbet taps incessantly at his nest in the dead tree in my front garden. This is one of the reasons I stay in Zimbabwe, another is the sudden and unexpected pride in your country which comes when you least expect it.

There haven't been many occasions in the last three years when I can say that I've been proud to be a Zimbabwean. That all changed this week when Henry Olonga and Andy Flower walked up to the press box at the Harare Sports Club shortly before the World Cup Cricket match against Namibia started. They were both wearing black armbands and presented a press statement explaining they were in mourning for the death of democracy in Zimbabwe. Their one page statement said it all, the hunger, oppression, torture and lawlessness which has become a part of every minute of every day in our country. Their bravery has been an inspiration this week and given us the strength to continue fighting for democracy. The closing sentence of their statement is echoed by us all and reads: 'We pray that our small action may help to restore sanity and dignity to our nation.'

It's not an easy thing to get over this huge shroud of fear that is suffocating our country. This morning our suburbs are littered with hundreds of pamphlets. Printed in red, on one side is a list of all the things that are wrong in Zimbabwe. On the reverse is a list of things we can do. The first thing is: 'Show courage and do not be afraid.' Passers-by are reading the pamphlets; some are being brave enough to pick them up and stuff them hastily in their pockets. It is a start. One of these mornings we will wake up and watch our majestic red dawn knowing that the madness is over. We pray it will be soon.

22 February 2003. Sucking salt

Recently I heard the shocking story of children sucking lumps of coarse salt to make themselves thirsty. The water they drink fills their stomachs, suppressing the pangs of hunger. While this is happening at home, our President caused an international uproar by attending the Franco African Summit in Paris. The press was full of reports of the luxury and extravagance of the Paris hotel where the Zimbabwean delegation were staying. Menus include black truffles, caviar and pâté. The entire 33 roomed wing of the hotel was reserved for Zimbabwe and the cheapest room per night costs the equivalent of three quarters of a million Zimbabwe dollars; enough to buy thirteen thousand loaves of bread to feed hungry children sucking salt.

More and more people are beginning to stand up for their rights. Last weekend seventy women were arrested at Valentine Day marches in Harare and Bulawayo. Handing red flowers to passers-by they carried posters reading 'Yes to Love,' and 'No to Violence.' Arrested for not having police permission to march, the women in Bulawayo were kept in police cells overnight. A friend wrote, describing how, barefoot and bra-less, they were sent to open-air cages before later being moved to dark, stinking cells with 18 women crammed into a 15 square metre room. During the night they were allowed food and effects from their families. My friend wrote: 'In the bag of goodies provided by my husband was a red rose, my most romantic Valentine gift yet. I clutched that poor rose all night.' Amongst those arrested were an 83-year-old woman, an elderly nun and a catholic priest.

In the World Cup cricket matches Andy Flower and Henry Olonga remain defiant, continuing with their silent protest. With each match the two have come under increasing attack for their courage and honesty. Olonga was expelled from his cricket Club, Takashinga. Both men were reprimanded by the Zimbabwe Cricket Union and told to take off their black armbands. At the next game they wore white wristbands in a call for peace and were again hauled in by cricketing authorities. Told to end their protest or risk being dropped from the selection, both men refused and bravely play on.

During the match against Australia, Catholic Archbishop, Pius Ncube and twenty others wore black armbands and ribbons in the grounds and issued a statement saying they were mourning the death of democracy in Zimbabwe.

Archbishop Ncube has given us more than a little reason to feel proud. On Thursday evening he held a service for victims of torture in Zimbabwe. A dozen people gave testimony about what had happened to them. Police were in the Church and the following morning the Archbishop was cautioned, told not to bring politics into Church.

Asked if the warning would deter him, Archbishop Ncube said: 'I cannot stop. As long as people are suffering I must speak out.' On Friday morning 22 pastors and clergymen marched to Harare Police Headquarters carrying a petition saying that laws which forbid gatherings without police permission are impinging on people's right to freedom of worship. At Police Headquarters 19 of the clergymen were taken in for questioning only released six hours later. Now, more than ever before, there is not a shadow of doubt in anyone's minds that the tragedy in Zimbabwe is not about land or the colour of our skins, but simply about a party clinging to power. No one is safe, not even men of God.

IN THE NEWS

~*26th February 2003* Industry Minister Amos Midzi says bottled water is half the price of petrol. The Minister doubles the price of petrol from $74.47 to $145.20 a litre. Diesel increases by 80% to $119.43 and aviation fuel, Jet A1, is quadrupled to $220.75 a litre.

~*5th March 2003* Cyclone Japhat hits parts of Manicaland.

~*6th March 2003* The Reserve Bank urgently supplies foreign currency to prevent the eviction of Zimbabwe's ambassadors to Rome and Switzerland, whose overseas rents have not been paid for the last five months.

~*6th March 2003* US President Bush imposes economic sanctions on President Mugabe and 76 other high-ranking government officials, accusing them of undermining democracy. The Order prohibits any transactions or dealings in all property and interests in the US or held by US citizens.

8 March 2003. Gold for trains

A month ago two of the most important African Presidents said they would not support a renewal of Zimbabwe's suspension from the Councils of the Commonwealth. Nigerian President Obasanjo and South African President Mbeki said they had been reassured by the Zimbabwean government that the land seizures were over. They were also told that all white farmers who had been thrown off their land would be given another farm in a policy of one farmer, one farm. They were lied to because in the last ten days no one's been given another farm, 13 more farms have been listed for seizure and 24 farmers have been served with 90 day eviction notices.

The African Presidents also said that they were satisfied with assurances from our government that public repression would stop. Again they were lied to because since their visit 280 people have been arrested under POSA ı (the Public Order and Security Act). This includes 73 women on a peace march;

19 priests and clergymen on a freedom of worship march; a human rights lawyer, Bishop and an American diplomat. A well-known civil rights leader was assaulted whilst in police custody and 26 MDC supporters were intercepted when they drove past State House. The 26 were taken into the grounds of State House, detained and assaulted for wearing MDC T shirts. Another 70 MDC supporters were dragged out of their homes by police in the early hours of the morning after having attended an MDC rally.

Africa's two most important and influential leaders were not the only ones who were taken in by lies. The International Cricket Council said they were satisfied with reassurances by Zimbabwean police that cricket fans would be allowed to demonstrate peacefully at world cup matches. In fact, 41 people were arrested for demonstrating after the match against Holland, 28 after the game with Pakistan and 5 after the game against Australia. In a number of cases those arrested were held for as long as four days, denied bail and many were assaulted, kicked and whipped whilst in police custody. People carrying independent newspapers were not allowed to take them into the grounds and one man was detained and interrogated because he wore a black armband. All queues, whether for food or fuel, were banned on roads leading to cricket grounds. The cricketers certainly didn't hear the National Railways announce the suspension of trains between Harare and Bulawayo, because of damage to the line. The damage was not caused by Cyclone Japhat but by illegal gold panners who have dug trenches for gold right under the main rail line. There was nothing at all peaceful about the world cup cricket matches that were held in Zimbabwe and frankly we are glad it's over.

15 March 2003. Ordered to kill his father

Last Saturday 500 women braved the wind and rain and gathered in the car park of the Bulawayo City Hall. It was International Women's Day and they were holding a peaceful demonstration about the crisis in Zimbabwe. When police arrived and attempted to arrest the organisers, the woman knelt down in front of the police vehicles, sang and prayed. Women, some with babies on their backs, were kicked and beaten by riot police wielding baton sticks. An elderly woman who lay on the ground begging for mercy was repeatedly assaulted by five policemen who took it in turns to beat her. In Harare at a similar Women's Day gathering, fifteen women were arrested, stripped naked and beaten on their backs and abdomens. Men inflicted the beatings, watched by policewomen who stood and laughed.

In another incident this week a young MDC activist was kidnapped in broad daylight in Nkayi. Mthulusi Moyo was putting up posters on a tree when he was grabbed and hauled into a government vehicle without number plates. He has not been seen since but all his clothes, including his underpants, have been found covered in blood. There are fears that the young man is now dead.

Other young men and women, graduates from the notorious Youth Brigade Training Camps are reported to be fleeing to South Africa in their hundreds. According to human rights organizations, law firms and churches in South Africa, youths as young as 15 are appealing for assistance. The youngsters say they have fled Zimbabwe because they are: 'tired of killing for nothing.' The youths report that training centres have been set up in secondary schools where students have no choice but to attend. They say they are trained to kill in ways that are 'silent and leave no evidence.' They speak of being given alcohol and cannabis to give them false courage before being sent out on missions of violence. Youngsters told how they had killed a man by breaking his neck and were ordered to burn the body. One Youth Brigade boy said he had been instructed to kill his own father. Others said they were told to kill close family members who belonged to the MDC.

How will Zimbabwe even begin to heal these wounds? As a nation we are traumatised by evil. I know that for my 10-year-old son, it has been a long and painful two years overcoming the trauma and memories of the awful things that happened on our Marondera farm in 2000.

Just a year and a half year before he starts senior school I had begun to despair that he would ever be able to spell. Teachers, counsellors and educational specialists told me that he had a mental block, that he had 'unlearned' basic spelling and writing principles and that it was a type of stress dyslexia. This week he came home wearing a Merit Badge for spelling. He has finally overcome the trauma and opened his mind again. We can only pray that it will be the same for all the victims of violence.

IN THE NEWS

~19th March 2003 The Iraq war begins with the invasion of Iraq by US and allied forces.

~21st March 2003 Cricketers Andrew Flower and Henry Olonga publicly announce their 'retirement' from international cricket.

22 March 2003. Fingers and toes broken

The MDC called for a two day national stay-away and it is estimated that as many as 80% of shops, businesses and factories were closed for the two days. At the end of the stay-away up to 500 people had been arrested for a number of obscure reasons. Included amongst those arrested was a newspaper photographer, held for two days without being charged and assaulted whilst in custody. When the Corporate Director of the Newspaper enquired at a police station as to the photographer's whereabouts, she was also arrested and then severely assaulted by the wife of the Commander of the Army, Jocelyn Chiwenga and her messenger. No one could understand what Jocelyn Chiwenga and her messenger were doing in a police station or why they were allowed to do what they did.

In Ruwa, 15km from Harare on an MDC MP's leased farm, armed men in army uniform, assaulted men, women and children who work and live on the farm over the two days of the stay-away. Three security guards at the farm had their fingers and toes broken; the farm manager and his wife were beaten as were at least eighty men, women and children resident on the property. Dozens had to be taken to hospital. One man, Steven Tonera, was literally beaten to death by men in army uniforms.

At the end of the two day stay-away, the MDC delivered a 15 point ultimatum to the Zimbabwe government. They have given the ruling party until the 31st of March to restore freedom and democracy to the country. They have demanded an end to the torture of people in police custody; the restoration of freedom of speech, worship and association; disbanding of the youth militias; repeal of repressive legislation and depoliticising of police and security personnel in the country. The MDC leader stated publicly that if these demands are not met by the end of March, 'mass action will escalate' and 'proceed on another level.'

Welcome diversions. Hammerkop snacks.

There is a frenzy going on outside. The sky is grey, heavy and oppressive. More rain looks imminent and while waiting for the heavens to open a hammerkop is in the garden having an extravagant breakfast after 34mm of rain overnight. First it patrols the pool: walks, bobs its head, walks, stops, bobs, turns and patrols back. On the third circuit the hammerkop finally starts to fish. Fat golden flying ants, patternedwing cicadas, shiny black beetles, glossy brown Christmas beetles and long, slim black ants with thin transparent, lacy wings. The hammerkop stands on the edge of the pool, feet apart, toes spread, claws gripping the lip of the edging stones. It steadies itself, bends and snatches the insects it can reach from the edge. It's a quick, mechanical process: bend, snatch, swallow, bend, snatch, swallow. When all the insects near the edge are eaten it moves to the snacks in the middle of the pool. This isn't such an easy meal as the hammerkop has to fly low, dip its beak into the water, scoop and then fly back to edge. It never misses, again and again the hammerkop skims and scoops; toes get wet but tummy gets full.

IN THE NEWS

~*23rd March 2003* Doctors treat over 250 people at one hospital alone who are alleged to be victims of reprisals by government forces after last week's national stay-away.

~*29th March 2003* Beer prices increase: a pint of Castle, Lion, Black Label or Pilsner, which used to cost $270 now costs $360.

4 April 2003. Freelance Revenue collectors

A few days ago a large and menacing Gymnogene circled lazily over my garden. The big grey bird of prey came to rest on a branch of a dead tree on the front lawn and immediately started trying to get a pair of crested Barbet chicks out of their nest. Using first its curved claws and then its bright yellow beak, the huge raptor tried to spear the helpless chicks. The Barbet parents were going mad, screeching alarm calls and hurling themselves at the raptor trying to stop it from getting their babies. The Barbets mobbed the Gymnogene, flying closer and closer to the huge bird, hitting it with their own bodies, trying to distract its attention. The Barbets are residents in my garden and having watched them build the nest and then incubate and hatch the eggs, the Barbets had become a part of my life. I ran outside to try and scare the

Gymnogene away. But it wasn't easy persuading the raptor to leave. Shouting didn't do it, waving my arms was pointless and it finally took a stone hitting the trunk just below the bird's feet to make the raptor leave. It didn't go far, perched in a tree across the garden and whenever the coast was clear renewed its assault on the nest.

For the last three years Zimbabweans have been very much like the crested Barbets in the garden. We've been shouting out for help and in the last month our calls have got more frantic but no one is hearing us. The invasion of Iraq has totally overshadowed the horrors in Zimbabwe. Day after day, the BBC, CNN and SKY TV give us the moment by moment developments in Iraq. Night after night Short Wave Radio Africa interviews ordinary men and women in Zimbabwe who tell of horrors so barbaric that they belong in 16th century history books. Our government are using the incessant international media coverage of the Iraq war as a smoke screen and behind it they are crushing all dissent in Zimbabwe.

Opposition supporters, activists and even MPs are being arrested and held for days without bail, charged with being involved in last month's two day stay-away. This week came more reports of men, wearing army uniforms and carrying rifles, forcing their way into people's homes, accusing them of supporting the MDC. One man told of a 12-year-old girl being gang raped in Chitungwiza and how friends and neighbours were beaten and forced to watch.

A visiting delegation of Southern African Foreign Ministers was in Zimbabwe this week. At the close of their nine hour meeting in Harare, a spokesman for the South African Foreign Ministry said: 'Our position is that the people of Zimbabwe must be the masters of their own destiny.' That's a bit like saying that two tiny, naked, helpless and flightless chicks should get rid of a massive bird of prey without assistance. This month is our 23rd anniversary of Independence and already the intimidation has started. In villages, suburbs, towns and cities government supporters are banging on gates and doors demanding that each household give them 500 dollars for Independence celebrations. If you refuse to pay they take your name off the lists for food distribution and say you may not even line up to buy maize when it is available. There are no receipts but no one stops these freelance revenue collectors and if you were hungry what would you do?

IN THE NEWS

~3rd April 2003 The Bulawayo branch of Dairibord is fined $1.5 million for repackaging milk into smaller sachets and increasing the price in contravention of the Control of Goods Regulations. The supply price of milk is $125 a litre while the government's controlled selling price is $79 a litre. The government have a 10% shareholding in Dairibord. *~9th April 2003* US forces seize control of Baghdad, ending the regime of Saddam Hussein.

~15th April 2003 The price of fuel increases by over 300 %. Leaded petrol increases from $145 to $450 (320%) a litre; unleaded petrol from $176, 53 to $500 (350%) a litre and diesel from $119, 43 to $250 (70%) a litre.

Are you serious? Surrender those uniforms

Actual announcement on ZBC Radio: 'The police appeal to the public for anyone in possession of army uniforms and equipment associated with the police force or army to immediately surrender them.' (ZBC Radio)

18 April 2003. Happy Birthday Zimbabwe

It is the 23rd anniversary of Zimbabwe's Independence. This morning President Mugabe spoke at Independence celebrations in Harare. The stadium was decorated with impeccably printed banners which read:

'Zimbabwe will never be a colony again.'

'We have 11 million hectares of reclaimed land in the bag.'

'We are now on solid ground.'

'Zimbabwe at 23: our land is finally in our hands.'

President Mugabe stood at the podium, unsmiling. His wife sat behind him, she wore dark glasses throughout and seldom was there a flicker of any emotion whatsoever on her face. Mr Mugabe spoke briefly from a prepared script. There was nothing surprising in his speech and no acknowledgement of the massive suffering of 11.6 million Zimbabweans. He ended his speech with the sentence: 'Never, never, never again will Zimbabwe become a colony.'

This evening Short Wave Radio Africa replayed President Mugabe's speech made at Independence in 1980. I sat with goose bumps listening to his words of 23 years ago. He called for tolerance and patience; said the time for retribution was over and that the wrongs of the past must be forgotten. In 1980 President Mugabe said that racism and oppression were iniquities that must never again happen in Zimbabwe. Two speeches, made by the same person, 23 years apart left me with only one question: What has happened?

Our 23rd anniversary of Independence was also a sad week as we heard of the death in Iraq of a young Zimbabwean who was serving in the Irish Guards. 20-year-old Christopher Muzvuru from Gweru was killed by sniper fire in Basra. He died helping to set Iraq free of a dictator. Just as he never saw Iraq's freedom, nor will he see his own country once it is under a new and democratic government. Happy birthday Zimbabwe!

IN THE NEWS

~18th April 2003 A Zimbabwean soldier in the British army, Christopher Muzvuru (21) who died this week serving in Iraq, is condemned as a 'mercenary' and a 'sell-out' by the state media. The Daily Mirror, owned by a Zanu PF member, urged that authorities bar Muzvuru's body from being returned home for burial. 'It should be buried in Britain, the country that he chose to die for,' the newspaper said.

Are you serious? Stock trespass sale

Actual notice in The Herald.
'Stock Trespass Sale. Livestock auction. Guruve Rural District council.
CATTLE

Black cow with sharp horns pointing forward and a brown calve. (sic) Black cow with white dots and black calve. (sic) Complete black hornless heifer.
GOATS
Large black and white he goat, white forehead, white right front leg and black and white bears with horns (sic)
White goat with blackish neck with horns. Complete black she goat with horns and two kids.
DONKEYS
White belly and brownish white female donkey.
Brownish white female donkey with white mouth.'
(The Herald)

26 April 2003. Lord of the manor

This week, for the first time in three years, I became a farmer again, although only for a day. Battling to survive the massive inflation and the price of food, I had reared 24 chicks from fluffy yellow day-olds to plump chickens for the table. Sam, the foreman on our farm before we were evicted, came to help me and we still work well together. He sat on an empty, upturned fuel tin and I on a blue plastic milk crate. We both had knives and buckets of water, his scalding hot, mine very cold. Sam chopped and plucked, I gutted and cleaned and all the time we talked.

Working in the sun side by side was something we had done hundreds of times before on the farm: dosing sheep, dipping cattle cutting off lambs tails and testicles, putting tags in calves ears, picking vegetables or working on a fire break together. I had forgotten how good it was to get utterly involved in a physical job and how satisfying when the task had been completed. I'd also forgotten how much I miss the ordinary gossip and chat that was so much a part of my life as a farmer.

Sam had lots of stories about what's happening now on our occupied farm and others in the neighbourhood since government supporters took them over. On our farm the borehole has been destroyed so there's no piped water anymore. The house looks scruffy and the garden unkempt. The solar water panels and tanks have been stolen and the huge water reservoir stands permanently empty. Most of the big gum tree plantations have been felled for firewood and the boundary and paddock fences, poles and wire have long since gone. The dairy no longer sees cows with udders heavy in milk but only lines of clothes hung up to dry on the milking stalls. The tobacco barns are derelict: doors, flues, furnace covers and bricks slowly being stolen bit by bit. A handful of huts are dotted in the fields alongside little patches of scraggly, yellowing maize plants which may feed a family for a few weeks at most. The people are hungry, the children go and beg from the kitchens of a nearby boarding school and the adults queue up for World Food Programme maize, beans and cooking oil when the big trucks come.

Over the road on the farm seized by Wind which just one year ago was a thriving beef and chicken farm, there is absolutely nothing going on. A local village Chief has moved into the beautiful house and there he lives entirely alone. He has not invited his fellow villagers to share and work the land with him, instead, he struts around arrogantly, Lord of his new

Manor. Neighbouring villagers are not allowed to walk through the farm or graze their cattle there; he says they are trespassing on his farm. Nothing at all is being produced on the land and slowly the bush is reclaiming the cattle dip and chicken runs, but the Chief is happy, in his eyes he is now the landowner.

Neither of the farms was ever served with acquisition papers by the government of Zimbabwe, both just seized by men hungry for power, backed by political heavyweights. Next door to these two farms there is still an overcrowded communal village whose people have not gained at all from the seizure of the commercial land. Edward, the war veteran who spearheaded the invasion of these two farms and a dozen others in the district, spends his days in the neighbourhood bar. He lives off his government war veterans' pension which was increased by 166% this week. He already has his own farm in another district, given to him by the government 6 years ago and his children's school fees are paid by the government. This is the result of our government's land re-distribution programme three years down the road.

IN THE NEWS

~*1st May 2003* The cost of a postage stamp for a local letter increases from $30 to $100.

10 May 2003. I am not the one

Zimbabwe's police commissioner, Augustine Chihuri has been appointed the Honorary Vice President of Interpol. A police spokesman in Harare said the award proves to the world that Zimbabwean police are professional and nonpartisan.

For three years the Zimbabwe Republic Police have used a string of phrases to excuse themselves from acting against rape, murder, torture, arson and looting. These phrases are: 'It is political,' 'It is my first time of hearing this,' 'I am not the one' or 'We have received no instructions.' For three years the police in Zimbabwe have ignored numerous High Court rulings. Over 200 people have been murdered in the country in the last three years and to date not one of the perpetrators have been apprehended or brought to trial. There are none so blind as those who will not see, including Interpol.

Are you serious? Digging up the money

'Two stock thieves stunned the court when they asked the presiding magistrate to grant them bail so that they could go home and dig [up] the money they hid in a hole before their arrest.

Collen Dehwe and Charles Chiimba made the request soon after they were each slapped with an effective six-year jail term after being convicted of stock theft by Harare magistrate Judith Tsamba. Dehwe and Chiimba said they wanted to go to their communal homes because nobody would find the hidden money, but Tsamba rebuffed their request and asked them to write letters to their relatives informing them of the whereabouts of the money.' (Daily News)

17 May 2003. Parked ambulances

This week some staggering statistics were published about the state of agricultural production in Zimbabwe three years after 90% of commercial farms were seized by the government. Prior to 2000 we produced 162 thousand tonnes of soya beans a year, which gave us enough for our own use and allowed for exports. Now we import soya beans, only growing 30,000 tonnes ourselves. Tobacco production has been reduced by more than half. Maize production has dropped from 2 million tonnes in 2000 to just 800,000 tonnes now and over 60% of our national herd has been slaughtered because commercial farmers had no land on which to graze their cattle.

The World Food Programme provided food for 8 million Zimbabweans last year and estimate the same number will need assistance again this year. Undoubtedly our government will blame drought but this week even Pope John Paul said that our land reform programme was: 'an error which would only create tension and discord.'

The most dramatic statistic to come out in the report was that prior to 2000, farmers bought 1,600 tractors a year but last year only 8 new tractors were purchased countrywide. The day after these shocking facts were released, a weekly newspaper reported that over US$100 million of agricultural produce from Zimbabwe is to be given to Libya in order for us to purchase petrol and diesel and pay outstanding fuel debts. Where are our government going to find agricultural produce to give to Libya when we cannot even feed ourselves?

The fuel situation has deteriorated throughout the country. By mid-week the national airline, Air Zimbabwe was refuelling in Zambia as aviation fuel here had run out. By Friday newspapers reported that in Harare only one of the city's 25 new ambulances was still running, the rest were parked alongside fire tenders with empty tanks and crews unable to attend emergency calls.

After a two decade break, I got on a bicycle and rode with my ten year old son to school and back every day this week. I guess the sight of me pedalling furiously over the bumpy track made people smile but I've already clocked up 24 kilometres and every bone, muscle and fibre of my body is screaming out for the comfort of a car. Imagine my utter speechlessness one morning when Richie shouted over his shoulder to ask if we could go out and do some 'fun riding' over the weekend. Hardly able to breathe, legs going madly on the pedals, freezing, melting mist dripping off my nose, I managed a sort of grunted: 'I think I'll be too busy' and pedalled even harder to try and catch up.

IN THE NEWS

~17th May 2003 Banks increase lending rates to between 65 and 75%.

~30th May 2003 Addressing journalists before taking early retirement, Reserve Bank Governor Tsumba says: 'Due to the sharp rise in inflation, a dollar in 1995 is worth just under two cents today.'

31 May 2003. Boxes of money

For over three years the question on everyone's lips has been: how long can this go on? There have been a score of different occasions when we didn't think that things could get much worse. Like when the government said they would seize 5 million hectares of farmland, increased that to 11 million hectares and then gave the best farms to government ministers and security officials.

Then we thought it was bad when we ran out of maize meal, bread, oil, sugar, flour, petrol and diesel. Then came the long electricity cuts, collapsing infrastructure, closure of hundreds of companies and the massive brain drain from the country. Then the end of internal Air Zimbabwe flights, first to tourist destinations and now even between Harare and Bulawayo as aviation fuel ran out. Now, forty months after the political mayhem began, the country has literally run out of money.

There are big queues everywhere you look, the short ones are for non-existent food and fuel but the really long ones are outside banks where hundreds of people are trying to draw out money. There are no big denomination bank notes left in our banks, it started in the capital city and over the week has spread across the country. Many companies can't get enough bank notes to pay their wages and employees can't cash their salary cheques. Big companies are paying out multi-million dollar wage bills in 20, 50 and 100 bank notes and people are leaving banks with boxes stuffed with small bills. Big bank notes have become so sought after that the joke in our town this week is that for $700 you can buy a $500 dollar bank note on the black market.

The person at the supermarket till in front of me had 47 thousand dollars' worth of groceries and was paying the bill with huge blocks of 50 and 20 dollar notes. The teller could barely cope with counting all these mountains of small bank notes and on his lap he had a cardboard box to put the money into as it wouldn't all fit into his till. He told me he needed a new box for every third customer and the manager's office looked like a bank-note warehouse.

The opposition, trade unions and civil society have united and called for a week of organised, peaceful protests, street marches and demonstrations calling for the resignation of President Mugabe. The opposition are calling this the Final Push and we fear bloodshed and violence. People have been advised to stock up on food and be prepared for all eventualities. The police and army have been put on high alert and all security personnel have been called back from leave.

Zimbabwe humour. Saving money the Zimbabwean way
I have so much more money in my bank.
For all of this, I have you to thank!
I'm saving money at a rate of knots.
By the time I'm 40, I'll really have lots!
I can't spend it on fags, fine food and fair.
'Cos when I go to TM, the shelves are all bare!
Other shops are quite empty of tempting treats.
Who needs dairy products, cokes or sweets?
Standing all day in the queue for maize meal.
Means I don't have to work – wow, what a deal!
I see all my mates there from days gone by.
We catch up on news and make plans for a braai!

I can't find any marge or oil in the shop.
My bathroom scales are starting to drop!
When I put on my jeans, they fall to the floor.
'Cos no sugar or flour, means no baking no more!
Now bread, it seems, is a thing of the past.
But I'm not worried, 'cos I'm losing weight fast!
There's no need to lose weight by going to a gym.
Just live in Zimbabwe and you'll get really thin!
I walk everywhere; there's no fuel in my car.
I'm really quite fit now, from walking so far!
I spend more time at home than ever before.
This is a good thing 'cos there's always a chore!
I take time for all the positive things in life.
Like my family, reading and staying out of strife!
I'm coping quite well; so it just goes to show.
That living with shortages is not such a blow!
 (Source Unknown)

7 June 2003. Baptism of fire

The week began and ended with opposition leader Morgan Tsvangirai being arrested. He joins hundreds of others who were arrested this week, from ordinary men and women to Mayors and MPs. Hundreds of people were beaten by police, army and state agents; at least two were killed and we have felt very much like a country at war. Harare and Bulawayo have been completely shut down; shops, banks and businesses closed. There have been air force helicopter gunships, tear gas, water cannons and literally thousands of security agents and militants deployed in and around our towns and cities to stop people attempting to march for democracy. There have been reports of horrific barbarity, of a new-born baby being tear gassed, of university students having their doors kicked down before being beaten, of a hospital being raided by armed police to stop victims of violence from talking to the press. One man, abducted from his home by state agents, was whipped, kicked, rolled in sewage, beaten again and then left to die. When his friend took him to a clinic, the nurses refused to treat him, saying they were only allowed to treat police and prison officials; the 33-year-old man died before an ambulance arrived.

Mid-week President Mugabe said it was 'sad' that his security officials had to use force to silence civilians and their 'British sponsored opposition party.' Information Secretary Nathan Shamuyarira admitted that the government had bussed over 2,000 youths into Harare to help stop any mass demonstrations before they started. These youths were camped out at the Zanu PF headquarters, and even in residential areas where they were deposited in deserted car parks. On the two days when calls were made for marches, there were reports of groups of 10-15 youths, accompanied by army or police, on every street corner.

Throughout the week the government have proclaimed that the stay-aways and mass action had been a monumental flop but with each pronouncement they have added a threat. Minibus drivers were ordered to get their vehicles back onto the roads or have their permits taken away. Company owners, from bankers to shop keepers, were warned to open their businesses or have their operating licences withdrawn. In my hometown police cruised around with loud hailers ordering businesses to open and people to go to work.

Our opposition MPs and activists have had a baptism of fire this week and yet they have not fought back but have remained dignified, proud and determined to rebuild Zimbabwe into the great country that it is. After 40 months of mayhem, the events in Zimbabwe this week have again shown the world that land and race are not the issues here but only the survival of a political party and its leader.

Welcome diversion. Snakes that climb out of windows

A neighbour in his late seventies was in his kitchen when he spotted a long black snake slithering down the passageway towards his study. The snake disappeared into his study so John closed the door and phoned the local National Parks office. It took them a few hours to get to the house which is just four kilometres away from their offices. Parks staff said none of their vehicles were working anymore so they had borrowed a Ministry of Health vehicle and John had to pay for the petrol. The two female National Parks officers didn't have a catchpole or a sack with which to catch or contain the snake but instead were armed with a shotgun and a little pill bottle containing a single green tablet. They said the tablet would put the snake to sleep although it wasn't clear if the reptile had to swallow it, eat it, or inhale it. After two hours of searching John's study there was a lot of mess but no snake so the experts left saying the snake had obviously 'climbed out the window.'

Three nights later at 8pm John saw the snake again. Sure that it was a black mamba, John kept his distance and watched the snake slither across the passageway from study to toilet and back again. It had 'gone to have a drink,' John said when he phoned for help. Armed with a .22 rifle and a golf club it took a friend an hour to locate the mamba which was tightly curled up underneath a bookcase. After two well aimed whacks with the golf club, the three metre long mamba was taken outside and permanently dispatched. John's sentiments that the snake had been drinking out of the loo left everyone who heard the story lifting their toilet seats before sitting down for a long time to come.

IN THE NEWS

~*7th June 2003* Police arrest more than 800 people across the country in an attempt to crush opposition protests.

~*10th June 2003* Funeral parlours in Harare condemn demands being made by many service stations in Harare to see dead bodies in coffins before they will sell fuel to undertakers.

14 June 2003. Alice in wonderland

Don't wear red! This week everyone is whispering to their friends and neighbours not to wear red clothes because if you do you will be beaten by government supporters. It's happening all over the country and in my hometown workers at a prominent butchery in the town were beaten by unknown men for wearing red clothes. Red is the colour associated with the MDC. In fact Marondera has been like a town out of Alice in Wonderland this week. Aside from people being beaten for wearing red clothes, scores of others have had their windows broken and been pulled out of their houses at night and beaten for being MDC supporters. For two weeks we've had no independent newspaper in the town; vendors have been threatened, papers seized and on one ludicrous occasion people seen reading the Daily News were forced to stuff pieces of the paper into their mouths and eat it. Our one and only sports club, which offers golf, tennis, squash and hockey to people of all colours, ages and sexes has been taken over by militant youths. The road has been closed off and no one is allowed in; the youths guarding the gate say it is now their club.

This week the President said that companies which closed down during the strike will be taken away from the owners and given to the workers while expatriate company owners will have their work permits withdrawn and will be deported. He said that the British High Commissioner, Mr Donnelly, will be expelled from the country because he is supporting the opposition.

Zimbabwe humour. Roses are red

Roses are red the MDC is too, If I had a brick I'd throw it at you.

IN THE NEWS

~*19th June 2003* Harare City Council adopts a $59.5 billion supplementary budget which will increase municipal tariffs by between 100 and 600% from July.

21 June 2003. Short memories

This week started in Marondera in complete silence. An electrical fire in our local telephone exchange left us cut off from the country and the world. It was amazing how something as simple as this suddenly gripped our little town with gossip, whispers and paranoia.

Government supporters and youths have banned all independent newspapers from our town so with no papers, telephones, emails or internet it felt very much like the end of the world.

Everywhere you went people were asking what had happened, what the news was and for two days and nights we had no communications at all which was very frightening. Not so long ago a quick trip to Harare would have put everything in perspective but with the unavailability of fuel we were a community in solitary confinement.

Each day the country waited with bated breath to hear if MDC leader Morgan Tsvangirai would be released on bail. Finally, fourteen days after his arrest, Mr Tsvangirai was released on a staggering Z$10 million bail and had to surrender his title deeds and assets to the value of $100 million in surety. With our banks still having no big bank notes, it was unbelievable to watch a line of men arriving at the Harare High Court all carrying big cardboard boxes stuffed with bank notes in order to meet the cash bail requirements of Mr Tsvangira

l. The release of Mr Tsvanagirai caused an almost audible national sigh of relief. Instead of seeing a man cold, broken and exhausted after two weeks in prison, we saw a man even more filled with resolve. His face wreathed in smiles, surrounded by journalists and friends, Morgan Tsvangirai said that after his detention his resolve to continue to struggle for democracy had only increased. If the government had intended to humiliate, intimidate or break the man, they ended up achieving exactly the opposite and made Morgan Tsvangirai more popular than ever before. Our present leaders have such sort memories as to how they themselves soared to popularity because of their incarceration.

IN THE NEWS

~3rd July 2003 Forty three people die of hunger in Bulawayo between April and May 2003. Most are children in the 5 to 14 age group.

12 July 2003. Sad

American President George Bush came, believed his South African counterpart who said talks were in progress, said the situation in Zimbabwe was 'sad,' and then left. Before George Bush had even left South Africa, both political parties in Zimbabwe categorically denied that there were any talks going on between them. There are other things that are also very sad about Zimbabwe this week.

President Mugabe awarded himself a 600% pay rise and now earns two million dollars a month. That's pretty sad compared to the government's stipulated minimum wage for a house worker in Zimbabwe which is $3,457 a month (less than five British pence a day). It's pretty sad that a new Bill has just been enacted making it an offence for MPs to leave

Parliament while President Mugabe is speaking; the penalty for doing so is to have 6 months' pay docked. It's pretty sad that the main Kidney Unit in Harare has run out of drugs to treat renal patients. It's also sad that on Monday the price of an ordinary loaf of bread went from $300 to $1,000. It's sad that an ordinary house worker can now only afford three loaves of bread and four eggs on their entire monthly wage.

It's very sad that the government of Zimbabwe haven't put in a request to the World Food Programme for assistance for 5–7 million people. Current food supplies run out at the end of August and the request, which has to be accompanied by crop forecasts should have been made two months ago. It's sad that we should even have to ask for world food aid when just three years ago we fed ourselves completely and sold surplus to Zambia and Mozambique.

What is even sadder is that there does not seem to be anyone out there with the guts to condemn torture, murder, oppression and rape. Speaking at the Maputu AU summit, UN Secretary General Kofi Anan said democracy was not just about winning elections. He said it was about abiding by the rule of law, obeying your own courts and not oppressing and abusing your own people. Strong words from Kofi Anan but they are just words because he and the UN have still not found the courage to actually name names.

IN THE NEWS

~*18th July 2003* Bank officials say the lengthy delay in the printing of cheque books is due to a shortage of paper.

Normally it takes 48 hours to process a cheque book, it now takes up to two months.

~*18th July 2003* The UN Human Development Report says Zimbabwe's standard of living is lower than it was 28 years ago at the height of the war. 52% of Zimbabweans are living below the poverty datum line and life expectancy has dropped from 61 years (1990 level) to 35 years (2000–2005 level)

Are you serious? Morgue workers nabbed

'A Harare mortician and his assistant lent an infant corpse to a black market fuel dealer so he could claim cheap diesel reserved for the bereaved burying their dead. Police spokesperson Inspector Cecilia Churu confirmed that Knocks Zvakwidza and his assistant, named only as Chikwanha, both of whom worked in the mortuary of a state hospital at Chitungwiza had been arrested on Thursday for 'violating a dead body' and for corruptly issuing burial orders. An unnamed illegal fuel dealer was also in custody.

The scarcity of fuel is so serious now it can be obtained at ordinary service stations almost only with special permits, including burial orders carried by undertakers or grieving relatives. Chikwanha issued a burial order for a month-old child to the fuel dealer on Thursday, and also gave him the use of the corpse in a tiny coffin. The dealer drove to the nearest service station where the production of the burial order and the dead baby got him instant attention. He drove back to the Chitungwiza mortuary to return the coffin and its contents but was stopped at the hospital gates by security guards whose suspicions were aroused when they saw that the same coffin which was taken away earlier for supposed burial was now re-entering the hospital.' (News 24)

19 July 2003. We apologise

It was my son's annual school play this week and he told me with great seriousness that they were doing an 'olden days' story called The Sound of Music and handed me the slip asking parents to contribute to the half time refreshments. I stared at the paper, wondering which of the options would be easiest to provide. There were three choices: cake, sandwiches or savouries. I didn't know whether to laugh or cry. If I made a cake it would mean using my precious reserve of flour, replaceable only on the black market. I would also have to use the outrageously expensive block of South African margarine I'd bought last week and my precious black market sugar. I turned my thoughts to the sandwiches option. Sliced bread is Z$1,500 a loaf if you can get it, again I'd have to use the precious margarine and then I'd have to find something affordable to use as a filling. With inflation having hit 365% this week and a single egg now costing over $130 dollars, I soon scrapped that option too. That left the savouries – all the same issues came to mind, flour, margarine, eggs. How can something as simple as a plate of snacks become such a nightmare?

Nothing's normal in Zimbabwe and while I pondered my choices I was listening to Short Wave Radio Africa. I felt ashamed to be worrying about something so pathetic when I heard of how 200 Kamativi villagers are hiding in the mountains to escape the violence of government youth militia who have hounded them out of their homes accusing them of not supporting Zanu PF.

I can hardly bear to think of how those people are surviving. It is the middle of winter and as my son and I cycle to school every morning wearing coats, gloves and woolly hats, the frost lies in thick white sheets along the roadside. What sort of government would knowingly allow their supporters to force people out of their homes and into the freezing elements? When the Radio Africa reporter phoned our Minister of Home Affairs for a comment, the MP simply said, 'there is nothing like that happening' and put the phone down. It is absurd that an MP can simply say that events being witnessed by hundreds of people are not happening.

The Zimbabwe Council of Churches issued a long overdue statement apologising for their inaction and silence this week. 'We have been witnessing to and buried our people who have starved to death due to food shortages... while we have continued to pray, we have not been moved to action. We as a Council apologise to the people of Zimbabwe for not having done enough at a time when the nation looked to us for guidance.'

Sitting under the stars on a freezing winter evening watching my 11-year-old son on a stage of grass with his classmates, I was filled with a feeling of such sadness at everything that has happened in Zimbabwe. All around me were parents and friends, black, white and brown. I could not help the tears from rolling down my freezing cheeks as the school said a formal goodbye to another wonderful family who are emigrating because they can no longer afford to stay here. We are all struggling to survive but every day go through the motions of being normal to secure the future for all our children.

IN THE NEWS

~19th July 2003 The GMB (Grain Marketing Board) increases the selling price of maize to millers by 1,600% from $9,600 a tonne to $211,756. The government controlled retail price of a 10kg bag of mealie-meal goes up from $1,500 to $6,800.

26 July 2003. Silly season

It's Silly Season in Zimbabwe. Municipal and local council elections are a month away and things have gone mad, as they always do with any elections in this country. Silly season anywhere else in the world is characterized by officials being polite, answering letters and attending to long overdue local issues in order to attract voters. In Zimbabwe silly season means blood, beatings, intimidation and violence. For the last fortnight, our town has been plagued by government supporters and youth militia. Like arrogant bullies in the playground, these young men in their late teens and early twenties have roamed around in groups and gangs. MDC candidates in Marondera have been abducted in broad daylight outside our main supermarket, taken away and beaten. Others have had their homes trashed, windows smashed and been threatened with death if they stand in the elections.

In Bindura militant youths put ten people in hospital, issued death threats and barricaded the road leading to the courts on nomination day, physically preventing candidates from filing their papers. Eleven MDC candidates were attacked in Chegutu. A mob of 400 youths roamed the town, ransacked the homes and stole documentation of opposition candidates, issued death threats and left one man with a broken neck. Assaults and death threats also occurred in Rusape and Karoi. When the nomination courts closed, the government announced they had already won 41 wards as opposition candidates had not registered in Marondera, Rusape, Bindura, Chegutu and Karoi: no prizes for guessing why.

Silly season increased after the price of bread more than tripled. The government said the increases were illegal, fined our local supermarket over a million dollars and now there isn't any bread to buy. The few bakers still managing to operate have resorted to sprinkling a few seeds on their loaves or twisting the dough into plaits and calling it 'Fancy Bread.' This bread with an astronomical price ticket, just sits on the shelves as most people can't afford it.

Compounding silly season is the chronic shortage of money. Everyday hundreds of people are queuing for hours outside building societies and banks to try and withdraw their own money. On the door of Barclays bank in Marondera today the sign reads: 'Today's maximum withdrawal: twenty thousand dollars.' That's enough to buy 10 litres of petrol on the black market, one litre of milk and two loaves of bread. The withdrawal limits are virtually pointless because the bank tellers have to wait for people to make cash deposits before they can start serving.

Are you serious? Snakes and rabbits

'Gweru: The Midlands show, the prime event on the Midlands agricultural calendar, has this year been reduced to a non-event due to the absence of traditional exhibitors. Agricultural experts say the show is a pale shadow of its former self which depicts the havoc that has been wreaked upon the once thriving agricultural industry by the government's policies.

Traditional cattle displays, a major source of attraction over the years, were absent this year and major players such as seed companies also shunned the event. However, small-scale farmers were in full force at the show exhibiting their rabbits and chickens while the National Parks chipped in with their snakes and crocodiles for exhibition.' (The Standard)

IN THE NEWS

~31st July 2003 In the last three years the government has spent over US$93.8 million in the upkeep of diplomats and supporting staff stationed in embassies in several parts of the world.

~31st July 2003 Zanu PF's Secretary for Information tells the Herald: 'President Mugabe said he would not allow people to have more than one farm. He advised those with multiple farms to choose one and give up the rest to the government for resettlement.'

~6th August 2003 The Zimbabwe dollar crashes overnight by 33% against the US dollar to trade at Z$6,000 to US$1 on the parallel (black) market. On the official market, the exchange rate remains pegged by the government at Z$824: US$1 but the banks say they have no US dollars to sell.

9 August 2003. Lost the plot

I have lost the plot about just exactly what is going on in Zimbabwe. The shortage of bank notes has not eased and riot police are continually being called to control crowds at banks. In response to the crisis the Ministry of Finance introduced internal traveller's cheques and said with great pride and massive propaganda that Zimbabwe is to become a 'cash-less society,' despite the fact that we already are! They urged people to rush out and buy travellers cheques but didn't explain the most obvious problems. Firstly you have to have cash or a bank account in order to buy the travellers cheques, which 90% of people don't have. Then there's the issue of change. If I present a $5,000 traveller's cheque for $4,000 dollars' worth of groceries, where is the change going to come from? It's laughable to think that bus drivers and vegetable vendors are going to accept traveller's cheques, let alone the black market dealers who have a stranglehold on all basic commodities from fuel to food.

To further compound the chaos is the fact that the traveller's cheques are printed on special paper with wire safety strips. This is paper which our government doesn't have so they had to raise foreign currency to pay a German company to print the traveller's cheques. This led to another massive demand for foreign currency and caused the black market rates to soar even higher.

IN THE NEWS

~*11th August 2003* Agriculture Minister Joseph Made blames white farmers for the collapse of the economy. 'They started exporting crops grown here, retaining foreign currency, banking it outside. They were growing flowers instead of food crops and they even slaughtered dairy cows and now they're burning pastures.' Made said the CFU who represented 4,500 farmers, was irrelevant. 'This group played mischief all the time because they think they are a special race,' he said.

~*11th August 2003* President Charles Taylor of Liberia resigns and flies to Nigeria, where the Nigerian government provide houses for him and his entourage in Calabar.

~*13th August 2003* A human resources consultant says 400 companies closed in Zimbabwe in 2002 leaving at least 350,000 people jobless. They estimate that over 800,000 formal jobs have been lost since 2000, mainly in the agriculture, construction and manufacturing industries.

Are you serious? 'Big Daddy' dies

'According to the news agencies, Idi Amin, a.k.a. 'Big Daddy' or, more formally 'His Excellency President for Life Field Marshal Al Hadj Doctor Idi Amin Dada, VC, DSO, MC, Lord of All the Beasts of the Earth and Fishes of the Sea and Conqueror of the British Empire in Africa in General and Uganda in Particular,' has died. After spending some time in Libya, Amin was granted asylum in Saudi Arabia. He thereby avoided trial in Uganda for the 100,000 to 300,000 murders committed by his regime, in the name of umma solidarity.' (Front Page Magazine)

16 August 2003. Pride and dignity

When I got to the front of the queue in the supermarket the teller remarked that I didn't have many groceries in my trolley. I laughed and said that was all I could afford. He said I shouldn't worry; I should just go and get what I need and then pay by cheque. The cheque will bounce, I replied. No problem the teller said, we'll send the bounced cheque to the government and tell them to pay the bill because they are the ones who took the farms, didn't pay for them or any of the assets and it was that mess that has left the whole country hardly surviving. The teller knows me well, I've been shopping there for fifteen years but this was an amazing little conversation. Normally people whisper these sorts of comments, look over their shoulders to see who may be listening or simply don't say things like this at all. The conversation came at a time when the government have just embarked on something called 'Operation Clean Sweep.' This is the listing, for state seizure, all the remaining white-owned commercial farms in the country. It comes less than a month before the planting season and when there are no seeds to buy. This week even the government controlled newspapers announced that seed companies could only provide 40% of national requirements.

Government propaganda continues to churn out file footage of people dancing in food – filled fields proclaiming: 'Our Land is Our Prosperity.' The adverts are aired every 30 minutes day and night on ZBC TV and radio. The irony is that moments after the jingles have stopped ZBC tell us that fields are not ploughed because government tillage units have no fuel. They tell us that Foot and Mouth disease continues to destroy the rapidly dwindling national herd and that there is insufficient seed, fertilizer and chemicals to grow staple crops this season. It is criminal to think that just four years ago there were more than enough inputs for our own needs and an excess to export to other African countries. It is even more criminal to have watched many hundreds of highly productive farms being seized, often taken only for the house itself while the lands lie untended. Worst of all is the sickening reality that it is not the starving masses that have been made prosperous by Zimbabwe's land seizures. Instead it is top government officials and supporters of the ruling party.

The ZanuPF government and their greedy supporters have destroyed so much and they may be the financial winners but have blood on their hands. The ordinary people are the moral victors and the one thing this government can never take from us is our pride and dignity.

Welcome diversions It's raining worms

There are fat pink worms everywhere, plopping out of the ceiling, squirming on the floors all over the house, writhing on the windowsills and wriggling in the bathroom. They are the larvae of insects that laid their eggs in the Musasa pods months ago when the plants were soft and green. Now that the pods have turned hard and brown they are cracking, splitting and exploding as they fall to the ground. The worms are being thrown out in every direction including through open windows and doors and even managing to slip down between the roof tiles. The fat orange worms are raining down like manna from heaven, providing a banquet for all the newly fledged thrushes, bulbuls and drongoes hopping around on the ground.

IN THE NEWS

~17th August 2003 Forty soldiers and police storm the Chitungwiza premises of Beverley Building Society, break windows and threaten tellers. After waiting in the queue for hours they became incensed when the Building Society announced it was running out of bank notes and would serve only four police who had been helping to maintain order.

~26th August 2003 The price of fertiliser increases by 75%. It is the third increase in four months resulting in a total rise of 275% since May.

~27th August 2003 The price of fuel increases by over 500% as the government announces a deregulation of the petroleum oil industry. Diesel increases from $200 (25 US cents) a litre to $1,060 (US$1.32) and petrol goes up from $450 (56 US cents) to $1,170 (US$1.46) a litre.

Are you serious? Food and grocery prices 1981, Jan 1999, Aug 2003
Shopping basket:

Item	Size	1981	1999	2003
Bread	Loaf	0.25	8.80	950.00
Mealie meal	5kg	0.51	29.35	4,180.00
Flour	2kg	0.66	31.30	2,660.00
Rice	500g	0.41	47.50	1,415.00
Milk	600ml	0.16	5.30	430.00
Cheese	1kg	2.28	150.00	12,150.00
Eggs	dozen	0.75	19.00	2,310.00
Potatoes	15kg	3.70	194.25	9,500.00
Onions	2kg	0.20	64.95	3,000.00
Jam	450g	0.72	22.66	1,680.00
Fillet steak	1kg	2.80	125.20	7,750.00
Bacon	500g	1.31	57.28	6,640.00
Tea	500g	0.24	21.09	1,462.77
Coffee	400g	0.88	75.15	5,340.70
Beer	375ml	0.23	10.05	800.00
Matches	×10	0.16	6.00	450.00
BASKET TOTAL		**$15.26**	**$867.88**	**$60,718.47**

6 September 2003. Next time we meet

Sitting in the sun on a low wall outside one of the main banks in Marondera this week was a man who has become familiar to me over the last year and a half. I don't know his name and he doesn't know mine but we always greet each other and bit by bit I've come to know of his story and circumstances. The man used to work on a farm just outside Marondera until it was taken over by war veterans. Like most of us that were once on Zimbabwe's farms, this man has seen his fair share of violence and brutality meted out by government supporters and war veterans. He has seen mobs marauding through the farm workers' village, pulling people out of their homes, burning possessions and thatched roofs, smashing doors and beating people. He saw his employer being arrested and going to prison for trying to keep farming and he's got the same sort of look on his face that I still sometimes see on my own face when I look in the mirror. It's a look which is a combination of shock, fear, disbelief, mistrust and a deep sadness at everything that has happened to us all regardless of what colour our skin is and whether we were employers or employees.

Every time I meet the man he asks me what I am doing now that I cannot farm, how I am surviving and how my son is. Likewise I ask him about his wife and their four young children, how they are coping, if he is working and if he has found somewhere to live. Like all the farm workers I've ever known, the man has a way about him, a sort of strength and quiet dignity which comes from having spent your life out of doors. His big hands are work hardened, his eyes crinkled up from being in the sun all the time and he's got the most wonderful smile. Every now and again the man asks me if I can help him with a bit of money for food but more often it's just chat about what he calls 'those good days that are gone now.'

When I came out of the bank this week, I saw the man and he smiled and rested his hand on the wall next to him. I sat down next to him and we passed the usual pleasantries. He still hasn't got a job and is surviving by sometimes pushing a hand cart filled with wood for people or hanging around outside factories on the chance of a day's casual labour. The bit of money he manages to earn just gives him enough to feed his family once a day but none of his children have been in school since the farm was taken over, he simply can't afford the fees, let alone uniforms or books.

In his hand, the man had a doctor's prescription and I asked him if he was unwell. He said the script was for a cream and he bent down and carefully lifted his trouser leg to show me his problem. Behind his knee and on his calf were about fifteen big blister-encrusted sores, seeping and oozing. He said it was painful to walk and that he didn't have enough money for the medication which was going to cost $3,500. He took a well-worn wallet out of his pocket and showed me the two five hundred dollar notes he had managed to earn towards the cost. I pulled out my wallet and gave him the balance and the man's eyes filled with tears. He patted my hand repeatedly as we sat there in the sun being stared at by passers-by. 'God Bless You,' he kept saying as he counted his and my money again and again to make sure it was enough. As we said goodbye he asked me to wait and watch him go into the chemist so that I would know he really was going to get the medicine. 'I will be strong next time we meet,' he called out as he limped away and I watched until he turned into the chemist. He looked back and smiled, waving the prescription and the precious pile of five hundred dollar notes.

Lots of things happened in Zimbabwe this week, President Mugabe is in Cuba, Vice President Muzenda is critically ill in hospital but it was my meeting with a proud, struggling ex farm worker which I will remember for a long time to come.

Are you serious? No cheques below a million

'In a notice seen at its banking halls on Friday, Barclays Bank tells its customers: 'Please be advised that we no longer issue bank cheques of below $1,000,000 and we have increased the service charges for bank cheques to $10,000.'' (Daily News)

IN THE NEWS

~9th September 2003 The price of passports increases from $1,500 to $5,000 for adults and from $700 to $2,500 for children.

13 September 2003. Plastic bag footballs

On a dusty siding near our local railway station, eight children were playing soccer this morning. On the surface it was a very normal sight but pulling over to watch the game for a couple of minutes I soon saw that, like everything else in Zimbabwe, nothing is ever as it seems. The children ranged in age from about seven to fourteen. All were wearing extremely tattered clothing, ragged trousers falling apart at the seams, vests with huge holes at front and back and all were barefoot. The football was not a ball at all but plastic bags wrapped around each other and tied together with bits of raffia and red knitting wool. The children danced and waved at me as I watched, showing off like crazy and I waved back and smiled at their dirty, thin little faces, wishing they were sitting in classrooms where they should have been.

The third and final school term of the year started in Zimbabwe this week and it has been utterly chaotic and left thousands of children playing football unattended on dusty roadsides. There is still no money in the banks which has meant that parents have been unable to pay school fees. Almost all the schools, government or private, have raised their fees by almost 100% this term which left even more children not returning to school. Parents who managed to pay their fees then had the problem of actually getting their children to school. There is only black market fuel available and two days after schools had opened, hundreds of children still waited for transport, sitting on their tin trunks in the sun, looking into the dusty horizon, hoping for a bus.

I'm still cycling to school with my son and we've been joined by four other kids. I've become an unofficial guardian to children whose parents, like me, simply cannot afford black market fuel and so we ride together every day. Often I feel a bit like the pied piper except that I'm never in front and it is quite touching as the kids race ahead until they are almost out of sight and then they all stop and wait for me to catch up.

One day this week we stopped to look at the most exquisite little antelope footprints in the sand, made by a steenbuck in the night. Seeing the spoor of wild animals in the dust used to be something we took for granted. Now it is a huge treat as bit by bit Zimbabwe's treasured wildlife heritage is also being destroyed by politics. In the last fortnight some horrific blows were dealt to Zimbabwe's wildlife and tourism industry. A retired Army Colonel took over the Lion and Cheetah Park outside Harare and wouldn't allow the owners to remove any of the animals, all of which are orphaned or abandoned, including lions, monkeys, elephants, giraffe, otters and jackals. Many of the animals are in cages and completely unable to fend for themselves. 3,000 school children used to visit the centre every month for educational purposes.

As I finish this letter news has just come in that police have closed down The Daily News saying they have not registered with the Zimbabwean government. The Daily News was challenging the constitutionality of recent legislation which dictates freedom of speech. The Daily News has been a lone voice of hope for millions in Zimbabwe. With its closure scores more people will be left without an income or the ability to support their families. I am just one of them.

20 September 2003. Then they came for me

Banks, building societies and ATMs continue to have no bank notes and the queues of people waiting for money are crowding pavements and spilling out into the streets. When a rumour circulates that a bank has received a delivery of cash, hundreds of people run to the doors hoping to be able to withdraw a few thousand dollars to survive for another day. It is now illegal to keep large amounts of your own money in places other than banks. Police have been given powers to stop and physically search you in the streets if they think you are carrying large amounts of money and confiscate bank notes in excess of prescribed amounts.

The Minister of Finance has said that our red $500 note will cease to be legal tender at the end of September but will be replaced by another colour $500 note which has not been released yet. The Minister seems to be completely unaware of the massive crisis people are facing as they struggle to survive 426% inflation without bank notes. The Minister's attempt to get us to use internal travellers failed dismally and now he tells us we are to use something called 'bearer cheques' which are like money but aren't money and are printed on something he called 'notepaper.' The 'bearer cheques' will only be valid until January 2004. If you are confused after reading this then join the club!

The week began and ended without our only independent daily newspaper The Daily News. Despite a High Court order which gave the Daily News permission to continue operating for another 60 days, the police refused to comply with the order. Earlier in the week they seized over 100 computers and other equipment from the Daily News but when it came time to obey the court order and give the equipment back, they said they had no transport to do so. The High Court Order instructed police to let Daily News owners and employees back into their offices but this also didn't happen as the police said they hadn't received a copy of the order.

Bit by bit our government have stripped us of our constitutional, legal and human rights. For the last three and a half years, thanks to the Daily News, at least we knew what was happening: which Ministers were grabbing multiple farms, which people were perpetrating violence on opposition supporters and what was happening to our national heritage and assets, now we are alone and in the dark.

'First they came for the Jews and I did not speak out because I was not a Jew. Then they came for the communists and I did not speak out because I was not a communist. Then they came for the trade unionists and I did not speak out because I was not a trade unionist. Then they came for me – and there was no one left to speak out for me.' (Pastor Niemoller, Nazi victim.)

IN THE NEWS

~*20th September 2003* Vice President Simon Muzenda dies.

27 September 2003. Just waiting

This week shortly after Vice President Simon Muzenda had been buried at Heroes Acre, President Mugabe, his wife and a large entourage flew to America for a meeting of the UN General Assembly. Almost the entire entourage are subjected to travel bans and targeted sanctions and have had their overseas assets frozen but they are protected by the United Nations. Whilst our leaders crossed continents we have not had fuel for such a long time that families less than a hundred kilometres apart go for many months without seeing their relations.

Recently it was my Mum's birthday and just going to spend that one special day with her turned into a marathon of planning and scheming, wheeler-dealering and ridiculous expense. It began with finding enough fuel to get to and from her home; going everywhere by bicycle to save the little fuel I had and looking for a trustworthy black market dealer who hadn't watered down the petrol and whose prices weren't too exorbitant. Finding the actual bank notes to be able to buy the black market goods was another story. Then there was the issue of the birthday lunch and a birthday cake. Finding and buying all the groceries on the black market and trying to include a few little luxuries to spoil my Mum was a mission. Then came the actual birthday present. I knew that the nicest thing I could give my Mum for her birthday was groceries she can't get or afford herself. This meant chocolate, real coffee and, the most precious gift of all, 20 litres of petrol to put in her car which had stood empty and unmoving for almost two months. The price tag for these three small items was absurd: one small bar of chocolate $2,000; one jar of real coffee $37,000, twenty litres of black market petrol $40,000.

The big day arrived and although we started out early for the journey to Mum's home, the first visit in six months, the sun was high in the sky before we actually hit the road. This was because we had been desperately trying, but failing, to get someone to stamp a piece of paper saying we were legally allowed to carry Mum's twenty litres of fuel on our journey. It has been made illegal to carry fuel in containers without police permission.

The trip was depressing as we passed mile after mile of deserted farms. Farms which have been seized by our government and supposedly resettled with thousands of people are derelict and deserted. Part of the journey is through a communal land and here there were people everywhere, scrawny cattle looking for grass on the roadside, children in tattered clothes pushing little wire toys in the sand and men sitting around a hut drinking beer from brown plastic bottles. Here too there was no sign of land preparation; people can't afford to plough, there are no seeds to buy and the sentiment is why bother to grow food when, if you just sit and wait, you can get it for free from international donors.

When we neared Mum's home there was a big police roadblock and I dreaded having the birthday present fuel seized, but the police ignored the container, saying they were looking for guns today. The day flew past and I cried as we drove away, not knowing when I would be able to visit again. I cried for the families that are no longer able to spend normal happy times together, the families who are spread out over continents and the huge sadness that has engulfed our country because of a political power struggle.

IN THE NEWS

~1st October 2003 Fuel prices increase by 70%.

4 October 2003. Can't afford to die

The government have issued 'bearer cheques' bank notes which are printed on ordinary paper, look like money on one side only and have expiry dates. Less than two weeks after entering the system there were widespread reports of fake bearer cheques already in circulation; economists say that they can be reproduced by something as simple as a colour photocopier or home computer with a laser printer. After months of incessant TV and radio propaganda jingles about how they have taken all the land back, suddenly the new advert is a song which begins with the words: 'Bearer's cheques, they are just for you.'

Just days after they'd been released, bearer cheques, were being called 'burial orders' and its very appropriate because we can't even afford to die anymore. The cheapest coffin you can buy is $78,000. For $120,000 an undertaker will do everything but you have to provide the fuel for the hearse. If you want a cremation there is a problem because there is a critical shortage of gas for the incinerators. There is a three week delay for cremations in Harare because undertakers have to wait until there are enough corpses so they can make maximum use of imported gas.

IN THE NEWS

~*18th October 2003* Commercial banks increase lending rates to over 100%.

18 October 2003. Falling through the cracks

After a fortnight of suffocating heat the clouds at last began to appear. It was so hot that even the scantest of clothing was too much; shoes were unbearable, walking was exhausting and the slightest exertion sapped all energy. At first the clouds were white wisps floating across a stark, almost painfully blue sky; gradually they changed to grey and then became great towers of deep purple. Faint rumbles of thunder in the far distance grew closer as the days passed and then came streaks of brilliant lightning, threatening rain, promising moisture but just teasing us, making us more exhausted than before. Finally huge drops fell, a short storm lasting less than five minutes but enough to cool the sand which had burnt our bare feet. When the rain stopped there came those few minutes of complete silence that always follow a storm; a silence which even the birds observe and then you breathe in that smell of the first rain, the long awaited freshness that settles six months of dust.

The next day the first big rainstorm came. From midday till sunset the clouds gathered and built up, lightning streaked down the sky and the noise from the thunder was so loud you could hardly hear yourself think. Just before dark the heavens opened; trees, roofs and windowsills were washed; gutters spluttered out muddy, leaf-filled water. The evening air was divinely cool afterwards, filled with the calls of a thousand frogs which appeared from nowhere, welcoming the new season.

This year, for the fourth season in a row, Zimbabwe enters its period of life and renewal surrounded by decay and suffering. Seized farms have become little more than weekend holiday retreats for political heavyweights while the fields lie derelict and unploughed. Our schools grow emptier as inflation soars and this term parents have been asked to pay a massive supplementary fee to keep the school open for the next six weeks. Our hospitals are critically understaffed, there are very few drugs, patients have to supply their own food. Pensioners have become prisoners in their own homes; they cannot afford to buy food or pay bills and there are increasing reports of elderly people committing suicide because they cannot afford to stay alive. On our back streets painfully thin dogs roam in packs looking for scraps on which to survive as their owners can no longer afford to feed themselves let alone their pets. Everywhere people are falling through the cracks.

IN THE NEWS

~24th October 2003 Zambia has more than doubled its maize harvest this season and will export 15,000 tonnes of maize to Zimbabwe, 5, 000 tonnes to Botswana and 4,100 tonnes to Namibia. Zambia produced 1.4 million tonnes of maize in 2002/03, more than double their previous 600,000 tonne crop.

24 October 2003. For the love of an elephant

'An elephant never forgets' is a very well-known saying and I shouldn't think there are many people who have had the opportunity to put the words to the test. I am one who has and it was an experience I will never forget. In the 1980s, shortly after Zimbabwe's independence, I spent nine years as the Estate Manager of a wildlife conservation centre on the outskirts of Harare. One of my duties was to hand rear orphaned baby elephants and calm them to a degree where they could safely be reintroduced into the semi-wild environment of Zimbabwe's game farms. In the four years that it took to rear a baby elephant until it could fend for itself, I became a surrogate mother. I taught it how to suck my fingers which had been dipped in milk and then to drink from a bucket. I learnt how to lance an abscess, how to discipline it the way its mother would by biting its tail, how to rescue it when it got stuck in mud, how to help it when it got bloat from eating too much cabbage, how to imitate its rumbling call and how to introduce it to other elephants. One of the elephants I reared was named Rundi and she took a piece of my heart the day she left my caring and loving hands to be relocated to one of Zimbabwe's most famous game farms.

Twelve years later and just before Zimbabwe's political madness began, I went to that game farm and saw Rundi again and yes, it is true, elephants do not forget. Standing in a group of a dozen other people, Rundi knew me immediately. By then she towered over me and had enormous tusks, but she walked past everyone and came straight to me, rested her trunk in my hair, sniffed my neck and face and rumbled softly before gently mouthing my arm.

Three and half years into Zimbabwe's land invasions I have lost track of Rundi but one very brave man is trying to keep up with what's left of Zimbabwe's wildlife. In 2001 Johnny Rodriguez went to the Minister of Tourism and offered his services for free to the Ministry. Johnny was concerned about shocking levels of fish poaching in Kariba and the Minister was delighted to accept his help. There were illegal nets to be seized, poachers to be caught, boats to be repaired and food and fuel needed for men conducting anti-poaching patrols. When Johnny discovered that a Minister's sister was at the head of the fish poaching ring, he was ostracized. Members of the CIO tried to have him deported, his house was raided and his life's work and possessions stolen. To add insult to injury, Johnny's partners asked him to withdraw from their small business saying they were being politically targeted because of Johnny's presence in the company.

Whenever he can Johnny goes out to what is left of our game farms. On one ranch he recorded the decline in animal numbers due to poaching and hunting since land seizures began. In 2000 there were 200 eland on the property, now there are 12. Zebras have declined from 120 to 35; giraffe from 60 to 9 and nyala from 30 to 0. On some game farms war veterans who have occupied the land, force owners to herd the game into small paddocks and bomas and feed them on stock feed. In one boma Johnny found a herd of 160 sable antelope waiting to be exported by a wealthy businessman who had 'acquired' them from an evicted game farmer. The sable were hugely malnourished and had badly infected feet from living for so long in cramped conditions on heavily soiled ground. Johnny's is a lone voice, for the love of an elephant or sable, a fish or a river.

IN THE NEWS

~24th October 2003 Government doctors go on strike demanding a 1,000% pay rise.

~24th October 2003 The Concorde makes its last commercial flight, ending the era of supersonic airliners.

~31st October 2003 Over 1,000 illegal Zimbabwean immigrants are being deported from Botswana every month.

~1st November 2003 The Reserve Bank says it has issued $153 billion worth of bearer's cheques onto the market.

~8th November 2003 The government increases nurses' pay by 800%.

~8th November 2003 The government instructs banks to retain 50% of foreign currency from individual FCAs (Foreign Currency Accounts). Individuals withdrawing foreign currency from their personal FCAs have to exchange half of it using the

official rate of $824 to the US dollar while the other 50% is remitted to the Reserve Bank.

22 November 2003. Millions, billions, trillions

We have become a 'zero' society and are struggling to keep up with all the digits. We look at prices and say to ourselves, 'is that a hundred thousand, or a million, or a billion?' My calculator has only got a 10 digit display so once I get to 9.9 billion I'm in trouble. My mind boggled when I sat listening to our 2004 budget which was all in billions or trillions of dollars and in desperation I turned to my dictionary to see just how many zeros there are in a 'trillion dollars. I wrote it down carefully and then counted digits. A trillion has 12 zeros.

Zimbabwe's budget for 2004 lost all credibility for me in the first half of the first sentence when the Minister of Finance began his presentation by saying: 'Sanctions imposed on the country have worsened the economic environment.' His statement was interrupted by jeers, groans and calls of disapproval from the House who know very well that it is only 79 top government officials who have had sanctions imposed on them and not the eleven and a half million people of the country.

Before presenting the budget, Finance Minister Murerwa outlined what can only be described as utter chaos. He talked about the near collapsed state of virtually every Government owned sector and asset including the airline and airports, railways, mines, schools, hospitals, grain marketing board, fuel procurement facilities, roads, water, sewage and government owned buildings. The Minister spoke of 'runaway inflation, rampant environmental degradation and collapsing infrastructure' across the entire country. He said inflation would rise to 600% by Christmas and to 700% by the end of April 2004 and said that this was not in line with inflation in other Southern African countries whose average inflation is just 14%. I sat forward in my chair with my pen poised as the Minister began to outline how he was going to rescue the country from this unspeakable disaster but didn't write much as I soon discovered that what he was presenting was a beer, football and strong arm budget.

The second highest amount of our national budget was allocated to the Ministry of Defence who were given $1.27 trillion. The Minister's words were met by such roars of disapproval that the Speaker had to repeatedly call for order in the House and then the sentence had to be read again. Unbelievably the Minister allocated $1.4 billion to the country's national football team for their match against Tunisia and said that tax on cigarettes and beer had been reduced. It seems that the solutions to Zimbabwe's problems are that we can smoke and drink ourselves to death and watch football on TV while being guarded by well-armed police and soldiers. Assuming of course that we can afford a television which now costs more than a four bed roomed house on an acre of land cost just two years ago.

Are you serious? Kicking the safe

'In 1911 Jasper Newton 'Jack Daniel,' a famous American distiller, died from blood poisoning as a result of an infection in one of his toes. The toe became infected after he damaged it while kicking his safe in anger because he could not remember the combination.' (Wikipedia)

29 November 2003. Fade away and die

This week, for the first time in many months, I managed to find a petrol queue in which I felt confident of reaching the front before stocks ran out. At the pump-head was a little piece of white paper stuck next to the cost-per-litre indicator. On it was written '×100.' In other words the price I paid last time I had queued here six months ago had to be multiplied by 100 to get today's price. On the rare occasions when petrol stations have fuel it now costs $168,000 to fill a standard sixty litre tank.

In the 2 hours it took for me to get to the front of the petrol queue there wasn't much to do and a young woman came to my car window carrying a large enamel bowl filled with wild mahobohobo fruits which she was selling. She greeted me by name, saying she was the sister of Chipo, a young lady I knew who died a few years ago. I asked about Chipo's baby son. The last time I had seen the child he had been a fat, gorgeous baby, smiling and dribbling in my arms. I remembered how Chipo had smiled and clapped with cupped hands when I gave her all my own son's baby clothes. 'I am sorry,' Chipo's sister said at my car window, 'the baby also died.'

AIDS is ravaging Zimbabwe. Official estimates are that 3,000 people are dying from AIDS here every week, many think the number is far higher than that. Seven out of ten people are unemployed in Zimbabwe and hundreds of thousands who are HIV positive cannot afford the antiretrovirals, let alone

one decent meal a day. Everywhere you look you see AIDS staring you in the face. The obituary notices in the newspapers and the dates on headstones in the cemeteries are filled with people who have died in their twenties and thirties. In almost every shop and street you see young men and women as thin as skeletons, with sunken eyes, grey hair, swollen feet and sores on their faces and necks. On hospital cards you read the doctors' reports of the sudden onset of epilepsy and arthritis or prolonged diarrhoea. The recommendations are always: 'improve nutrition, needs milk, eat fruit and vegetables, take vitamin supplements.' To anyone living in a country with 525% inflation these words are a joke. Milk, fruit, eggs and vegetables have become unaffordable for the majority of people and so, young women like Chipo and her beautiful son, just fade away and die.

Since October 2000 when government supporters chased my family off our farm, three of our seven employees have died of AIDS. Twb others are HIV positive. The daily assistance I used to be able to give to those employees with milk, fruit and vegetables from the farm, stopped in 2000. The free condoms I used to give out every month stopped too. The nearest farm clinic was long since closed down by government supporters grabbing land for their political masters. This letter is dedicated to the lives, loves and in memory of the men and women who worked on our farm and have now died of AIDS: Emmanuel, Josephine and Wilfred and also to a friend, Chipo, and her baby son.

Are you serious? Chastity tassels

'On June 28, 2002, King Mswati III of Swaziland, in an attempt to protect his people from the spread of AIDS and return them to more traditional values, passed a number of edicts. Young women were to put off sex for 5 years and to wear traditional chastity tassels as an outward display of their sexual status. According to Swazi tradition girls under 18 should wear blue and yellow tassels to discourage sexual advances, while older women who are still virgins should wear red and black tassels. Also, women were warned that any woman wearing pants could face the possible punishment of having the pants publicly torn off by soldiers and torn to pieces.' (BBC News)

IN THE NEWS

~*11th November 2003*. The pro-land reform jingle, Sendekera Mwana Wevhu is costing the taxpayer about $1.1 billion a week. The jingle is played an average 72 times a day on all ZBC radio stations.

~*29th November 2003* Agriculture minister Joseph Made blames commercial farmers issued with compulsory acquisition notices for destroying the economy. 'We know the saboteurs. They are now hiding combine harvesters in warehouses. Yes, ladies and gentlemen, former farmers are holding on to them to sabotage the country.'

8 December 2003. Homemade pots

The Commonwealth Heads of Government meeting in Nigeria has begun. Zimbabwe was not invited to attend. At the same time, the annual congress of Zanu PF opened in Masvingo. All around the massive tent are impeccably printed posters proclaiming what Zanu PF thinks about the rest of the world.

'Flush McKinnon in a Blair toilet.'

'To hell with the racist white commonwealth.'

'Blair the toilet, Howard the coward, McKinnon the Liar.'

It is with these slogans that Zimbabwe faces the world. But these are not the faces of ordinary Zimbabweans who don't care about political posturing; they care about the appalling quality of our lives and the desperate plight of the country because of a political party's determination to stay in power.

I met one ordinary Zimbabwean who is a nurse and had just come back from a trip to Beatrice which used to be one of the most agriculturally prosperous parts of the country. Again and again Hope said that what she had seen was 'pathetic.' She urged me to travel so that I could see for myself what is happening on the farms that have been 'taken' by Zanu PF. Hope described farm after farm that she had passed as being either deserted or just squatter camps where the settlers sit on the roadsides and beg. 'They are starving,' she told me. 'Those huge farmhouses are being stripped and sold, bit by bit. Roofs, window frames, doors, fences: everything is just being taken off and sold.'

Hope said that the new 'settler' farmers are sitting doing nothing, waiting for world food aid to be delivered. I asked her if she saw crops at all, or irrigation. Hope said she saw only hungry beggars who are stripping million dollar irrigation pipes and hammering them out into home-made pots and pans. Hope said that as a nurse she could see immense hunger, malnutrition and disease just waiting to eradicate thousands upon thousands of people. A nurse in a crumbling health system, Hope's own future is bleak and she told me thousands of nurses are leaving the country every month, they cannot survive here anymore. Hope wiped away a tear and said she will also be forced to leave if things don't change soon.

Are you serious? Chinese clearing Zimbabwean farmland

'The China International Water and Electric Corporation (CIWEC), the company contracted by the Government to clear 150,000 hectares of land for irrigation at Nuanetsi Range in Masvingo, has moved in some of its equipment to start clearing the land. The Chinese company is now expected to start clearing the land any time soon after the Government supplied it with fuel for the bulldozers.' (The Herald)

IN THE NEWS

~*13th December 2003* Former President of Iraq, Saddam Hussein is captured in Tikrit by the US 4th Infantry Division.

~*December 2003* School fees will rise by 2,500% in January 2004. In some schools, fees will increase from $500 a term to $50,000 while in private schools, they go from $19,000 per term to $250, 000.

20 December 2003. Previously prosperous

In the first month to Christmas, the government gave to me:

Police torturing lawyers, judges grabbing farms, long sugar queues and inflation of 175%. Our leader left for Indonesia but the TV said to me, no worries,
'Our Land is Our Prosperity.'

In the second month to Christmas, the government gave to me: Priests in prison, long petrol queues and 8 million needing world food aid. Our leader left for Ethiopia, France, Malaysia, Thailand and Singapore but the TV said to me, no worries,
'Our Land is Our Prosperity.'

In the third month to Christmas, the government gave to me: World Cup cricket, black armbands, scores of arrests, women being beaten and men having their toenails torn out. Our leader left for Sudan but the TV said to me, no worries,
'Our Land is Our Prosperity.'

In the fourth month to Christmas, the government gave to me: Women raped by guns, soldiers beating people and petrol prices up 320%. Our leader left for South Africa but the TV said to me, no worries,
'Our Land is Our Prosperity.'

In the fifth month to Christmas, the government gave to me: No fuel for aeroplanes, long electricity cuts, postal workers fired and inflation of 269%. Our leader left for South Africa and Nigeria but the TV said to me, no worries, 'Our Land is Our Prosperity.'

In the sixth month to Christmas the government gave to me: Hundreds of arrests, water cannons, riot police and helicopter gunships. Our leader left for Libya and Egypt but the TV said to me, no worries,
'Our Land is Our Prosperity.'

In the seventh month to Christmas the government gave to me: Tripled bread prices, banks that were broke and more of Mbeki's quiet diplomacy. Our leader left for Mozambique and Nigeria but the TV said to me, no worries,
'Our Land is Our Prosperity.'
In the eighth month to Christmas the government gave to me: Fires on farms, filthy water and police taking my own money from me. Our leader left for Swaziland, Malaysia and Tanzania but the TV said to me, no worries, 'Our Land is Our Prosperity.' In the ninth month to Christmas the government gave to me: Banning of the Daily News, journalists in gaol and money with expiry dates. Our leader left for Cuba and America but the TV said to me, no worries,
'Our Land is Our Prosperity.'
In the tenth month to Christmas the government gave to me: No tractors to plough, no seeds to plant, war vets barricading the SA High commissioner and yet more of Mbeki's quiet diplomacy. Our leader left for Namibia but the TV said to me, no worries,
'Our Land is our Prosperity.'
In the eleventh month to Christmas the government gave to me: A billion dollars for a football game, striking nurses and doctors, police seizing foreign money and inflation of 526%. Our leader stayed at home this month but the TV said to me, no worries,
'Our Land is Our Prosperity.'
In the last month to Christmas, the government gave to me: Permanent exit from the Commonwealth, Presidential decrees to grab tractors, 619% inflation and 1,000% increases

in rates, rents and school fees. Our leader left for Switzerland, Egypt and Ethiopia but the TV said to me, no worries, 'Our Land is Our Prosperity.'
Happy Christmas from a previously prosperous Zimbabwe.

Part Five 2004

Dear Family and Friends

3 January 2004. Who let the dogs out?

New Year arrived very noisily in my neighbourhood as the clock ticked into the first half hour of 2004. A group of youngsters took to the streets banging drums, whistling, screaming and singing. Their song was simple, loud and a clarion call for all who were still up to hear it. 'Who let the dogs out?' they sang. 'The people let the dogs out,' they shouted back, answering their own question. With these extremely apt words the youngsters went around the neighbourhood in the noisiest New Year celebrations heard around here for over three years. It was very strange to hear people doing something so normal in such abnormal circumstances. As the voices faded I sat quietly thinking about the motivation of people brave enough to celebrate New Year but not able to stand up for their rights in a country where oppression and repression have dominated for three years and ten months.

It certainly wasn't hard for Zimbabweans to think of New Year's Resolutions this year. All those traditional vices like alcohol, cigarettes and chocolates that people vow to give up every year have already been given up by most of us as they have become unaffordable. This year the things we promise to give up or cut down on, are done from economic necessity and not choice, like meat, cheese, bread and milk. We have resolved not to get sick this year as our health system is on the verge of complete collapse. Zimbabwe's doctors, in the third month of their strike, were called to a meeting this week where the new Commander of the Army, General Chiwenga told the doctors that they should return to work. 'If you refuse to co-operate we can take you to the army barracks and detain you and you will see what will happen.' The General went on to brag that he had fought and won 45 battles since he was a teenager and compared the doctors struggle over their pay to 'a cup of tea' that could be resolved in a matter of minutes.

IN THE NEWS

~3rd January 2004 The official exchange rate is Z$815: £1 while the black market rate is Z$7,000: £1. Reports say some banks are buying hard currency from the Reserve Bank at the official rate and selling it on the black market, making huge profits in the process.

~5th January 2004 Private doctors increase their fees by over 500% and demand up-front cash payments. A consultation with a GP is now $50.

~6th January 2004 Shops begin refusing cheques from six major commercial banks.

10 January 2004. Condemning a generation

Zimbabwean schools re-open this week in the most diabolical of circumstances. In 2000, the fees at a government junior school were $250 for one child for a term. In 2004 the fees for the same child, still at the same junior school are $45,000. In addition, each child must pay $4,000 towards the school's electricity costs and provide all their own exercise writing books. These little writing books cost $1.10 in 2000 and are now $1,240. Each book has to be covered, in both brown paper and plastic or they will not be allowed in the classroom.

School uniforms are mandatory. In 2000 a girl's complete school uniform, comprising two dresses, two pairs of socks, a jersey, hat and school shoes cost $2,800. In 2004 a pair of girl's brown school shoes alone is $90,000. Also required on the list from the school is sports kit: shorts, T shirt, track shoes and coloured socks. The need for a swimming costume has gone as the school pool has been emptied because the chemicals are too expensive. Also gone is the need for a tennis racquet as the school cannot afford to replace the tattered net and the court has been completely taken over by weeds and grass.

Fees for a child attending a rural government senior school for a term are $250,000 dollars and they come with a letter signed by the Headmaster. Parents are required to 'donate' bricks, cement, roof sheets, candles, jam, bread, maize meal, soap and even sugar for staff teas.

The situation is the same in almost all rural government schools and once beautiful government schools are falling apart at the seams. The buildings are unpainted, gutters gone or falling off, windowpanes broken or missing, sporting facilities closed or in tatters and exhausted, underpaid teachers barely surviving on pathetic wages. Our government's response to this crisis is to complain about greedy headmasters, greedy uniform manufacturers and the cost of importing fabric for school uniforms. They say nothing about the 620% inflation which has caused this state of affairs or about the fact that Zimbabwe used to grow all its own cotton to make school uniforms until farms were grabbed in 2000.

Hundreds of thousands of Zimbabwean children will not be returning to school this year because their parents cannot afford to educate them. Zimbabwe's political and economic mayhem is condemning a generation of children to poverty and misery.

IN THE NEWS

~10th January 2004 It is revealed that Hear The Word Ministries in Borrowdale gave President Mugabe a $30 million gift raised through a collection at the church. 'The scriptures say that we should honour our leaders,' Pastor Tom Deuschle said.

17 January 2004. Little begging girl

Catholic Archbishop Pius Ncube said this week that people in Zimbabwe are going for four or five days without a meal and he estimates that as many as ten thousand people died of malnutrition during 2003. The Archbishop's words pounded in my head as I watched a little girl this week and knew for sure that she too would soon be dead. Standing barefoot and in a filthy, torn dress, a wild eyed, desperate looking little girl of perhaps eleven stood in the middle of four lanes of traffic. The girl's hair was matted and had the characteristic orange colour that indicates malnutrition. On the little girl's back, wrapped in a towel, was a baby. It cannot have been her own baby but was perhaps her brother or sister. The little girl just stood, counting filthy twenty dollar notes in the middle of the road as luxury cars streamed past her. Perhaps she was trying to work out that she would need 100 of those dirty notes to buy the baby one litre of milk, or 125 to buy just one loaf of bread. For an eleven year old girl begging on the highway, a loaf of bread or litre of milk would represent a miracle.

For days, the image of the little girl has haunted me and I cannot banish it, particularly after the news of the Z$30 million donation given by Hear the Word Ministries (formerly Rhema) to President Mugabe. That money could have bought 12 thousand loaves of bread or 15 thousand litres of milk and saved the lives of hundreds of little begging girls standing in the middle of busy highways. That same $30 million dollars could have been given to school children who are now sitting at home because their parents cannot afford the fees or to people dying of AIDS who cannot afford anti-retrovirals.

Are you serious? Blame it on the weather

'New farmers interviewed on ZBC TV about failing crops accuse the Met department of inaccurate forecasts resulting in farmers growing the wrong varieties of crops.' (ZBC TV)

24 January 2004. Aye or should it be nay

Parliament tried to push through more amendments to the 'fast track' land acquisition act in an attempt to add paper legality to a totally illegal land grab. A parliamentary legal sub-committee presented an adverse report on the amendments saying they were unconstitutional. When Justice Minister Chinamasa tried to counter the adverse report he was called up on a point of order by opposition MP David Coltart.

Coltart said Chinamasa could not be involved in the discussion because the Justice Minister had a personal financial interest in the issue. Coltart said that the Justice Minister and many other Zanu PF MPs in the House were named as being multiple beneficiaries in the government's allocation of seized farms and should therefore recuse themselves. The Justice Minister immediately shouted out that Mr Coltart was a 'racist liar' and pandemonium broke out in the House resulting in three MDC MPs being thrown out of Parliament for arguing.

The legal sub-committee's adverse report was debated and the Speaker called for a vote: 'All those in favour say Aye.' As one, the Zanu PF MPs all shouted 'Aye' and then realised that they had actually just voted against themselves. By voting Aye, they had just agreed that the land acquisition amendment was in fact unconstitutional. In breach of all parliamentary procedures, the Zanu PF chairman ignored the rules of the House and called for a second vote, as if the last shout of Aye had been an illusion, and this time the Zanu PF MPs all voted 'Nay.'

With President Mugabe's signature, the amendments will become law. One of the amendments says that the government no longer has to serve the landowner with a notice of acquisition, now it just has to state its intention to take the land in the government gazette. The first that the landowner or smallholder will know about the loss of their home, livelihood and land will be when the men arrive at the gate. This comes at a time when international organisations have said the number of people needing food aid has risen from five to seven and a half million, well over half our population.

IN THE NEWS

~*2nd February 2004* The price of bread increases to over $3,500 a loaf as local wheat supplies are exhausted and bakers import wheat and flour from South Africa.

~*3rd February 2004* Passport fees increase from $5,000 to $30,000 for adults.

~*4th February 2004* Thirteen heads of schools are suspended for increasing fees without approval from the Ministry of Education.

~*5th February 2004* The Supreme Court rules 4–1 that the government's Media and Information Commission is constitutional and that laws prohibiting journalists from practising without accreditation are legitimate.

7 February 2004. Hairy caterpillars

In an intricate and close knit zipper pattern, about 100 pale green and bright orange caterpillars are clinging to a Musasa tree in the car park at my son's junior school. Lying side by side in a great swathe which is almost a metre long and half a metre wide, the caterpillars have very long hairs and their united gathering is enough to scare away the most determined of attackers. In contrast to the unity of this great congregation of Musasa moths, we are all wandering around in a state of dazed paralysis after a week of turmoil.

It began on Wednesday when the results of a parliamentary byelection in Gutu were announced. The seat fell vacant on the death of Vice President Simon Muzenda last September. Out of 59,000 registered voters in Gutu, only 28,000 voted. In the run up to the election, the government gazetted 10 commercial farms in Gutu for state seizure. The MDC were unable to hold even one rally in Gutu and their candidate was held hostage for several hours by over a hundred government youths who attempted to get Mr Musoni to withdraw his candidature. A villager said that traditional chiefs warned residents that if Zanu PF didn't win people would be evicted from their homesteads. A chief said that he and his colleagues had been warned by government officials that they would be stripped of their positions and have their monthly allowances withdrawn if the MDC won. The MDC said that 7,000 names of people from other constituencies had been added to the voters roll and when voting began maize was being distributed by government officials. Zanu PF declared victory and retired Air Chief Marshall Josiah Tungimirai polled 20,699 votes.

On Wednesday, the Minister of Education announced that headmasters from 35 schools across the country were to be suspended and prosecuted for raising school fees without government permission. Many of the schools listed are Zimbabwe's finest private institutions and, ironically, it is to these schools that government ministers and top Zanu PF officials send their children. Included in the list was the headmaster of a government school in Marondera. Because of his suspension this headmaster was unable to take the school vehicle to collect food for boarding pupils, prohibited from even signing cheques for daily bread deliveries.

IN THE NEWS

~*February 2004* Municipality charges increase in Marondera: rates go up by 1,615%; water by 1,650% and refuse removal by 1,150%.

~*14th February 2004* The Presidential Powers (Temporary Measures) (Amendment of Criminal Procedure and Evidence Act) regulations are gazetted, giving police powers to detain suspects for seven days without trial for economic crimes including corruption, money laundering and illegal dealing in foreign exchange and gold. The new regulation prevents courts from granting suspects bail for seven days and give police the power to detain people suspected of 'subversion' for a month without trial.

Are you serious? Tourism earnings

'Tourism is Zimbabwe's third largest earner of foreign exchange after tobacco and gold. But a plethora of self-inflicted misfortunes has resulted in the shrinkage of earnings from US$770 million in 1990 to US$152 million in 2004.' (The Standard)

14 February 2004. For Viola

This week I visited a newly opened supermarket in Marondera. I had neither a trolley nor a basket in my hands, just a scrap of paper and a pen to write down prices. In the aisle where female sanitary products are displayed, six men stood in a bunch, made crude comments and laughed loudly. Tears welled up at the disgusting behaviour of bored bullies but the real pain in my heart was for the women. Women who grit their teeth, ignore the taunts and count their dollars to see if they can afford to keep themselves clean this month. There were neither tampons nor cotton wool to buy and a pack of ten sanitary towels was $17,000. This is the equivalent of almost seven loaves of bread, so for a woman with hungry children at home, the decision about what to buy is non-existent. Standing next to me in the supermarket was a very pretty young woman who picked up the small packet of sanitary towels, looked at the price, sighed, shook her head and then put them back and left.

The lives of Zimbabwe's women are a series of agonising decisions. Do we pay a bill or feed our children? Do we buy a bra or get soap, shampoo and toothpaste for the family? Do we stem the flow of nature's functions or buy bread for breakfast? This week women attempted to make their plight known to the men who run our country. Led by Janna Ncube, 70 women from the Women's Coalition marched through Harare to expose the horrific increase in rape. In the last month in Harare alone 137 girls and women were raped and when tested, 90% of them were found to be HIV positive. It is not known how many of these girls are pregnant as a result of being raped.

WOZA women were also due to gather today to attempt to walk peacefully in Harare, Bulawayo and Victoria Falls. WOZA women were going to wear white, carry and give out flowers and call for love and peace in Zimbabwe. Less than 24 hours before the event, police in Harare and Victoria Falls cancelled permission previously given for the walk. Police in Bulawayo denied permission for the peaceful walk and when WOZA challenged the ruling, the High Court deferred making a judgement saying it was 'not urgent.' Jenni Williams and WOZA will not break Zimbabwe's oppressive laws but will stay at home on Valentine's Day.

If you would like to support WOZA or help women and girls in Zimbabwe, post whatever you can spare from your bathroom cupboard. Nothing will be wasted. A bag of cotton wool or packet of sanitary towels will be a treasured gift to a woman who has to choose between bread and hygiene. I continue to wear my yellow ribbon in support of victims of Zimbabwe's political mayhem and this week it is for three young women. Viola (18) was raped by men who call themselves war veterans in Chimanimani a few days ago and her two friends Spiwe (15) and Melody were sexually molested that same night.

IN THE NEWS

~16th February 2004 The Tobacco Association of Zambia says their production has risen from 3 million kgs in 2002 to 7.2

million kgs in 2003 due to white Zimbabwean farmers who have recently resettled in Zambia.

~*21st February 2004* In a ZBC TV interview on his 80th birthday President Mugabe says: 'In five years I will be here still boxing, writing quite a lot, reading quite a lot and still in politics. I won't leave politics but I will have retired, obviously.'

13 March 2004. Of bolt cutters and an orange boat

Events in Zimbabwe this week have left us all open mouthed and shaking our heads in disbelief, surprise and shock. Every day and every hour the talk has been of mercenaries, conspiracies, terrorists and coup plots. An aeroplane landed in Harare with people, described by ZBC TV as 'burly, heavily built men' of assorted nationalities. At first the talk was of 64 mercenaries, later in the week it became 67. Reports as to what these men were doing here varied from collecting mining equipment, going to guard mines in the Democratic Republic of Congo or buying guns to overthrow the government of Equatorial Guinea. None of the facts were clear and nothing became clearer as the week wore on.

The government talked of the UK, US and Spain being involved in a plot to overthrow an African government while the Minister of Foreign Affairs warned of capital punishment for the 67 men. Night after night our television screens showed the same footage again and again of the cargo on board the aeroplane. There were radios and cell phones, loud hailers and bolt cutters, one very large sledgehammer and one very small pepper spray, sleeping bags, trousers, white shirts and something which the newsreader called a 'bright orange dinge.' (sic) This turned out to be an inflatable dinghy and it all made for a most peculiar cargo for men who the State media called mercenaries and terrorists. On Friday, speaking to BBC radio, the lawyer appointed to represent the 67 men said he had still not spoken to most of his clients because the police had not been given clearance by 'higher authorities' to allow interviews. The Herald newspaper reported that an eight man team had arrived in the country from Equatorial Guinea to 'exchange notes' about the 67 men.

While conspiracy theories abounded the story that should have been making world news was lost. A report issued by The Zimbabwe Institute in Cape Town said that 50 opposition MPs and 28 parliamentary candidates were interviewed and between them 616 incidents were documented. More than 90% of the MPs had experienced jail, violence and threats; 25% had survived murder attempts; 42% had been physically assaulted and 16% said they had been tortured whilst in police custody with electric shocks to the genitals and beatings on the soles of their feet. The Zimbabwe Institute said that of the 616 incidents, half had been blamed on police, army and the CIO and the other half on men calling themselves war veterans and members of Zimbabwe's youth militia. Most shocking of all was the statement that not one single perpetrator had been arrested, charged or tried for any of the 616 incidents.

IN THE NEWS

~14th March 2004 Intermarket Building Society, the Discount House and the Banking Corporation are all placed under curatorship.

~16th March 2004 The Supreme Court declares unconstitutional legal provisions that give the president powers to eavesdrop and intercept mail, telephone conversations and other electronic telecommunications devices.

~17th March 2004 Barbican Bank is placed under curatorship and Barbican Asset Management is closed for a number of breaches of regulations.

~20th March 2004 An IMF delegation say the Zimbabwean economy can take no more than seven commercial banks: less than half the 17 commercial banks presently registered.

~27th March 2004 A BBC documentary on Zimbabwe's youth training camps alleges that rape, instruction in torture, human rights violations and victimization of MDC supporters are being used.

Welcome diversion. Genets and flying ants

For a few days, the intruder alarm has rung early in the morning and getting up to investigate I saw a Genet sitting in the fork of a big Musasa tree near the house. The animal's camouflage was superb, its spots disappearing into the silhouettes of dawn making it almost invisible. It was a fleeting view of a cat I hadn't seen since being evicted from the farm.

A few days later the Genet appeared at about 6.30 in the evening, just before it got completely dark. Running on the lawn in the front garden, jumping, twisting and twirling in circles, the Genet was catching flying ants in the twilight. I stood right at the window watching but the genet didn't seem to be concerned, intent on snagging flying ants that didn't have a chance against the cat's agility. What a beautiful little creature it is with spots all over its body and stripes down its tail. For the next three evenings and within fifteen minutes either way of 6.30 pm the Genet appeared from under the eave on the roof of my study, scratching and stretching, yawning and observing the garden before setting out on its nocturnal adventures.

IN THE NEWS

~*27th March 2004* New salaries and allowances are gazetted for the Presidency. Backdated to January 2004 the President will earn $73.7 million (increased from $20.2 million). Cabinet and General allowances double to $2.8 million and $1.6 million a year, respectively.

~*2nd April 2004* Medical doctors increase their fees for the second quarter of the year by 50%, dentists by 55% and private hospitals by 100%.

3 April 2004. Romping

On Monday night ZBC TV announced that the Zanu PF candidate in the Zengeza by-election had 'romped to victory.' What a romp it had been with numerous reports of violence, intimidation and harassment in the weeks prior to the poll.

Hospital officials said they treated at least 50 people for injuries immediately prior to and during the two days of voting. Other reports told of 200 people being attacked and chased away from a voting queue by a 'riotous' group of Zanu PF youths. In one incident on the first day of voting the opposition said four truckloads of Zanu PF youths stormed the house of the MDC candidate. Twenty two year old MDC supporter Francis Chinozvinya was shot in the chest and pronounced dead on arrival at hospital. In the same incident Arthur Gunzvenzve was shot and injured. The Zimbabwe Electoral Support

Network said the atmosphere was extremely tense and intimidatory and there was 'not a chance this can be called a free and fair election.' Only 32% of registered voters cast a ballot in the Zengeza by-election.

IN THE NEWS

~*15th April 2004*. The EU pledges €15 million in humanitarian aid for Zimbabwe. The money will go towards maintaining aid programmes which provide water, sanitation and health support.

~*15th April 2004* 1,500 farm workers are evicted by the government which seizes Kondozi Farm. The 224ha horticultural exporting property is a registered export-processing farm.

~*16th April 2004* Zimbabwe has the fastest shrinking economy in the world. In 2004 it is projected to shrink by 13.2% while Mozambique's economy is expected to grow by 14%.

17 April 2004. Foxes in the chicken coop

Every day in the week leading up to Zimbabwe's 24th anniversary of Independence the propaganda on our radio and television has been unrelenting: anti-white, anti – west, anti-world. Each night the main evening news on ZBC TV has been preceded by 25-year-old film footage of aeroplanes dropping bombs and white soldiers running through long grass shooting at people. The news bulletins have all begun with a lecture. On Thursday night, with deadpan expression, the newsreader said: 'Let us all come together and sing the same song: Zimbabwe will never be a colony again.' On another night this week the propaganda message was: 'With the success of the third chimurenga, Zimbabwe is ready to feed the world.' We couldn't help but wonder what the World Food Programme would make of this as they continue to feed more than half of Zimbabwe's population.

Two days before Zimbabwe's 24th anniversary of Independence the weather was grey, cold and damp in the small town of Marondera. Pairs of police reservists in blue uniforms stood on every street corner and the highway in and out of town had police roadblocks. On tractors and trailers and in Municipal vehicles, teams of men were going around the town tying plastic flags around lamp posts, telephone poles and on all government buildings. In the back of one open government truck a young man sat with a plastic flag wrapped around himself to keep out the cold and rain.

In every direction trucks driven by men with big hats and long overcoats were laden with beer and bread being taken to Independence day rallies. For the last month every house, shack and hut in every village has been visited. Occupants have been told to each pay $2,000 towards Independence celebrations. Money must be given to the village Headman who records names and contributions. People were told that if their names are not found on the list they will be 'visited again after Independence to explain their unpatriotic behaviour.' Everyone gives the money; they are too scared not to and everyone goes to the rallies because they are too scared not to.

Two days before Zimbabwe's 24th Anniversary of Independence we learned that our press restrictions, constitutional violations, torture and human rights abuses will not be discussed by the UN Human Rights Commission. Yet again a 'No Action Motion' has been passed. A fortnight ago the UN said that never again would it sit back and watch another Rwanda unfolding and yet, for 50 months they have watched us slip, slide and fall and will still not even talk about events in Zimbabwe. I can think of no more appropriate way to end this letter than by using the words of Jose Vivanco, the Director of Human Rights Watch, who describes members of the UN Commission for Human Rights as: 'the foxes in charge of the chicken coop.'

IN THE NEWS

~22nd April 2004 Australian Indigenous groups are invited by President

Mugabe to attend a land reform conference which Didymus Mutasa says intends to 'strengthen the struggle against colonialism remnants.'

~25th April 2004 Finance Minister Christopher Kuruneri is arrested following allegations he was illegally exporting hundreds of thousands of rands, pounds and euros to South Africa.

~25th April 2004 South African Archbishop Desmond Tutu urges England's cricketers to boycott a planned tour of Zimbabwe in October.

~1st May 2004 One of Zimbabwe's largest horticultural exporting companies, Kondozi, relocates to Mozambique.

Are you serious? Dinosaur footprints

'A professor who risked life and limb searching for dinosaur footprints in Zimbabwe has been told that a unique footprint discovered by himself and his colleagues was recently destroyed by a herd of elephants. University of KwaZulu-Natal palaeontologist Professor Theagarten Lingham-Soliar and Zimbabwean geologists Ait-Kaci Ahmed and Tim Broderick discovered the 150 million-year-old footprint of the Brachiosaurus in December 2001. The Brachiosaurus was the biggest plant-eating dinosaur on earth. It could grow as tall as 16m and weigh as much as 10 fully grown elephants. This dinosaur resembled a giraffe, with a long neck and front legs which were longer than its hind ones.

The footprint of the dinosaur's back left foot was found in the Chewore area of northern Zimbabwe. Broderick recently informed Lingham-Soliar that the footprint, the first to be discovered in subSaharan Africa, had been destroyed. Broderick, who took pictures of the destroyed footprint, said:

'The smoothly rubbed and rounded banks in the close vicinity are distinctly elephant traces and strong indications are that the agent of the destruction was a herd of elephants.'

Only three toes of the footprint remain. Lingham-Soliar said the irony was that the track of the largest extinct land animal was destroyed by its largest existing counterpart. At the time of the discovery, Lingham-Soliar and his team were unable to make a mould of the footprint as there was no latex available in Zimbabwe. However, they did photograph it. 'The footprint was large, about a metre-long and 22cm deep,' said Lingham-Soliar.' (Sunday Times SA)

2 May 2004. Kipper-fish

Can you imagine a country running without a Minister of Finance? And we're not talking about a normal country with a normal economy, we're talking about Zimbabwe whose economy is shrinking faster than almost anywhere else in the world. A country which has hyperinflation of almost 600%, a massive shortage of foreign currency, a booming black market and unimaginably large international debts. All the talk this week has been about the arrest of Zimbabwe's Finance Minister on charges of dealing in foreign currency and holding two passports. A few weeks ago the South African Press exposed the story that a R300 million luxury mansion was being built in Cape Town for Finance Minister Christopher Kuruneri. At first we thought the story of such enormous wealth and extravagance by one of Zimbabwe's Ministers would just get buried, like so many others have, but Kuruneri, only sworn in 2 months ago, was arrested and remanded in custody with applications for bail being refused.

Everyone wants to know how Zimbabwe's politicians have made so much money so quickly. Apparently there are now more Mercedes and luxury cars in Zimbabwe in proportion to the population, than anywhere else in the world. The contrasts between the leaders and the people are stark, particularly evident recently in an evening petrol queue. Finally finding petrol just before dark and watching the gauge rapidly soar into multiple thousands of dollars, a scruffy little boy stopped near my car and put a small tin plate down on the ground at his feet. In the dish were tiny smoked fish, less than 10cms long. 'Are they bream?' I asked. 'Kipper fish' he said, 'only one thousand dollars each.' As the fancy cars lined up behind me at the petrol pump and the little boy went window to window with his little fish, so many questions came to mind. Why was such a little boy selling 'kipper fish' at dusk on a cold winter evening when he should be at home having a warm bath, did he have a home to go tonight and has he got enough blankets? He is just one of hundreds of thousands of victims of Zimbabwe's turmoil; what horrors has he seen and what has led him to be an adult in a child's shoes?

IN THE NEWS

~5th May 2004 The Kwara State government allocates almost 200,000 hectares of prime agricultural land to Zimbabwean commercial farmers wishing to relocate to Nigeria.

~*6th May 2004* The National Association of Dairy Farmers says year on year production in the dairy sector has declined by 40% since 2003.

8 May 2004. What are we going to do Mum

One week into the new school term my 11-year-old son, along with 30,000 other Zimbabwean children was still sitting at home. His school was one of 45 private schools that were not allowed to open this week under orders from the Ministry of Education. It has been the week from hell which began for me a little before 5pm on Monday the 3rd of May. My son's friend is a border and I was to drop him at the school hostel late in the afternoon. We arrived to find the hostel gates closed and children and parents milling around outside in the gathering dusk. There were many desperate faces and raised voices. A man came to the window of my car and said: 'You are not allowed in; the school is closed.' He handed me a letter signed by the Headmistress which read: 'Under direction from the Minister of Education in Harare, the police have closed our school down. We do not know when we will be allowed to open.' It took some persuading to get the man at the gate to let me in to collect a trunk, bedding and tuck (sweets and food) which had been left at the school earlier that day. The order to close the school had only been made late in the afternoon, hours after many children had been dropped off by parents.

I drove away in shock, my heart pounding, tears in my eyes. I had to stop the car halfway home, not to pull myself together but to tell my son and his friend to stop raiding the sweets they had extricated from the school trunk. By Wednesday the propaganda had reached hateful levels. Education Minister Chigwedere said that he had closed 'racist schools which throw Africans out simply by hiking their fees.' He did not say that enrolment in Zimbabwe's private schools is made up of 80% black children or that virtually all Zimbabwe's government ministers and civil servants send their children to private schools. He did not say that President Mugabe's own children attend private schools in Zimbabwe. He did not say that school fees have gone up because of hyper-inflation. As with everything in Zimbabwe, it was easier to not address the real issues and their causes but to yet again play that ugly racist card.

On Thursday, the Headmistress of my son's school was arrested, at night, from a prayer group meeting and spent the night in a police cell. She heads a small non-profit making Christian school which has only seven white children in its enrolment of over two hundred pupils. The school remained closed and two policemen patrolled the road in front of the locked gates. Driving past the Marondera Police Station my son and I saw our town's only anaesthetist, who is also the Chairman of the Board of Trustees of Richie's school, locked in an outside cage which serves as the holding cell in the police camp, he too had been arrested. Tears were in my eyes and Richie's lip was quivering. 'What have my school done wrong Mum? Why don't they like us? It's just like on the farm again. What are we going to do Mum?' I couldn't answer any of his questions.

This scene was being played out in schools across Zimbabwe and as the Minister yelled 'racism' the children became more and more traumatized. All private schools were told that unless they signed a 'Certificate of Compliance' in which they agreed to a number of regulations, including massively reduced school fees, they would be taken over by the government and nationalized. This comes at a time when Zimbabwe's inflation hovers at around 600%, electricity charges have gone up by 400%, rates and water by 500% and in the same week that the price of a loaf of bread went up by 50%.

30,000 children who can afford to go to school were denied their basic human right to do so this week. Hundreds of thousands of other children who cannot afford to go to either private or government schools continue to play on our streets. Some used to go to farm schools which ceased to exist when farms were taken over. Others used to go to government schools but with inflation at 600%, food comes before reading and writing. The private schools will re-open but on unsustainable budgets and none of us know how long they will be able to pay their bills or keep their teachers.

IN THE NEWS

~*12th May 2004* Zambia offers leases on 100,000 hectares of land to foreign and local farmers, including some from Zimbabwe.

~*13th May 2004* A new maize producer price of $750,000 per tonne is announced by the government. Farmers unions say the price will result in farmers making a $1.8 million loss per hectare.

On the lighter side. The Ant and the grasshopper

The original story – in the finest tradition of oral cultures.

An ant and a grasshopper live in the same field during the summer. The ant works day and night bringing in supplies for the winter. He prepares his home to keep him warm during the cold winter months ahead. Meanwhile the grasshopper hops and sings, eats all the grass he wants and multiplies. Come winter, the grass dies, it is bitterly cold. The ant is well and warm in his house, but the grasshopper has not prepared for the winter, so he dies, leaving a whole herd of little grasshoppers without food or shelter. The moral of the story is that you should work hard to ensure that you can take care of yourself.

The Zimbabwean version – in the unique tradition of Zimbabwe's behaviour.

The first part of the story is the same but being Zimbabwe there are a few complications. The starving, shivering offspring of the grasshopper demand to know why the ant should be allowed to be warm and well fed, while next door they are living in terrible conditions without food or proper clothing. A TV crew shows up and broadcast footage of the poor grasshoppers, contrasting this with footage of the ant, snug in his comfortable home with a pantry full of food. The public is stunned. How can it be in this beautiful field that the poor grasshoppers are allowed to suffer like this while the ant lives in the lap of luxury?

In the blink of an eye the ZGU (Zimbabwe Grasshopper Union) is formed. They charge the ant with species bias and claim that the grasshoppers are the victims of 30 million years of green oppression. They stage a protest in front of the ant's house and trash the street. TV crews interview the ZGU who state that if their demands are not met they will be forced into a life of crime. In a show of strength they loot the TV crew's luggage and hijack their van.

The TRC (Take and Redistribute Commission) demand that the ant apologises to the grasshoppers and make amends for all the other ants in history that may have discriminated against grasshoppers. The government introduces the POG Act (Protection of grasshoppers). The ant is fined, forced to back-pay grasshoppers for half a century and then has his home confiscated by government for redistribution to grasshoppers.

When winter comes again the grasshoppers are still starving. They have sold all the seed, given away the tractors the government gave them and stripped the ant's house of all the moveable and fixed assets. The government imports food. The ant packs his things and moves to another field where he starts a highly successful food company and becomes a millionaire by selling food to the grasshoppers on the field where he came from. (Source unknown)

15 May 2004. Exact estimate

Since the end of February 2000 Zimbabwe has been a country in crisis. Hundreds of thousands of farm workers, managers and owners were thrown off their properties to make way for people who at first were called 'peaceful demonstrators,' then 'land invaders,' then 'settler farmers' and are now called 'new farmers.' Homes were taken over, farmers and their workers were murdered, assaulted and terrorized, private property was looted, burnt or seized, and agricultural equipment and machinery became the property of the State. To make what our government calls this 'Agrarian Revolution' look OK in the eyes of the world, Presidential Powers were used, the constitution was changed, court rulings were ignored and legislation and statutory instruments were gazetted in favour of the actions of the Zanu PF government.

Zimbabwe's maize crop has not yet been harvested but for the last two weeks the government have announced that we are in for a "bumper harvest." At first they said we could expect 1.7 million tonnes and now our Agriculture Minister Joseph Made has fine-tuned his estimate to very precise and exact numbers and says that Zimbabwe is about to reap two million, four hundred and thirty one thousand, one hundred and eighty two tonnes of maize. If the Ministers figures are correct, you would think our government would be throwing the borders open and inviting journalists, camera crews and agricultural experts from all over the world to come and see just exactly what an awesome harvest has been achieved. They are not.

A fortnight ago the Zimbabwe government ordered a UN crop assessment team to leave the country after it had been in the field for only four days. The World Food Programme said they had written approval to carry out the assessment but Minister Made said they were here without his approval. The UN described Minister Made's estimated harvest figures as 'impossible' and 'a fantasy,' the FEWS Foundation warned of 'an impending famine' and the CFU estimated a crop of around 700,000 tonnes. This week the Minister of Social Welfare said Zimbabwe does not need any more World Food Aid but our eyebrows are raised because everything in Zimbabwe is dictated by politics, even harvest figures, and elections are getting near.

IN THE NEWS

~*25th May 2004* The Deputy Sheriff attaches a bus belonging to Air Zimbabwe after the airline fails to settle a $745 million debt owed to a senior flight attendant who was unlawfully dismissed.

29 May 2004. Are you sitting comfortably?

In the last fortnight the situation in Zimbabwe has deteriorated dramatically. It began with an altercation in Parliament where the opposition MP of Chimanimani finally lost his temper at the personal abuse being thrown at him and pushed a Zanu PF Minister to the floor. The opposition MP happened to have a white skin and his action was exactly what the Zimbabwean government have been waiting for. Since the incident in Parliament there has been a blatant whipping up of rhetoric and anti-white sentiment in the media. RACIST,

RACIST, RACIST are the screams. In a country of 11 million people generous estimates put the number of white people still here at about 70 000 people – it is a miniscule proportion of the population but for four years and three months people with white skins have consistently been blamed for everything that has gone wrong in the country. We have become the easy targets, the incessant and obvious scapegoats.

Since the incident in Parliament the MDC offices in Harare have been attacked, windows smashed and property destroyed. A 35-year-old white farmer has been abducted, tortured and beaten black and blue on his back, legs, arms and buttocks. Another white farmer is in hospital with two broken arms, stab wounds and a charge of murder hanging over him. The MDC offices in Chimanimani have been attacked, windows smashed and roofing destroyed. A white woman has had her house stoned and been paraded through the streets, publicly humiliated and hugely traumatized. After the horrific events in Rwanda, the UN and the world said that never again would they sit back and watch genocide and ethnic cleansing. Are you sitting comfortably in the UN?

IN THE NEWS

~3rd June 2004 Ostrich production has declined by 75% since 2000. *~8th June 2004* RBZ Governor Gono goes on a tour of the US, Europe and South Africa promising Zimbabweans in the diaspora a good exchange rate if they send money back home through the Homelink system, which is administered by

the RBZ. Gono says he aims to realise US$1.2 billion a month from diaspora remittances.

12 June 2004. Highway robbery

Zimbabwe made international news this week with the announcement by Minister John Nkomo that all land is to be nationalized. Title Deeds are to be made null and void and the State will issue 99 year leases for agricultural land and 25 year leases for conservancies. Minister Nkomo said that the government did not intend to 'waste time and money' on disputes with people who had Title Deeds, Court Orders and other legal documents which confirmed they are in fact the legal owners of the land.

What didn't make international news was the Acquisition of Farm Equipment and Materials Bill. Despite the fact that the Parliamentary Legal Committee unanimously declared 5 clauses of the Bill unconstitutional and all opposition MPs walked out of the House in protest when it came to the vote, the Bill was passed by Zimbabwe's parliament this week. This Act now allows the State to compulsorily acquire farm equipment and materials and forbids farmers from selling, dismantling, removing or destroying their own private property. This includes tractors, ploughs, irrigation equipment, machinery, seed and fertilizer. The mind just boggles at where this highway robbery and blatant disregard of people's private property rights will end and who or what will be next.

Are you serious? Impounding pushcarts

'The Harare municipal police have impounded 2,350 pushcarts that were obstructing the flow of traffic in the city centre. This also includes grocery trolleys that were being abused by vendors outside shops.

'We are hoping to intensify the clean-up campaign of the city centre's roads,' said municipal police chief security officer Mr Tavanana Gomo. He said owners of the pushcarts would be fined a $60,000 administration fee and another $25,000 which will go to Zimbabwe Republic Police licence inspectorate. The pushcart owners would also have to pay an additional $1,000 for storage. (The Herald)

10 July 2004. Total bombardment

Almost since the beginning of Zimbabwe's land seizures in late February 2000, we have been bombarded with propaganda jingles on state controlled radio and television. Every half hour, day and night, the adverts are aired telling us that now the land has been taken away from white Zimbabweans, life is wonderful.

This week a new propaganda jingle started and every half hour, day and night, it is being played on ZBC radio and TV. This time the new jingle isn't about land but about electricity. According to the lyrics it doesn't matter where you are, be it a castle or a cave, in a city or under a tree in the middle of nowhere, electricity is going to be available for all Zimbabweans. The irony of this jingle is that in the same week as it was launched, electricity supplier ZESA announced that due to chronic power shortages, load shedding was being introduced across the country. Even more ironic is the fact that ZESA ı can afford to advertise over 50 times a day on TV and radio and yet it has an outstanding debt of US$51 million to electricity suppliers in South Africa, the DR ı Congo and Mozambique. So while we sit in the dark with candles waiting for the power to come back on and women stream out of the bush with firewood on their heads because they can't afford electricity, the jingles go on and on and on.

IN THE NEWS

~*11th June 2004* The weekly Tribune has its license revoked by the government.

~*12th June 2004* Zimbabwe rejects an extradition bid attempting to bring deposed Ethiopian dictator, Mengistu Haile Mariam, to justice for human rights violations during his rule.

17 July 2004. For Christopher

Through thick mist and an icy wind, a friend and I went visiting in a high density suburb on the outskirts of town. In two long, thin buildings that face each other and had once been pink but were now dirty brown, there were twenty four doors, and we stood outside one waiting to go in. I looked around, not so that I could soak in the sight but to force my brain to accept what my eyes would not believe. There was one leaking tap in a muddy hollow in the barren yard. This is the water supply for twenty four families – for washing, cooking, cleaning and bathing. There was one outside concrete sink in which people do all their washing. It does not have a drain and the dirty water simply pours out onto the ground and sits in filthy, slimy puddles in front of the block of communal toilets.

When the door opened we saw Christopher. He is dying of AIDS and being nursed through his last days by his wife. Christopher was too weak to even raise his head from the bed but he tried to smile and greeted us in a whisper, leaving his wife to do the talking. This one room, perhaps three by three metres, is their entire home. It does not have water, a bathroom or toilet and has only one small window in the back wall. At the bottom of the bed was a huge pile of soiled bedclothes, waiting to be washed in the concrete sink outside. In a bucket of cold water by the bed were Christopher's soiled clothes, also waiting to be washed outside. There was no spare linen to put back on the bed and no plastic sheeting with which to protect the mattress and so Christopher lay on top of a folded cloth, rags wrapped around his waist, a thin blue blanket on top of his skeletal body. On the floor was a small tin bath from which Christopher's wife would try and bathe him. She has only one disposable glove and carefully took it off as we stood talking.

Christopher is 36 years old and is the father of five children, four of whom have been sent to live in the rural areas with their grandparents. Christopher does not take anti-retrovirals, he could never afford them and now his body is too weak to be able to handle them. He used to support his wife and children working as a security guard until he became too sick to continue. Then his wife supported the family, selling tomatoes and bananas on the roadside, but now, all day, every day she is at home, caring for her husband, watching him die. They have no income, no drugs, no support and only the food given to them by well-wishers. Christopher is one of the lucky ones because he has someone to care for him. There are thousands more like him, lying in their own faeces and vomit behind filthy doors in freezing, dark rooms, alone, unseen and waiting to die.

Are you serious? Ox drawn ambulances

'The Ministry of Health and Child Welfare yesterday received nine ox-drawn ambulances and three regular ambulances worth about $550 million from the United Nations Children's Fund. The ox-drawn ambulances, an idea initiated by the ministry based on the commonly used scotch-carts for rural transport, would be distributed to Makoni, Wedza, Seke, Mwenezi, Mberengwa, Umguza, Zvimba, Gwanda and Guruve districts. While all community members would have access to the carts, priority would be given to pregnant women and children. The communities themselves, with a carts minder responsible for maintenance, would manage the ox-drawn ambulances. The carts would be based at the homestead of the headmen.' (The Herald)

31 July 2004. Reap where they did not sow

As winter comes to an end, a kind of desperate urgency has appeared within our government to do something about the complete chaos that continues on Zimbabwe's farms. The issue under the spotlight at the moment is that of government Ministers and high ranking officials who have got, taken or been given more than one farm. For four years President Mugabe has been saying 'one farmer one farm' and recently appointed John Nkomo to the position of Minister of Land Reform and Resettlement. Ministers who have got more than one farm since 2000 have started receiving 'withdrawal letters' advising them that the land was being taken back. According to the Zimbabwe Independent some of the Ministers with 'extra land holdings' are: Information Minister Moyo; Local Government Minister Chombo; Agriculture Minister Made; Justice Minister Chinamasa and Transport Minister Mushowe.

One of the Ministers concerned said the withdrawal letters were 'preposterous and annoying.' He said of the multiple farms credited to him, one had been reallocated to his cousin and another to his mother.

So far Minister Nkomo is standing firm and has said he won't be 'intimidated, perturbed or frustrated by those causing all this hullabaloo.' Responding to a tirade against him in the Herald newspaper, Nkomo said the angry outpourings by those 'defending the indefensible would not scare him or frustrate his efforts to retrieve the farms.'

Also speaking out on the chaos surrounding Zimbabwe's farms is the Governor of the Reserve Bank Gideon Gono. Referring to the recent seizures of highly productive horticultural and export processing zone farms, Gono said: 'We now have a new set of farmers who want to reap where they did not sow.' Gono called them 'fly by harvest time farmers' who pitch up on a property just when a crop is ready to harvest and declare the harvest, land, house and farm equipment as their own.

IN THE NEWS

~*1st August 2004* The government gazettes new regulations requiring Zimbabweans born in the country but whose parents and ancestors were born elsewhere to fill in special renunciation forms to restore their Zimbabwean citizenship.

~*4th August 2004* Police arrest five men, including a white farmer for attempting to take farm equipment to Zambia.

~*5th August 2004* Royal Bank is shut down for six months; all deposits are frozen and a curator named.

~*7th August 2004* Approximately 800 auditors have emigrated in the past year according to the Institute of Chartered Accountants of Zimbabwe. This represents 60% of the 1,400 members of ICAZ.

7 August 2004. Inflation and education don't mix

Zimbabwe's schools have been teetering on the edge of collapse for the last three months since our Minister of Education declared that private schools were too expensive and stipulated that schools could only charge what his Ministry decided was an acceptable fee. This ruling disregards what parents have agreed to pay to School Associations and Boards.

Despite the fact that inflation is presently at 400%, the Minister of Education refused to back down on his ruling about school fees. During this school term, postage and telephone costs have risen by over 400%. Last term when my son's school needed to send me an important letter (one that wouldn't get buried at the bottom of his suitcase), it cost $500. Now it costs $2,300 for just the stamp on the letter. If each parent at my son's school was to get just one posted letter a month from the school, the cost of the stamps alone would consume $1.2 million. The Minister of Education has stipulated that this same school cannot charge more than $1.4 million per child per term. So one student's entire school fees for a three month term, is enough for each parent to receive one letter a month but nothing else: no teachers, lessons or sports.

Last term when my son was taken ill and the school had to phone me, the call cost $120. This term that same three minute call costs $585. Last term if my son was taken sick I knew the school would give him ear drops, a bandage or a pain killer. This term I know that none of those things are guaranteed anymore. When you extrapolate the dollars and cents of the most basic services into the number of students at an average small private school, it is physically impossible for any schools to run on the fees the Minister of Education has stipulated.

No one really knows why Zimbabwe's Minister of Education has decided to do what he is doing to our private schools. The Minister continues to shout about racism in the 1960s and the privileged white elite, but he still chooses to ignore the fact that the enrolment at all Zimbabwe's private schools in 2004 is comprised of at least 80% black children. The Minister is adamant that no private schools may increase their fees again in 2004, completing ignoring the existence of 400% inflation. Last week one private school, established in 1911, declared its necessity to go into provisional liquidation as it simply cannot pay its bills anymore. It's almost as if the Minister has just decided that inflation doesn't affect education, that they don't mix.

Are you serious? Goblins at work

'A self-styled traditional healer popularly known as tsikamutanda, was on Monday seriously burnt by a suspected goblin, which he was allegedly trying to get rid of during a cleansing ceremony at one of his client's homestead in Lalapanzi. Asst Inspector Mukwiza said Mr Mangisi's family and other villagers were called and gathered in Mangisi's kitchen and the tsikamutanda started beating drums and singing. Mr Musiiwa Denhere is said to have stood at the kitchen door and said that he had managed to get hold of the goblin and wanted to burn it.

'Musiiwa looked like he was struggling with something and then said he had thrown it into the fire. He then said he had been burnt himself,' said Asst Insp Mukwiza.

On checking the injuries on Mr Musiiwa, it was observed that he had been burnt on the right thigh, private parts and stomach and the police were called in and they ferried him to the hospital where his condition was said to be stable. The Mangisi family had called him because they suspected that there was a goblin at the homestead as they were losing a member of the family every year.' (The Chronicle)

IN THE NEWS

~13th–16th August 2004. The 2004 Summer Olympics are held in Athens. Kirsty Coventry wins 3 medals: gold, silver and bronze for the women's 200 metre backstroke, 100 metre backstroke and 200 metres individual medley respectively.

28 August 2004. Lost their reason for being

This week Zimbabwe's opposition made a monumental decision. Their Executive announced that the MDC would not be taking part in any more elections at any level in Zimbabwe. In a carefully worded statement the MDC talked about 'suspending participation until political space had been opened up and a legal, institutional and administrative framework had been established.'

At each and every election since 2000, Zimbabwe has turned into a bloodied battlefield. Belonging to the opposition has been a literally life and death decision. Carrying an MDC membership card, wearing their T shirt or being openly involved in their party in any way has incited the wrath of government and its supporters. People have been beaten, burned, stoned, tortured, raped, maimed and murdered. People's homes have been torched by petrol bombs, looted by mobs and had every window, door and roofing sheet smashed.

At every election in the past four and half years the Zimbabwe government have changed the rules. They have changed constituency boundaries at the last minute, reduced the number of polling stations in congested areas and increased them in remote areas, changed static polling stations into mobile ones and denied the opposition their right to inspect the voters roll. Obviously, the MDC had no choice but to finally stop giving legitimacy to Zimbabwe's elections. We don't know what lies ahead but for now the overwhelming feeling is one of immense relief that the bully boys who are already hanging around on our street corners have lost their reason for being.

For the past two weeks the winds of natural change have been blowing very strongly though Zimbabwe. The trees have been raining leaves. The Musasa woodlands stood bare for what seemed like a day and now they are glorious as they take on their new summer colours: crimson, red, burgundy, chocolate, lime and hot-green. Zimbabweans long for more than seasonal change, but it feels as elusive as ever. We long for some way to shake off the old and start again with new colours. We long for a political summer, it has been winter too long.

IN THE NEWS

~*1st September 2004* Chechen terrorists take up to 1,500 people hostage, mostly children, in a school in Belsen. Two days later Russian forces end the siege at the school leaving at least 335 people dead and 700 injured.

4 September 2004. Numbers louder than words

I feel almost ashamed to write about Zimbabwe's problems after such horror at a school in Belsen in Russia. My letter this week is about numbers, they speak louder than any words I can write.

Zimbabwe Tobacco production: 2000: 237 million kilograms
Zimbabwe Tobacco production: 2004: 64 million kilograms
One packet of 20 cigarettes in 2000: $22.
One packet of 20 cigarettes in 2004: $4,500.
Zimbabwe wheat production 2001: 314 thousand tonnes
Zimbabwe wheat production 2003: 50 thousand tonnes
One loaf of bread in 2000: $21.
One loaf of bread in 2004: $3,500
Zimbabwe milk production 2001: 160 000 tonnes
Zimbabwe milk production 2003: 100 000 tonnes
One litre of milk in 2000: $15.
One litre of milk in 2004: $2,600
One dozen eggs in 2000: $36
One dozen eggs in 2004: $7,500.
One bag of sugar in 2000: $40.
One bag of sugar in 2004: $5,303
Harare Agricultural show total livestock exhibits 2004: 9 cattle, 2 goats, 3 sheep.
Zimbabwe Tourism Earnings 1999: $200 million.
Zimbabwe Tourism Earnings 2003: $44 million.
And the last number comes from the Zimbabwe Independent: 'Baton wielding riot policed on Wednesday broke up pro-democracy demonstrations in the capital arresting at least 44 activists.'

IN THE NEWS

~7th September 2004. The government seizes Mutumwa Mawere's multi-million dollar Shabanie-Mashava Mines

under the new Presidential Powers (Temporary Measures Act) Reconstruction of State-Indebted Insolvent Companies) Regulations. The new Regulation allows the state to convert into equity debt owed by a private company if there is evidence the company is unable to meet debts.

~*10th September 2004.* British national Simon Mann, the alleged ringleader of a plot to stage a coup in Equatorial Guinea, is sentenced to 7 years in prison in Harare for trying to illegally buy weapons from the Zimbabwe Defence Industries. 65 other suspected mercenaries are sentenced to 12 months in jail.

~*16th September 2004* Police set up roadblocks to search for maize being moved from rural to urban areas. All commuters are ordered to disembark; their possessions are searched and maize is confiscated and forfeited to the state.

Are you serious? Lion in the loo

'Excuse me, there's a lion in the loo,' Zimbabwean safari operator Peter Calera politely informed his colleague Steve Pope by telephone. Residents of Nyamhunga, a township near Kariba, were trying to drive three lions out of town last week by throwing stones when a young male took refuge in a public toilet. Veterinarian Rob Rees agreed to shoot the animal with a tranquilizer dart, but he was in Harare, a three hour drive away. Pope and Calera trapped the lion in the bathroom with a game capture net and for the next three hours, took turns shining a light into his face to keep him from lunging. The story had a happy ending, with Rees finally arriving and sedating the animal, which was then loaded into a truck and released back into the bush." (UPI / Washington Times)

IN THE NEWS

~17th September 2004 The 2004 Summer Paralympics begin in Athens. Zimbabwe's Elliot Mujaji wins a gold medal in the 100 metre sprint. *~22nd September 2004* The Zimbabwe Government officially informs Western donors that it has had a bumper harvest and will not need food aid for the foreseeable future.

Are you serious? Wheat production statistics

2000 – 45,000 hectares planted
2001 – 56,000 hectares planted
2002 – 25,000 hectares planted
2003 – 10,999 hectares planted.
Central Statistical Office. (Zimbabwe Independent)

25 September 2004. Live blanks

It was the annual Marondera Show last weekend and part of the entertainment involved displays by the army and air force including a mock battle. Under normal circumstances there would be helicopters and a lot of noise and smoke but there shouldn't be blood or injuries. Like everything else in Zimbabwe, there was nothing normal about what went on in Marondera last Saturday. No one really knows what happened but the mock battle started and somehow a few live bullets had been loaded instead of blanks and suddenly people in the crowd of spectators were being shot.

Eyewitnesses said people were screaming and running in all directions and there was utter chaos. A teacher accompanying school students at the show said she saw a woman who had been shot in the chest and a man who appeared to have been shot in both legs. Two teenage girls standing next to the army display were both shot in the legs. Others reported seeing two soldiers being covered with white sheets and loaded onto a helicopter but no one knows the condition of these men. There has been very little news in the state media about the event, but at least 14 people were shot, four of whom appear to have been children.

All week the gossip and rumour in Marondera about the shooting has escalated and the quieter the government and army are, the more we have speculated about what really went on. No one can understand how live bullets accidentally got mixed in with blanks, or how any trained soldier could mistakenly load a live cartridge instead of a blank. Some people think it was just gross incompetence or negligence but others believe it was actually an assassination attempt on the provincial Governor who was one of the spectators.

The Commander of the Zimbabwe National Army, Major General Sibanda, visited the injured at Marondera Hospital during the week and, according to the Herald newspaper gave the patients Bibles, fruits and get well soon cards. He said: 'What happened was an accident which has never happened before since Independence. We have come here because we are human and feel for the people who were injured in the accident.'

Are you serious? Mermaids and floodlit lakeside ceremonies

'A bogus traditional healer who persuaded a businesswoman to hire 'mermaids' and accommodate them in a Harare hotel to help find a stolen car was convicted of theft by false pretences, court officials said Tuesday. Harare magistrate Sandra Nhau found Edina Chizema guilty of swindling a businesswoman of her savings with promises that mermaids would help recover the luxury car in 2004 and solve the businesswoman's unspecified 'personal problems.'

In Zimbabwe, where tribal superstition is deeply entrenched, prosecutors said Chizema persuaded Margaret Mapfumo to pay 200 million Zimbabwe dollars to hire mermaids, feed and accommodate them in a Harare hotel, buy power generators for a floodlit lakeside ceremony and invoke ancestral spirits to find the missing car.' (AP)

IN THE NEWS

~*30th September 2004* 42 women are arrested and charged with disturbing the peace. The women (members of WOZA) were on a 450 kilometre march to protest proposed laws that would ban human rights organizations.

2 October 2004. Skin colour is irrelevant

In the last three weeks some diabolical things have been going on in Zimbabwe but still our African neighbours cannot find their voices. Hundreds of black peasant farmers and their families have been forcibly evicted from the land they themselves seized from white commercial farmers since

February 2000. Evictions have apparently been undertaken by soldiers and police who have set light to people's homes and left peasant farmers with their wives, children, furniture and livestock stranded on the side of main highways. Quoted in the Zimbabwe Independent last week, one evicted peasant farmer said: 'We are convinced that the government is now evicting us from the farms to pave the way for Zanu PF officials.'

White commercial farmers lived in fear and were powerless when the Zimbabwean government came and grabbed their farms in 2000. Black Zimbabwean farmers are now also living in fear for the powerlessness that is about to engulf them as our government kicks them off the farms too. Skin colour is irrelevant, we are all victims.

IN THE NEWS

~8th October 2004 Only 32% of land normally planted has been prepared this season. Less than 200,000 hectares has been prepared in the commercial sector and 220,000 hectares in communal and newly resettled areas. In normal circumstances, crop production should take up 1.3 million hectares.

~10th October 2004 All six of the controversial Youth Training centres are closed due to lack of funds.

~13th October 2004 The army takes charge of telephone and postal services after workers go on strike.

~15th October 2004 The Minister of Agriculture says the GMB has impounded 108 tonnes of maize at roadblocks manned by police since April.

16 October 2004. In memory of Dave

By all accounts Friday the 15th of October looked like it was going to be an historic day for Zimbabwe. From as early as 7am radio news bulletins were heightening the tension and ratcheting up the fear with warnings from police that unruly behaviour would not be tolerated. This was the day the verdict would finally be handed down in the treason trial against opposition leader Morgan Tsvangirai. Newspaper headlines were: 'Police put on high alert,' and the atmosphere was tense with reports of roadblocks throughout Harare and police standing in pairs or groups at every intersection in Harare.

When the 'not guilty' verdict was handed down just before midday, there was a national sigh of relief. Although no one could see how any court would find Tsvangirai guilty with the evidence the way it was, we don't take anything for granted in Zimbabwe. Tsvangirai said he had been hoping for the best and preparing for the worst. He said the verdict signalled a 'good basis for national reconciliation.

I end this week with a message of condolence to the families and friends of six Zimbabweans who were tragically killed in an air crash in Canada a few days ago. Happy times from years gone by will never be forgotten and I write this letter in memory of Dave.

IN THE NEWS

~22nd October 2004 The Confederation of Zimbabwe Industries (CZI) say the influx of cheap imported goods mainly from China forced 40 companies to close in 2003 resulting in the loss of 3,858 jobs. 25 firms are expected to close in 2004 with 2,575 job losses.

~22nd October 2004 A group of depositors led by Harare lawyer Edwin Manikai storm the National Discount House after the firm failed to meet its obligations to them.

~22nd October 2004 Of the $339 billion allocated to the Ministry of Home Affairs in the budget, the police had used 77% of the ministry's total allocation by June.

23 October 2004. Until we meet again

My letter from Zimbabwe this week comes from my Mum who came to this country in the mid-1950s. I have added nothing to her words as they speak for themselves and express the pain that 3 million other families have gone through as they too have been forced to leave Zimbabwe.

My name is Pauline and I am proud to say that I am Cathy Buckle's mother and the grandmother of her son about whom she has written so movingly in many of her letters and in the two books which describe the horrors of the past four and a half years in our beloved Zimbabwe. In two weeks' time I am very reluctantly leaving Zimbabwe. There is such turmoil of feelings going on inside me but above all there is sadness at all the goodbyes. Goodbye to the country which has been my home for so long. Goodbye to the people, the wonderful ordinary people of Zimbabwe that I shall miss more even than the beauty of the land. Goodbye also to all the hundreds – if not thousands – of students I have taught over the years and particularly in the past ten years since I have been living in a small rural centre some one hundred kilometres from Cathy's home in Marondera.

There are so many memories that I shall take with me, some happy and some sad and painful. Like everyone else, I have watched in disbelief as this beautiful country has become entrapped in a web of violence and hatred as if a huge and all-pervasive evil had spread over the land. Every morning I would wake early and stare out at the soft grey gomo behind my house and wonder how it was possible that a landscape so beautiful could contain such evil. I would watch as the kids trotted happily to school and wonder what the future held for them in a country which was rapidly falling into total ruination around them. Friends and students would come to the house, for tutoring or just to share friendship, laughter, discussion and ideas. They stopped coming for a while when things were really bad and we spoke only in lowered voices for one never knew who might be listening. It's always like that in the run-up to or aftermath of an election but now we seem to be in permanent election mode in Zimbabwe.

In spite of the problems, there are good memories and I shall always treasure the absolute acceptance all those friends showed me, a woman of a different culture from their own.

Now that I am leaving I am overcome by a deep sadness that Zimbabwe should come to this. I have lived through and fought in my own way the hideous racism of the Smith regime which swore 'never in a thousand years' would the people take overpower in their own country only to see now the savage cruelty of a dictator and his party, apparently drunk with power and determined to hold on at all costs regardless of the suffering of their people. Politics dominates every sphere of life in this country. It seems that we have learnt nothing from history.

I want to thank all those dear and special friends who have made the past ten years so memorable for me. I shall never forget them or Zimbabwe which remains forever in my heart. It is they, the people of Zimbabwe who hold the power to change their lives for the better. I pray that they find the will and the courage to do that.

IN THE NEWS

~28th October 2004 The Reserve Bank closes Time Bank, bringing to five the number of banks that have closed as instability rocks the financial sector.

30 October 2004. Judge and jury

The South African trade union were due to come to Zimbabwe on a fact finding mission, to meet their counterparts in the ZCTU and representatives from a wide range of civic society organisations. We were sure that COSATU would say it like it is. They are not the sort of organization who would be intimidated or harassed so with bated breath we followed every step of the saga. COSATU were told by our government that their visit was unacceptable and that they would not be welcome but the Union representatives said they were coming anyway. The 13 member COSATU delegation arrived in Harare but was detained by state security agents at the airport for almost two hours. The COSATU delegates were told that they would only be allowed in if they agreed in writing not to meet certain Zimbabwean groups on the grounds that these organizations were opposed to the Mugabe government. (One of the groups mentioned was the Council of Churches!)

The COSATU delegation stood firm, refused to sign anything and were eventually allowed into the country. Their visit did not last long. The next morning CIO agents descended; they were joined by riot police to enforce a Cabinet ruling to deport the COSATU team. The Ministry of Information attacked the COSATU visit describing it as 'a treacherously calculated assault; a challenge to (Zimbabwe's) sovereignty; a provocative visit (by a group) with alien interests.'

While the propaganda raged, the COSATU delegation was being shoved unceremoniously out of the country. There were no farewells from the airport but a six hundred kilometre drive in the middle of the night to literally dump the Union leaders at the Beit Bridge border. Exhausted, hungry and stressed, the COSATU vice president said it had been a 'nasty, horrible experience,' and that 'there is simply no law and order in Zimbabwe.'

While this was going on Parliament voted to jail opposition MP Roy Bennett for 15 months with hard labour for pushing over Justice Minister Patrick Chinamasa in Parliament in May. Roy Bennett didn't deny shoving the Justice Minister and apologised to the Speaker of The House. There is no doubt in anyone's mind that the incident was the culmination of almost five years of extreme provocation. Events which represent a litany of horror and abuse which include repeated violent invasions of his farm; illegal arrests; murder of one man, shooting of another; rape of three women; slaughter and theft of cattle; theft and sale of over 150 tonnes of the Bennett's coffee; the looting and trashing of his home; six court orders that had been ignored and the death of Mr and Mrs Bennett's unborn child.

Zanu PF did not waste any time debating these horrors, their parliamentary majority turned them into judge and jury and already MP Roy Bennett has been locked up. Roy Bennett has shown us all the meaning of courage and true patriotism and we thank him for the hope he has given us for the last five years.

IN THE NEWS

~2nd November 2004. George Bush is re-elected President of the United States of America.

~3rd November 2004 Under the Ex-political Prisoners, Detainees and Restrictees Bill, the government will pay once-off payments, expected to be in the region of $10 million, to each of an estimated 20,000 people who were either imprisoned or detained for their political activism during the independence struggle.

~12th November 2004 The GMB makes a loss of $302 billion in the year ending March 2004 after selling maize and wheat below cost. The GMB buys locally produced and imported maize for $750,000 and $1.6 million a tonne respectively but sells to millers at $650,000. The GMB pays local and foreign wheat producers $1.7 million and $1.8 million per tonne respectively but sells it at $900,000.

Welcome diversion. Roll over

I was alerted to the fact that something was going on overhead by the unusual number of white splats in the dust on the driveway. Even though I looked straight up, it took a long time to see them and what a sight it was. Three little baby Drongos were sitting squashed up in a nest on a branch of a Musasa tree. They looked so quaint sitting in their little cup of a nest swaying in the hot October wind and then I noticed the activities of their overworked Mum. Poor thing, she kept flying off and coming back with little edible offerings for the chicks. Every time she arrived there were always three little craning necks, gaping beaks and squeaking voices: more, more, more, they demanded.

Once I knew they were there I kept looking for the nest and watching the progress of the chicks who were squashed up tighter than sardines in a tin. Seeing them like that reminded me of the little song we used to sing when we were kids:

'There were three in a bed and the little one said: roll over, roll over. So they all rolled over and one fell out.

There were two in a bed and the little one said: roll over, roll over...'

A few days later the Drongo chicks were all sitting on the branch of the Musasa tree and the nest had gone. Now there was no option, they had to fly and I wondered if it was Mum that had dislodged the nest, maybe just rolling it over the edge.

20 November 2004. The darkest of days

On Friday afternoon the long, hot dry spell which had lasted for five weeks finally broke in true African fashion with the most ferocious storm. In the middle of the day it grew very dark, a fierce wind arrived and lightning streaked down the blackening sky every few minutes. The power went off almost as soon as the rain started and I surveyed all the bounty on the floor around me.

For almost three months I had been tracking a donation which had been left on the other side of the country. Three boxes, one suitcase and a bucket was the description of the donation and at last, thanks to the kindness of a whole string of people, it had finally arrived in Marondera. On the side of an 8kg bucket in big print it said: 'Old Fashioned Blueberry: Frozen gourmet muffin batter.' Inside the bucket was something far more valuable than muffin mix: scissors, tweezers, toothbrushes, soap, disinfectant, linen savers and antiseptic – everything that could be used to give some comfort and dignity to desperately poor people living with HIV and AIDS in Marondera.

There are over 700 unemployed and virtually destitute people with HIV and AIDS in Marondera. In addition there are over 900 orphans in the town and 21 child-headed households. In all cases these men, women and children are almost entirely dependent on the goodwill of strangers, on food and clothing handouts and charitable donations from NGOs (Non-Governmental Organizations).

There are thought to be in excess of 3,000 NGOs in Zimbabwe employing over 20,000 people who literally help millions of people in need in Zimbabwe. There are NGOs working to help the very young and the very old, the sick, hungry and downtrodden. There are NGOs working in the cities, towns and remotest of villages. This may well be the last week that a large number of these NGOs continue to operate in the country. This week parliament began forcing the NGO Bill through the required stages. Despite an adverse report by the parliamentary legal committee which said the Bill contradicted the constitution on 12 counts, it now seems inevitable that the NGO Bill is about to become law. NGOs are frantically making preparations; some will go underground; others will relocate to neighbouring countries and many more will simply cease to exist. Welshman Ncube, the Chairman of the parliamentary legal committee described the NGO Bill as a 'pervasive attempt to curtail and extinguish the fundamental freedoms of the people of Zimbabwe.' He said the Bill 'does not seek to regulate but to control, to silence, to render ineffective and ultimately shut down nongovernmental organisations.'

These are the darkest of days in Zimbabwe. So many people get from one day to the next thanks to the kindness of strangers and the goodness of charitable organisations. No one knows how they will survive once these organizations are outlawed.

IN THE NEWS

~*20th November 2004* A parliamentary committee surveying food stocks finds the government's forecast of 2.4 million tonnes of maize to be hugely inflated. The committee says the country could end up with a maximum of only 574,000 tonnes of maize this season.

~*20th November 2004* The Solidarity Peace Trust says an estimated 70% of Zimbabwe's working population, or 3.4 million people, have left the country to escape the political and economic crisis.

Are you serious? Christmas cards

'No one is sending Christmas cards from Zimbabwe this year because the stamp for a single page letter to the UK costs the same as 20 loaves of bread.' (Eddie Cross, Bulawayo)

27 November 2004. Don't give a damn about cricket

This week Zimbabwe made international news almost every day as the English cricket team hovered over the border while the politicians and assorted spokesmen argued and threatened, issued ultimatums and huffed and puffed about who would and would not be allowed into the country. Finally, by Friday, it looked as if the cricket matches were going to happen and the reporters were going to be present and while it was good that Zimbabwe was in the world news again, it was for all the wrong reasons. Most ordinary Zimbabweans don't give a damn about cricket and long after the shouting, batting and bowling is over and the cricket players have gone home, nothing will have changed. We will still have 80% unemployment, soaring inflation and a life expectancy of just 35 years. I don't know how many multi millions or billions of dollars these cricket games have involved but for sure they could have got people out of rickety wooden shacks and into decent brick houses with water and electricity and maybe, luxury of luxuries, a flushing toilet.

Are you serious? Life expectancy in Zimbabwe

1980 – 55 years

1988 – 61 years

2004 – 37 years (Institute of War and Peace Reporting)

IN THE NEWS

~1st December 2004 Postage rates increase by 1,280%

~1st December 2004 Seven senior Zanu PF officials are suspended from the party after a secret meeting in Tsholotsho to oppose President Mugabe's choice of Joice Mujuru as his potential successor. Those suspended are provincial chairmen July Moyo (Midlands); Mike Madiro (Manicaland); Themba Ncube (Bulawayo); Daniel Shumba (Masvingo); Lloyd Siyoka (Matabeleland South) and Jacob Mudenda (Matabeleland North). War veterans' leader Jabulani Sibanda is also suspended for four years.

4 December 2004. No prizes

This week our schools limped to the last day and shuddered to a stop at the end of what has been an impossibly difficult school year. It was my son's last day at junior school and I sat with other parents at the final assembly. Since nursery school I have never missed a gala, sports day, play or concert and I knew that Richard's last day at junior school was going to be emotional. It was also prize-giving day and one by one children came up grade by grade to receive awards for their excellence. There were the usual English, Maths and Arts prizes but also awards for achievement, consistent effort and Christian conduct.

As each child came up there were the usual claps, cheers and ululation's from parents bursting with pride and I found tears in my eyes on more than one occasion. I clapped and cried for myself as a single Mum, an ex-farmer and outspoken writer. I was not actually sure how I had survived these 57 months of turmoil, fear and penury and made it to this day. I clapped and cried for Richie who had changed schools, worked through learning problems, lived through horrors on an invaded farm and fought his fears and nightmares. I was not sure how Richie had made it to this day either or how either of us would cope with the phenomenal changes which lie ahead. I clapped and cried for the school, particularly after listening to the annual reports by the Headmistress and the Chairman of the Board of Governors. Even though I had been in and out of the school all year and had attended almost all of the meetings, listening to the litany of horrors in one speech really bought home to me what an enormous achievement it was that this little school had managed to stay open at all.

The year had begun with inflation of over 600% and yet the government had pegged the school fees at a rate which did not take economics into consideration. In May, first the headmistress and then the Chairman of the Board had been detained in police cells. The Police closed the school down and patrolled the premises preventing our children and their teachers from entering. As the year went on, the finances of the school became more and more precarious. All parents had agreed to make donations to the school to keep the standards up, but when it came to it, many did not do so. The feelings at parents' meetings got tenser and angrier as those parents who had made large donations to the school knew that their money was supporting the children of other parents who had promised to pay but didn't. Three weeks before the end of the term and in the heat of mid-summer, the school was forced to close the swimming pool down as they could no longer afford to keep it operating. And now, on prize-giving day, not a single child actually received a prize because the school simply could not afford to buy the usual book prizes. The children got certificates and applause, huge applause, from parents and teachers who knew what an achievement it was and what sacrifices had been made again and again for and by the school to get to this day.

Are you serious? So how much money did we lend you?

An actual printed, official notice on the wall outside the Marondera Post Office:

'RBZ LOANS REPAYMENT

All Mashonaland East farmers who were supplied with irrigation equipment under the winter wheat programme should urgently come and confirm the true figures of their loans before their loan statements are submitted to the RBZ. [Reserve Bank of Zimbabwe]. Ministry of Agriculture, Dept of Irrigation, Olympia House, Office Number 19, Pine Street, Marondera.' (18th Dec 2004)

11 December 2004. Termites among us

It is just weeks now until Zimbabwe's parliamentary elections and things are not looking at all good. The MDC have still not said if they are going to participate in the polls and the electoral playing field has not shown any signs of improving with three more pieces of repressive legislation rammed through parliament this week.

There is little doubt that all is not well within Zanu PF as we approach elections; in-fighting and power struggles seem to be the order of the day. Zimbabweans have been watching wide eyed as even the state media has been reporting on 'plots,' 'secrets meetings,' 'the tug of war for succession,' and 'the night of the long knives;' the latter referring to the secret meeting in Tsholotsho by senior Zanu PF officials. For a change none of these dire and dirty deeds are being committed by our usual enemies who the State say are The British, The Americans, The Rhodesians, The Selous Scouts or The Neo Colonialists. This time the evildoers are people within Zanu PF itself. The easiest way to describe the atmosphere is with quotes from the just ended Zanu PF Congress.

At the opening of the Zanu PF congress, Reverend Obediah Musindo set the tone by saying: 'It's my prayer that President Mugabe should live longer to deliver us to the Promised Land.'

Referring to suggestions that Mr Mugabe should step down, Vice President Joseph Msika said: 'Mugabe go? Go Where? He should rule even if it means he is walking with the aid of a walking stick. He is the father of our nation; he is entitled to rule us forever.'

President Mugabe, speaking about the top party officials he suspended because they tried to oppose the appointment of Joice Mujuru at a secret meeting in Tsholotsho, said: 'minds that can be bought, hearts that can be sold, are political prostitutes. This party has no room for political prostitutes.'

Jonathon Moyo's response to accusations about the secret meeting at Tsholotsho: 'Ugly lies. Pure fiction. It was a mere speech and prize giving ceremony.'

Enos Chikowore, reporting on Zimbabwe's top ministers and politicians who grabbed multiple farms, said: 'Top members of the party ignored even calls by the presidency to surrender the extra farms. There are termites within our party, they are not people.' Reporting on the dismal production on Zimbabwe's seized farms, he said: 'I am calling for attitudinal change within our newly resettled farmers. Under the regime of Ian Smith and up to 1999, 4,000 white farmers produced enough food for the nation and had more left over for export. Today, after the land reform programme, there are over 12,000 farmers (A2) but they are failing to do what their predecessors did.'

And, for anyone who thinks Zimbabwe has a chance of a free and fair election in March, we question why the budgetary allocation to the CIO (secret police) has been increased from $62 billion this year to $395.8 billion for the coming year.

IN THE NEWS

~*11th December 2004* A special government notice is issued which increases President Mugabe's annual salary from $73.7 million to $83.8 million.

~*18th December 2004* Minister of Justice, Legal and Parliamentary Affairs and leader of the House Patrick Chinamasa and junior Minister of Information and Publicity Jonathan Moyo, are left out of Zanu PF's newly announced politburo.

~*20th December 2004* The Reserve Bank puts CFX Bank under the management of a curator for six months.

~*26th December 2004.* A magnitude 9.1 earthquake hits the Indian Ocean with its epicentre off Sumatra. Enormous tsunami waves crash into coastal areas of Thailand, India, Sri Lanka, the Maldives, Myanmar, Bangladesh and Indonesia. The death toll in the affected countries is estimated between 87,000–230,000 with a further 45,000 missing and 1.69 million people displaced.

Are you serious? Shopping basket December 2004

A government school teacher takes home between seven and eight thousand dollars a month. Work out what they can buy:

Item	Price Z$
Matches (one box)	300
Candle (one)	1,300
Biscuits (pkt)	3,500
Cooking oil (2l)	26,500
Sugar (2kg)	5,000
Flour (2kg)	9,000
Tea bags (100)	6,400
Margarine (500g)	5,700
Potatoes (15kg)	80,000
Toilet paper (1 roll)	1,500
Bread (loaf)	3,500
Egg (one)	1,000
Banana (one)	1,000
Orange (one)	1,000
Chicken (1kg)	27,000
Plum jam (jar)	12,000
Pasta (500g)	6,000
Cabbage (one)	3,800

18 December 2004. The courage to go on

Christmas 2004 is an incredibly difficult time for most Zimbabweans as we struggle to cope financially with additional burdens and emotionally because families are spread out across continents due to the ongoing turmoil in the country. I would like to use this Christmas letter to thank some of the people who have made life bearable, others whose leadership and determination has been inspirational and yet others who, just by being there in the background, day after day, week after week, have given me the courage to go on.

Mostly I would like to thank Zimbabwe's opposition political party who have managed, for five years, to stop our country from descending into civil war. The MDC have fought with words, with court battles and with dignified determination. Every single one of the MDC MPs have made supreme sacrifices for the country. They have almost all been arrested; they and their families have been harassed, abused and intimidated; some have been tortured, others beaten and detained and some have even lost their lives in the fight for democracy. MDC MP Roy Bennett will spend this Christmas in prison and our thoughts will be with him because we know that the sacrifices he and his family made were for us all and for Zimbabwe. Some days I look at film clips of armed militants in Sudan, Ivory Coast, the Congo and other African countries and think that if it were not for the determined non-violent stance of the MDC, which could so easily be us.

This Christmas I would also like to thank the growing number of people inside the country who have formed and joined civic action groups and raised their voices for Zimbabwe. I hesitate to list them for fear of putting them at risk but they all lead by their bravery and example. Most of them have suffered appalling indignities and outrageous injustices and have put their lives and families on hold as they fight for democracy in Zimbabwe.

Lastly this Christmas I would like to thank the people outside the country who continue to fight for Zimbabwe. The staff of

Short Wave Radio Africa who are banned from returning to Zimbabwe but who faithfully report to us every night; without them we would be lost in a fog of propaganda. There are MPs in country's all over the world who continue to lobby their own governments to speak out about events in Zimbabwe. There are human rights organizations and associations, writers, reporters and lobby groups who speak out for Zimbabwe. There are groups who hold vigils, marches, protests and demonstrations in the UK, USA ı and South Africa. And then there are the ordinary people, the men and women all over the world, who care about Zimbabwe. The people who send emails and letters, sign petitions and join marches. People who write to their MPs, tell their friends about what's happening in Zimbabwe and add their voices to the rising international discontent. There are many people who take the time, every week, to read my letter from Zimbabwe and then pass it on to others to read. I thank you all for your support and compassion, and for your generosity to the people in need that I have written about. I wish all my family and friends a wonderful, peaceful and happy Christmas and thank you for everything you have done to help Zimbabwe.

Source list: Part One

AFP
BBC NEWS
CFU sitrep
The Daily News (Zimbabwe)
The Financial Gazette (Zimbabwe)
The Herald (Zimbabwe)
IPS
MDC Weekly Brief
News 24 (South Africa)
Reuters
The Standard, (Zimbabwe)
Xinhua News Agency
The Zimbabwe Independent
Zimbabwe Situation
ZWNews

Source List: Part Two

Business Day (SA)
The Cape Argus (SA)
The Cape Times (SA)
CBS News (Canada)
The Daily Telegraph (UK)
The Financial Gazette (Zimbabwe)
The Guardian (UK)
The Herald (Zimbabwe)
The Independent (UK)
News24 (SA)
Reuters
Sapa-AP
The Standard (Zimbabwe)
The Times (UK)
United Press International
The Zimbabwe Independent
Zimbabwe Situation
ZW News

Source list: Part Three

Africa Confidential (UK)
The Age (Australia)
BBC News
Business Day (SA)
The Daily News (Zimbabwe)
The Daily Telegraph (UK)
The Financial Gazette (Zimbabwe)
The Guardian (UK)
The Herald (Zimbabwe)
The Independent (UK)
IOL (SA)
Mail and Guardian (SA)
Natal Mercury (SA)
News 24 (SA)
The Observer (UK)
Reuters
SABC News
Sunday Telegraph (Australia)
Sunday Times (UK)
The Standard (Zimbabwe)
The Star (SA)
The Times (UK)
VOA i News
Wikipedia
The Zimbabwe Independent
Zimbabwe Situation
Zvajokes.com
ZWNews

Source list: Part Four

Botswana Daily News
The Daily News (Zimbabwe)
The Daily Telegraph (UK)
The Financial Gazette (Zimbabwe)
Front Page Magazine
The Herald (Zimbabwe)
IOL
News24 (SA)
Reuters
The Standard (Zimbabwe)
The Times (UK)
VOA
The White House (USA)
The Zimbabwe Independent
The Zimbabwe Situation

Source list: Part Five
ABC (Australia)
AFP
AP
BBC
The Chronicle (Zimbabwe)
Daily News online
EUpolitix
The Financial Gazette (Zimbabwe)
The Guardian (UK)
The Herald (Zimbabwe)
IOL
IRIN
The Mail and Guardian
New Zimbabwe.com
Reuters
SAPA The Scotsman
Sky TV News (UK)
The Standard (Zimbabwe)
The Sunday Mail (Zimbabwe)
The Sunday Times (SA)
SWRadio Africa
The Telegraph (UK)
This Day (Nigeria)
UPI
VOA
ZBC TV News (Zimbabwe)
The Zimbabwe Independent
Zimonline
The Zimbabwe Situation

Printed in Great Britain
by Amazon